Mystery Cats of the World

To my family – past and present – for love
and unwavering support.

Mystery Cats of the World

From Blue Tigers to Exmoor Beasts

Karl P.N. Shuker

ROBERT HALE · LONDON

First published in Great Britain 1989

Robert Hale Limited
Clerkenwell House
Clerkenwell Green
London EC1R 0HT

British Library Cataloguing in Publication Data

Shuker, Karl P.N.
Mystery cats of the world: from blue tigers to Exmoor beasts
1. Mysteries. Unidentified Felidae
I. Title
001.9′4

ISBN 0–7090–3706–6

Photoset in Times by
Derek Doyle & Associates, Mold, Clwyd.
Printed in Great Britain by
St Edmundsbury Press Ltd, Bury St Edmunds, Suffolk.
Bound by WBC Bookbinders Limited.

Contents

Illustrations

PICTURE CREDITS

The following photographs have been reproduced by kind permission of:
Trevor Beer: 4, 8, 11; Lena Godsall Bottriell and Paul Bottriell: 17, 18; Sandy Brander: 13; *Daily Mail*: 15, 23; Dudley & West Midlands Zoological Society: 10; Fortean Picture Library: 1, 3, 5, 16, 19, 20, 24, 25, 27, 28, 32, 33, 34; William Heinemann Ltd/Kenneth Gandar Dower: 21; Dr Bernard Heuvelmans/Monique Watteau: 31; International Society of Cryptozoology: 29; Marwell Zoological Park: 30; *The News* (Portsmouth): 6; Royal Museum of Scotland: 12; *The Scotsman*: 2; *Sunday Independent*: 9; Syndication International: 22; Professor Charles Thomas: 14.

Figures and Tables

Acknowledgements

I owe a great debt of gratitude to a considerable number of persons, societies, organizations and publications for their very kind interest and most generous assistance in relation to my mystery cat researches and preparation of this book; in particular, I would like to express my most sincere thanks to the following:

Victor Albert; ASSAP Library; Bill Bailey; Dr Michael Bassett; *BBC Wildlife*; Trevor Beer; Dr David Beeston; Phil Bennett; *Birmingham Evening Mail*; Birmingham Libraries; Janet and Colin Bord; Lena and Paul Bottricll; Sandy Brander; Bill and Ken Brewer; Bristol, Clifton & West England Zoological Society; British Library; British Museum (Natural History); Owen Burnham; D.N. Clark-Lowes; Coffee Books (Stratford-on-Avon); Mary Cotterill; *Courier Mail* (Brisbane); *Daily Express; Daily Mail; Daily Mirror; Daily Record*; Mike Dash; Dudley & West Midlands Zoological Society; Dudley Libraries; Dr Anthony Eve; Excalibur Books; *Express & Echo* (Exeter); *Express & Star* (Sandwell and Wolverhampton); *Fate; Folklore Frontiers; Forres Gazette*; Fortean Picture Library; *Fortean Times*; *Glasgow Herald*; Michael Goss; Geoffrey Greed; Richard Greenwell; Edith and Florence Griffin; Adam Hart-Davis; Heads 'n' Tails Taxidermists; David Heppell; Dr Bernard Heuvelmans; Highland Wildlife Park; Daphne Hills; Peter Houston; *INFO Journal*; International Society of Cryptozoology; Shereen Karmali; the Rt Rev. Mgr Michael Kirkham; Dr James Kirkwood; Andrew Kitchener; J.M. Knowles; Lorna Lloyd; Dr Peter Lüps; Ruth McArthur; Dr Roy P. Mackal; David McKinley; Marwell Zoological Park; Marcus Matthews; Dr Ralph Molnar; David Morgan; Dr Desmond Morris; National Museum of Wales; *The News* (Portsmouth); Edward Noble; North Queensland Naturalists Club; *The Observer*; Richard O'Grady; Edward Orbell; *Pursuit*; Queensland Museum; Radio Devon; Radio WM; Michel Raynal; Bob Rickard; John Rimmer; Royal Museum of Scotland; Sandwell Libraries; *The Scotsman*; Paul Screeton; Mary Shuker; Paul Sieveking; Malcolm Smith; Society For Psychical Research; Dora Stokes; *The Sun; Sunday Express; Sunday Independent; Sunday*

Mirror; Swara; Syndication International; Prof. Charles Thomas; Ernest and Gertrude Timmins; Dr Frank Turk; University of Birmingham; University of Leeds; *The Unknown*; Dr G.R. Cunningham van Someren; Walsall Libraries; Wednesbury Typewriter Service (Wednesbury, W. Midlands); *Western Morning News*; Prof. Ron Westrum; Wolverhampton Libraries; Gerald Wood; Zoological Society of Glasgow & West of Scotland; Zoological Society of London.

And in deep gratitude for their encouragement and faith in my book, I wish to express my especial thanks to my publishers, Robert Hale Ltd.

Author's Preface

I am too much of a sceptic to deny the possibility of anything.
Thomas Henry Huxley – Letter written in 1886

Once all-too-commonly derided and dismissed as a subject for dreams and for dreamers, cryptozoology – the scientific investigation of animals still awaiting formal discovery or identification – nowadays attracts substantial and serious international interest. So much so, in fact, that in 1982 the world's first scientific society devoted to mystery creatures was established – the International Society of Cryptozoology (ISC), based at Tucson, Arizona. Its board of directors comprises some of the world's most distinguished professional zoologists, and its president is the French zoologist Dr Bernard Heuvelmans, a renowned cryptozoological researcher and the person responsible for actually coining the term 'cryptozoology'.

It is not difficult to understand their interest and belief in the existence of such creatures. All of the following large-sized animals, for example, were unknown to science until the twentieth century: the okapi (relative of the giraffe – discovered in 1901); mountain gorilla (the world's largest ape – 1901); giant forest hog (over eight feet/240 cm long – 1904); Komodo dragon (the world's largest lizard at up to ten feet/300 cm in total length – 1912); kouprey (new species of wild ox – 1937); Shepherd's beaked whale (radically new species – 1937); coelacanth (large fish belonging to group hitherto believed extinct for 64 million years – 1938); cochito (new species of porpoise – 1959); Chacoan peccary (pig-like creature believed extinct since the Ice Ages – 1975); megamouth (world's third-largest shark species – 1976); bilkis gazelle (alive and well in Qatar – 1986). And these are only a few such discoveries!

Huge expanses of forested, mountainous, desert and polar areas still await scientific exploration and are currently known only from aerial photographs. The zoological content of much of the inland waters of the world is very incompletely known too, and that of the immense oceans is shrouded in mystery. In short, the potential for new and significant zoological discoveries is tremendous – a fact which cryptozoology's critics attempt lamely to deny by dismissing this century's major animal finds as irritating exceptions, and by conveniently overlooking the world's vast untraversed, unexplored regions – an attitude which is happily and ever increasingly ridiculed by every new animal discovery which takes place.

Astute students of cryptozoology will note readily that a considerable number of unknown animals fall into one of three main categories, and for good reason – namely that these animals have the greatest chance of remaining undetected. They are: Category 1 – aquatic creatures, whose natural habitat is not conducive to meticulous, sustained searches (especially the larger inland stretches of water and the voluminous oceans); Category 2 – higher apes and primitive humanoid forms, whose high intelligence would keep them well away from modern man; and Category 3 – mystery cats, whose inherent elusiveness is a primary requirement for their entire way of life.

Several books devoted to aquatic 'monsters' and unknown primates have already been published, and more continue to emerge. Never before, however, has a book appeared which is devoted to mystery cats of the world. I have been interested in such animals for many years, and my personal researches have yielded a considerable archive of relevant material – a notable proportion of which has not received serious cryptozoological attention before. Additionally, many items have not been previously published, while others have never before appeared in an English-language book. In recent years, mystery cats from many lands have gained very notable attention – the notorious Beast of Exmoor, the cheetah-like *onza* shot in Mexico, the resplendently striped king cheetahs filmed in southern Africa, Scottish specimens of a black gracile cat hitherto unrecorded by science, and the sleek panther-like creatures which roam almost every state not only of the USA but also of Australia. Journals specializing in mysterious phenomena are devoting ever-increasing amounts of space to reports of unidentified and strange cat forms too.

Consequently it seemed an appropriate time for me to prepare an entire book dealing with mystery cats worldwide – but *not* an exhaustive, rigidly formal work. For this subject is supported by such an immense body of material, documented and undocumented, that, quite frankly, a really detailed account would require several hefty volumes! Indeed, as we shall see, entire books have already been devoted to certain specific examples.

In fact, as my cryptozoological researches progress, I do plan to produce a specialized series of scientific treatises on selected mystery felids. At the present time, however, I feel that something rather different is needed first of all, for it is only too clear that the phenomenon of mystery cats worldwide is a subject which currently fascinates people worldwide – and with an appeal not limited to any single type of person. Specialists and non-specialists, scientists and the general reading public: all are very greatly intrigued by the numerous reports of a vast variety of cat-like creatures which continue to appear and which continue to baffle, involving feline fauna being sighted in regions where such animals are not supposed to exist, or fitting the description of no species known to exist anywhere!

With this in mind, I have therefore sought to produce a concise (but not superficial) and relatively informal *guide* to these animals, which brings together all of the principal mystery cat forms of the world within a *single* volume, and which defines and displays the scope and essential components of the subject. Hence my book has been designed to fulfil the following functions: to demonstrate the number and diversity of mystery cat forms; to provide for each of these a resumé of its basic history (which concentrates upon the more lucid and informative of reports currently available, rather than attempting an unselective blanket coverage); to offer an analysis, whenever possible, of likely zoological identity involved; and to produce a comprehensive reference list of all sources used in this book, which can be consulted by readers wishing to pursue any aspect further.

Incidentally, felids once mysterious but nowadays relatively well known and well studied (e.g. Rewa-type white tigers, Timbavati-type white lions) are treated only briefly here; additionally, unusual and out-of-place forms of domestic cat (e.g. sphynx, 'winged' cats, West Australian ferals) are not referred to at all.

One further point. It has been frequently suggested that certain mystery cat forms (notably the black pantheresque felids of Britain and continental Europe, Australia, and North America) are not corporeal beasts at all, but paranormal entities instead. A variety of identities of this type have been put forward for such cats, ranging from were-panthers, thought-forms (tulpas) and spectres, to UFO occupants, and denizens of a subterranean world at the Earth's core. As far as I am concerned, however, all of the mystery cat reports contained in this book are ones which I firmly believe can be satisfactorily explained by straightforward cryptozoological reasoning, following traditional scientific principles. Having said that, I am nonetheless aware of certain additional reports which describe cats that do appear to be more akin to the phantasmal 'Black Dogs' of British folklore than to any corporeal cryptozoological cat. Such creatures include, for example, the eerie devil cat of India, exhibiting a propensity for eldritch shrieks and a notable fear of holy water (Morrison, J., *Fate*, Vol. 8, pp. 23–25 (February 1955)); a ghostly black cat said to haunt Northern Ireland's Mount Pellier (Dunne, J.J., *Haunted Ireland* (1977)) and a comparable creature allegedly frequenting the ruins of Suffolk's Borley Rectory (McEwan, G., *Mystery Animals of Britain and Ireland* (1986)); and China's deadly devil tiger – more like an amorphous animated cloud than any form of animal (Bentley, E.G., *Fate*, Vol. 13, pp. 72–75 (July 1960)). Even if such bizarre entities as these really do exist, their origins and identities are evidently subjects that pass far beyond the realms of cryptozoology – consequently they are not dealt with in this book.

The past few years have witnessed the publication of cryptozoological books on a hitherto unprecedented scale. Worthy of especial note here is that a high proportion of these are still in print, demonstrating that there is indeed an appreciable public interest and demand for books dealing with cryptozoology. Similarly, the two-day ISC Annual Members Meeting held in July 1987 at Edinburgh's Royal Museum of Scotland attracted three times the audience present at previous years' meetings. Long may this upward trend continue, so that cryptozoology itself can flourish and thereby enable its researchers to succeed in carrying out those activities common and intrinsic to all scientific disciplines – transforming the myths and superstitions of the past into the facts and realities of the future.

Foreword

by Paul and Lena Godsall Bottriell

This thoughtful work of scholarship by Karl Shuker is an ideal book with which to enter the 1990s; he has performed an admirable service. As the century pitches inexorably towards the year 2000, humankind's awareness of the world's environment has taken a dramatic leap forward. Significantly, an increased appreciation of nature's limitless ability to bring forth life has accompanied it – a new comprehension of evolution happening around us. Suddenly those vestiges of wilderness that remain are being viewed as more than just the marvels of nature, without which our spirits would be the poorer. It's not only the untold benefits the preservation of our tropical forests offer, in cures for terminal diseases, that's coming home to humanity: rocketed into the spotlight by environmental events and resultant pronouncements on changes in weather patterns and the ozone layer, it is the compelling significance of what preserving the symbiotic processes of nature, with its remarkable interdependence of species, represents for the modern world.

Amid this new thinking can be glimpsed the budding of a universal realization that the saving of individual species is not a romantic, Franciscan whim reserved only for impractical eccentrics, but the concern of everyone; that it's not only possible to discover new species of flora and fauna, but animals once taken to be just attractive aberrations or compelling myths may be new races evolving – and new races evolving to survive, for reasons linked directly to the changing fortunes of the earth's environment. Legendary animals like the king cheetahs, for example – for the 're-discovery' of which we're privileged to be deemed responsible. It's here this exemplary treatise best sits; an intelligent study of a neglected subject that doesn't sensationalize information to fit personal theories. With an investigative, systematic flow of research details, Karl Shuker reviews his data critically and constructively, leaving room for readers to add their own analysis, and by extension, follow-up research and fieldwork.

Equally worthy is an attractive, uncomplicated style which makes it an enjoyable read, and thus as accessible to laymen as to zoologists.

In *Mystery Cats of the World*, Karl Shuker treads worthily in the footsteps of Bernard Heuvelmans. As a reliable, up-to-date reference, this is a book that both professionals and amateurs should carry in their hip pockets. Perhaps a sequel on another group of mysterious animals may be forthcoming from the author in the not-too-distant future. We avidly await it.

L.G.B. & P.B.
England
March, 1989

I saw a proud, mysterious cat.
Vachel Lindsay, *The Mysterious Cat*

Introduction

> Cats, no less liquid than their shadows,
> Offer no angles to the wind.
> They slip, diminished, neat, through loopholes
> Less than themselves.
>
> A.S.J. Tessimond, *Cats*, II

Cats are amongst the most elegant, aloof and awe-inspiring of all animals – they are at once ubiquitous and evanescent, docile and deadly, familiar and mysterious. Their ensemble includes the majestically maned lion, black-and-gold tiger, richly rosetted leopard and jaguar, gracile cheetah, densely furred ounce or snow leopard, mountain-haunting puma, keen-eyed lynx and a host of small species, not least of which is the tabby tiger which lies curled up in front of many a hearthside fire. A total of thirty-six wild modern species are currently recognized by science[1] (see Table 1). However, a vast body of information exists – ranging from anecdotal reports and native lore to unidentifiable paw-tracks (spoor) and even the very occasional preserved pelt or specimen – which implies very strongly that additional cat forms also inhabit our world. Some seem to be forms undescribed by science (at least in the living state); others appear to be felids already known to science but occurring in unexpected, non-native localities. All are awaiting discovery by anyone with sufficient interest and persistence to traverse little-explored terrain and peruse dusty, obscure journals in pursuit of conclusive evidence for their existence – evidence which can then at last be submitted for formal scientific analysis to determine these animals' identities.

Such cats comprise the subject of this book and include amongst their numbers: Tanzania's donkey-sized, brindled *mngwa*; Colombia's large-fanged striped cat; Fujian's blue tigers; East Africa's spotted lions; Australia's Emmaville panther and Queensland tiger; southern Africa's elegant king cheetah; northern Scotland's black, gracile Kellas cat; Mexico's equally gracile, puma-like *onza*; the Ile du Levant's fierce wildcat; Angola's water lion and Patagonia's water tiger; North America's mysterious maned lions; Guyana's white-chested *jaguarete*;

Ethiopia's tiger-like *wobo*; England's Surrey puma and Exmoor Beast; and many others too.

In order to set the stage for such animals and to appreciate their especial significance, however, we should first familiarize ourselves with the *known* cats, via a concise consideration of cat characteristics, form, evolution and present-day contingency, emphasizing those aspects particularly relevant to the investigation of mystery cat forms.

Characteristics and Form

Taxonomy is the scientific classification of organisms. Cats belong to the taxonomic order of mammals known as Carnivora, whose families comprise the canids (dogs, foxes, wolves), ursids (bears), procyonids (raccoons, coatis, cacomistles, kinkajou, olingos), ailuropodids (pandas), mustelids (weasels, polecats, otters, badgers, skunks, martens, wolverine), otariids (eared seals), odobenids (walruses), phocids (earless seals), hyaenids (hyaenas, aardwolf), viverrids (civets, genets, binturong, mongooses, fossa) and felids (cats).

Incidentally, 'feline' is often used wrongly as a noun. 'Felid' is a noun, but 'feline' is an adjective. Consequently, expressions such as 'the mystery feline' and 'unknown felines', which frequently occur in newspaper reports and popular-format items, are grammatically incorrect. In short, the cat is a felid, its behaviour is feline.

When dealing with mystery cats, it is essential to recognize that felids are undoubtedly the most perfectly evolved of all mammalian carnivores for flesh-eating and predation, in terms of both anatomical specialization and hunting behaviour – their prowess as predators and their inherent elusiveness are legendary. Hence we should not be surprised to discover that mystery cats possess these same qualities.

Except for certain absolute and relative size differences, all modern cat species are remarkably similar structurally, as the following blueprint of the felid 'hunting-machine' demonstrates.

The felid's head comes complete with large, highly developed eyes, mobile, acute ears, a sensitive, albeit smallish nose and touch-responsive whiskers (vibrissae). Coupled with a brain that possesses large cerebral hemispheres – responsible for well-co-ordinated, intelligent behaviour (an absolute requirement for a successful hunter) – all of these contribute significantly to very efficient prey-detection.[2-4]

Its jaws are relatively short and contain thirty teeth that comprise a dentition specialized to accomplish the two principal functions required of a successful predator's teeth – seizing and tearing the living prey, and then cutting its carcase into manageable pieces for swallowing. Consequently a cat's canines are long, strong and sharply pointed to carry out the first of these functions. The second is served by specialized teeth characteristic of mammalian carnivores[3] – the large carnassials. These comprise the last pair of upper premolars and the only pair of lower molars and are modified by the possession of sharp, blade-like edges that slice through meat when brought alongside each other like shears by the closing of the jaws. The remaining teeth are reduced in size and used mostly for holding the food in position (the incisors) and chewing (those premolars and molars not adapted as carnassials).[2-4]

The felid tongue is long and bears many horny, backward-pointing projections called papillae, used to prise meat away from bones (felids do not normally break the bones of their prey whilst eating) and to wash the felid effectively.[2-4]

The felid body is both flexible and strong – the vertebral column (backbone) is exceedingly so, especially in the lumbar (waist) region; and its intricate muscle system in combination with its powerful and supple limbs is co-ordinated superbly to yield the graceful, fluid gait and movements epitomizing all forms of cat and integral to their hunting-technique.[2-4]

The mode of hunting carried out by most felids consists of a short series of creeping runs (referred to as 'stalking runs'), bringing the cat ever closer to its prey, interspersed by pauses for renewed observation of the latter from behind cover (the 'watching posture'). When the cat ultimately reaches its intended victim, it then pounces with forelimbs outstretched to strike.[5]

Although the cat's long tail can certainly assist balance whilst jumping and climbing, it is clearly not indispensable – the short tails of lynxes do not seem to impair their agility in any way. In fact, probably its most important function is as a signalling device to other cats; it is also an indicator of felid behaviour – its movements and position vary according to the cat's mood and intentions.[2-5]

Spoor – Paws and Claws

Cat spoor (paw-print tracks) have certain characteristics which enable them to be differentiated in many instances from those of dogs or other mammals. Thus, if an unidentified mystery carnivore leaves behind spoor, this provides the investigator with important clues for determining the creature's basic identity. Such evidence has been obtained in relation to a number of beasts currently held to be mystery cats. Hence a short guide comparing felid and canid spoor will follow shortly.

Figure: Comparison of Cat and Dog Spoor (Typical Examples)

The illustrations of domestic cat and domestic dog spoor given below are reproduced from Trevor Beer's book *The Beast of Exmoor: Fact or Legend?*, by kind permission of Trevor Beer. The illustration of the spoor ascribed to the Queensland tiger given here is adapted from the original sketch produced by A.A. Hull and published in 1872 within the *Proceedings of the Zoological Society of London*.

large-sized domestic dog

Domestic dog spoor varies greatly in size and shape between breeds. For example:

In the alsatian:
Length = 3¾-4 inch/9.4-10 cm
Width = 3¾ inch/9.4 cm

In the beagle:
Length = 2¾ inch/6.9 cm
Width = 2¼ inch/5.6 cm

medium-sized domestic dog

Both examples of dog spoor are from forefeet – in dog spoor produced by hindfeet, posterior edge of plantar (palm) pad is convex, not concave.

In the West Highland White Terrier:
Length = 1½ inch/3.75 cm
Width = 1¼ inch/3.1 cm

Queensland tiger?

Length = 2½ inch/6.25 cm
Width = 2½ inch/6.25 cm

domestic cat

Length = 1 inch/2.5 cm
Width = 1-1¼ inch/2.5-3 cm

Though very similar in shape to domestic cat spoor, wildcat spoor is twice as large, lynx spoor (almost circular) three times as large, puma and leopard spoor four times as large, and lion spoor five times as large. Also worth noting is that in large felid species, the two members of a given toe pad pair sometimes differ from one another in size.

First of all, however, a few words concerning feet. Mammals such as ourselves, as well as bears and monkeys, walk on the soles of the feet and are termed 'plantigrade'. Conversely, dogs and cats are 'digitigrade', i.e. they walk only on their toes. This latter mode of locomotion is of benefit to those animals to which running and springing are of such great importance, e.g. hunters, because the act of moving on one's toes actually increases the length of the limbs, and hence the length of each stride taken.[2-4]

Cats and dogs possess five toes on each front foot (forefoot), but the first toe or pollex (corresponding to our thumb) is extremely small and is positioned well above ground-level so that these animals walk on only four toes on each of their forefeet. The same is true for their hindfeet, though with these the first toe or hallux (corresponding with our big toe) is missing altogether.[2-4]

The spoor of dogs, foxes and cats all yield paw-prints each containing four toe pads and one posterior plantar (palm) pad, but certain differences also exist. With foxes, the distinctly perceived toe pads are elongate; all four produce clear claw impressions; the two front toe pads are positioned very close to one another; the plantar pad is two-lobed, and its rear edge is concave on the forefeet, convex on the hindfeet; and the overall spoor outline is elongate. Dog spoor, regardless of breed, is very similar to the above, except of course for overall size, which varies according to the breed concerned. In addition, the overall outline of dog spoor is rounder than that of foxes, and the two central toe pads are not positioned so far forward.[6] See also the figure on p. 20.

Cat spoor, though varying between species in size, remains much the same in appearance, but is recognizably different from that of canids. Its overall outline is almost circular, enclosing four clearly separate, oval toe pads which point straight ahead, plus a large three-lobed plantar pad with convex rear outline on all paws. Moreover, cat spoor does not contain claw marks *under normal conditions*[6] – there is very good reason for emphasizing these three words, as we shall now see.

The terminal bone of each of a cat's eighteen toes bears a sharp claw, which can be fully retracted by all known felids except the cheetah and serval.[4] Numerous books and articles contain the statement that cats retract their claws when moving, and hence do not leave pawprints possessing claw marks. This is at best ambiguous and at worst suggests a lack of understanding concerning not only felid behaviour but also felid anatomy. For such a statement implies that claw-retraction is an active process, i.e. one requiring effort on the cat's part, without which its claws would automatically extend. In fact, the very reverse of this is true, for when its paws are in a relaxed state (i.e. unexerted, with no current use for the claws), the claw-bearing terminal bone of each toe is positioned completely off the ground, held on top of the bone immediately behind it by a retractor ligament, so that each claw is retracted. Conversely, when the claws are needed, a flexor muscle actively contracts, pulling upon a tendon that in turn lowers the claw-bearing terminal bone of each toe so that the claws then become fully protracted and in contact with the ground, i.e. they are extended.[7]

While it is certainly true that a cat's claws remain retracted *under normal conditions* when it moves (thereby keeping them razor-sharp for predatory purposes), they do not stay retracted under *all* conditions whilst the cat is moving; claw-extension occurs if conditions necessitate. For example, as any cat-owner will verify, when a cat leaps from an above-ground surface, e.g. wall, tree branch, even a chair, it extends its claws to secure a firm grip on the ground when it lands, thereby ensuring its continued stability. Similarly, if a cat is moving across a hazardously uneven or slippery surface, in order to maintain its stability it will once again extend its claws to obtain a better grip. In short, a cat's claws are used not only for seizing prey but also for coming to the rescue of its stability when moving. Needless to say, in a situation in which claws have been employed for the latter purpose, any spoor left behind will contain clear claw marks.

Consequently, the frequent tendency of mystery creature investigators to eliminate immediately a felid as a possible identity in a case involving clawed prints is clearly incorrect. Instead, whenever clawed prints are discovered in such a situation, an assessment of the ground's surface – is it slippery, rough, at a steep gradient? – should be made before any thought is made of dismissing a felid identity for the creature concerned.

Evolution

It will be seen in the chapters which follow that certain mystery cat forms apparently resemble various felids officially believed to be long extinct. If these mystery cats are ultimately discovered and are indeed found to be supposedly demised forms, it would be exceedingly significant scientifically, yet in fact it would not be overly outstanding; for many creatures supposedly long extinct have been discovered alive and well in remote regions – creatures such as the coelacanth, the Chacoan peccary and the marsupial *Burramys*, to name but three extremely important rediscoveries of this type made in the past fifty years alone.

Thus, in view of this exciting possibility, the following brief history of felid evolution is presented to illustrate and identify the major cat forms of the past (and present?).

All modern Carnivora are descended from a family of weasel-like creatures called miacids, of which the typical genus *Miacis* lived about 50 million years ago during the Eocene epoch.

Felid development from this humble ancestor occurred very rapidly. By the late Eocene/early Oligocene epoch (36 million years ago), the first recognizable felid subfamilies had already appeared, beginning with the nimravids or false sabre-tooths. They were so named because their upper canines were somewhat larger than the fairly normal lower canines. Examples included the puma-sized *Dinictis* and the gracile *Nimravus*, both from the North American Oligocene epoch.[4,8,9]

Early on in nimravid evolution, a side-branch diverged, giving rise during the Eocene epoch to a second subfamily, the hoplophoneids. These were the first true sabre-toothed cats, characterized by upper canines very greatly enlarged and lower canines greatly reduced in size. This highly specialized dental arrangement meant that the jaws and teeth of the hoplophoneids functioned by stabbing (though the precise mechanism used varied from species to species[10]), their enlarged upper canines being used to puncture the lower neck and throat of their prey; conversely, the jaws and more comparably sized upper and lower canines of the nimravids functioned not by stabbing but by biting. Hoplophoneids included *Hoplophoneus* of the North American Oligocene epoch and the initially Eurasian *Eusmilus*.[4,8,9]

During the Pliocene epoch (5-2 million years ago), the entire nimravid subfamily died out. Before its demise, however, it had given rise to two further subfamilies, the machairodontids and the true felids.[8,9]

The machairondontids comprise those familiar but formidable, large-fanged sabre-tooths popularly nicknamed 'sabre-toothed tigers' (even though they are only remotely related to true tigers). Like the hoplophoneids, they possessed greatly enlarged upper canines and very reduced lower ones, yielding a specialized stabbing apparatus (which again varied between species relative to certain morphological modifications[10]); and, indeed, it was once believed that the machairodontids had descended directly from the hoplophoneids. Conversely, recent researches indicate that this is not so; instead, the hoplophoneids apparently died out during the Pliocene epoch (*Barbourofelis* was one of their last representatives), while the machairodontids emerged as an independent side-branch of the nimravids – in short, the second time that this latter subfamily had given rise to a group of sabre-toothed cats.[9] *Machairodus* was a machairodontid from the Pliocene epoch, of near-ubiquitous distribution and of leonine stature.[8] By the Pleistocene epoch, the dirk-tooth *Megantereon* had appeared.

This was a panther-sized form, initially inhabiting Europe but extending its range during this epoch into Asia, Africa and ultimately America, where the most massive of all machairodontids evolved – the enormous and awe-inspiring *Smilodon*, larger than a lion and with colossal upper canines that measured 6 in/15 cm in length.[9,11] An interesting machairodontid side-line was *Homotherium*, the scimitar cat,[9,11] which we shall meet again in Chapter 2. Despite their variety and impressive form, however, with the demise of *Smilodon* in North America about 12,000 years ago the machairodontids *officially* died out.

The second subfamily to emerge from the nimravids just before they died out comprised the true felids, which include all thirty-six wild species of cat known to be alive today. Such emergence must have involved secondary reduction of the nimravids' somewhat large upper canines. Some authorities do not believe that this reduction occurred, and suggest that the true felids arose instead from some other, separate, obscure cat group not currently known from fossils.[4,8,9] But regardless of their origin, by the Pleistocene epoch (2 million years ago) many true felids existed, including not only modern species but also a host of exotic forms no longer with us (*officially*), such as the giant American lion *Panthera leo atrox*, Owen's panther *P. pardoides*, once found in Britain, the lion-sized cheetah *Acinonyx pardinensis* and a huge form of tiger from China. While the hoplophoneids and machairodontids were stabbing cats, the true felids, like the nimravids, were and are biting cats, with normal-sized lower canines.[4,8-11]

Present-Day Cats – Big and Small

The modern species of true felid are split into two groups: 1) the highly specialized cheetah *Acinonyx jubatus*, and 2) all the remaining thirty-six cat species. This second group is in turn divided into three, each comprising a single genus. The first is *Panthera*, represented by five species: lion, tiger, leopard, jaguar and snow leopard, known collectively as 'the Big Cats'. The second genus is *Neofelis*, containing only the clouded leopard. The third genus is *Felis*, containing the remaining thirty modern cat species, ranging from the puma and lynxes to the domestic cat and tiny black-footed cat, known collectively as 'the Small Cats'.

In popular literature, the term 'Big Cat' is used indiscriminately to describe any cat of large size. Items appertaining to mystery cats often include phrases such as 'Mystery Big Cat', 'Surrey's Big Cat' or even 'British Big Cat'. Unless the taxonomic identity of the cat concerned is known conclusively to be that of a *Panthera* species, however, it would be most desirable not to use the term 'Big Cat'

Table 1: Wild Cats of the World

In addition to the domestic cat *Felis catus* of worldwide distribution, science currently recognizes the modern existence of thirty-six species of wild felid.

Common Name	Scientific Name	Distribution
Wildcat	*Felis sylvestris*	EU, AF, AS
Sand cat	*F. margarita*	AF, AS
Black-footed cat	*F. (Microfelis) nigripes*	AF
Chinese desert cat	*F. (Erinailurus) bieti*	AS
Jungle (Swamp) cat	*F. (Chaus* or *Catolynx) chaus*	AF, AS
Pallas's cat (Manul)	*F. (Otocolobus) manul*	AS
Northern lynx	*F. (Lynx) lynx*	EU, AS, NA
Spanish lynx	*F. (L.) pardina*	EU
Bobcat	*F. (L.) rufus*	NA
Caracal	*F. (Caracal) caracal*	AF, AS
Serval	*F. (Leptailurus) serval*	AF
Marbled cat	*F. (Pardofelis) marmorata*	AS
African golden (Tiger) cat	*F. (Profelis) aurata*	AF
Asian (Temminck's) golden cat	*F. (P.) temmincki*	AS
Bay (Bornean red) cat	*F. (P.* or *Badiofelis) badia*	AS
Leopard cat	*F. (Prionailurus) bengalensis*	AS
Rusty-spotted cat	*F. (P.) rubiginosus*	AS
Fishing cat	*F. (P.) viverrinus*	AS
Flat-headed cat	*F. (P.* or *Ictailurus) planiceps*	AS
Iriomote cat	*F. (P.* or *Mayailurus) iriomotensis*	AS
Ocelot	*F. (Leopardus) pardalis*	NA, SA
Margay	*F. (L.) wiedi*	NA, SA
Geoffroy's cat	*F. (L.* or *Oncifelis) geoffroyi*	SA
Kodkod	*F. (L., O.,* or *Noctifelis) guigna*	SA
Little spotted cat (Oncilla)	*F. (L., O.,* or *N.) tigrinus*	SA
Pampas cat	*F. (Lynchailurus) colocolo*	SA
Mountain (Andean) cat	*F. (Oreailurus) jacobita*	SA
Jaguarundi	*F. (Herpailurus) yagouaroundi*	NA, SA
Puma (Cougar, Mountain lion)	*F. (Puma) concolor*	NA, SA
Clouded leopard	*Neofelis nebulosa*	AS
Leopard	*Panthera pardus*	AF, AS
Jaguar	*P. (Jaguarius) onca*	NA, SA
Lion	*P. (Leo) leo*	AF, AS
Tiger	*P. (L.* or *Tigris) tigris*	AS
Snow leopard (Ounce, Erbis)	*P. (Uncia) uncia*	AS
Cheetah (Hunting leopard)	*Acinonyx jubatus*	AF, AS

Abbreviations: EU = Europe
AF = Africa
AS = Asia
NA = North America
SA = South America

In earlier days, the felids were split into numerous genera (included here in brackets). Most of these are nowadays treated merely as sub-genera, although certain authorities still recognize various of these as full genera.

in this manner, confining it instead to its correct scientific definition, thus preventing ambiguity.

In fact, body size is *not* the feature which differentiates Big Cats (genus *Panthera*) from Small Cats (genus *Felis*). Even though it is true that all five species of 'Big Cat' are big, not all 'Small Cats' are small – the puma, for example, is equal in size to a leopard. Instead, the character responsible for splitting these felids into these two genera is the composition of a structure called the hyoid apparatus, located in the throat region and incorporating a bony arch or suspension.

In the Small Cats (and also in the cheetah and clouded leopard), this arch is composed wholly of bone (fully ossified), thereby restricting the movement of the larynx (voice-box), retaining it close to the skull, and in turn yielding a high-pitched voice. Consequently, Small Cats, although capable of purring continuously and emitting various yowls and screams, cannot produce deeper sounds – they cannot roar.[2-4]

Conversely, in the Big Cats, one segment of the arch comprises an elastic ligament, i.e. the arch is *not* made completely of bone (incompletely ossified). Consequently, in these species the larynx is held less rigidly and thus has greater mobility, yielding more resonant, deeper voices, exemplified by the Big Cats' diagnostic and most familiar vocalization – roaring.[2-4] They also purr on occasions, but only between breaths, not in the normal continuous manner typical of the Small Cats.[2-4]

The structure of the hyoid apparatus should be of interest not only to felid anatomists and taxonomists but also to mystery cat investigators, for it enables deductions to be made regarding the basic identity of a mystery cat in the field – even when the cat in question cannot be seen. Any felid heard purring continuously in the typical manner can be confidently identified as a Small Cat, whilst any felid giving vent to full-throated roars can be identified with equal certainty as a Big Cat.

Another fundamental difference between these two felid genera is that the eye pupils of Small Cats can be contracted into vertical slits, whilst those of Big Cats (and the taxonomically perplexing cheetah) remain round in shape.[4]

In this book, usage of the terms 'Big Cat' and 'Small Cat' will be restricted to their respective scientific meanings whenever possible, and when used in this way will be printed with initial capital letters. Correspondingly, terms such as 'large', 'sizeable' and 'small' will be used when simply describing a cat's size.

Morphs, Subspecies and Coat Colour Genetics

Some animal species exhibit several strikingly different, separate

Table 2: Geological Time Appertaining to Mammals

The first mammals did not arise on Earth until the early Triassic Period, which began 23 million years ago. This marked the commencement of the Mesozoic Era – popularly referred to as the Age of Reptiles, in which the dinosaurs reigned supreme, while the mammals were small, inconspicuous creatures. By the close of the Cretaceous Period, however, the dinosaurs had died out, and the mammals had gained ascendancy. They have maintained their prominent position in the complex scheme of life on Earth ever since, so that the Cenozoic Era is referred to as the Age of Mammals.

	Era	Period	Epoch	Millions of Years Ago
Age of Mammals	Cenozoic	Quaternary	Holocene	0.01
			Pleistocene	2
		Tertiary	Pliocene	5
			Miocene	24
			Oligocene	36
			Eocene	54
			Palaeocene	65
Age of Reptiles	Mesozoic	Cretaceous		140
		Jurassic		195
		Triassic		230

morphological types all within a single interbreeding population. For example, in addition to its normal spotted form, the leopard *Panthera pardus* can produce individuals with black coats (melanistic), white coats (albinistic), red coats (erythristic) and several other coat colour types too. Such morphological types as these are termed morphs but, as they are merely genetic variants, they have no taxonomic significance and do not usually receive formal scientific names[12] (though in earlier days some morphs were mistakenly assumed to be full species). Species such as the leopard, exhibiting several morphs, are termed polymorphic.

The greater the frequency of a morph's occurrence within a population, plus the greater the number and the wider the distribution of populations containing it, the more common that morph will be; some morphs of a given species may occur over most of its distribution range. Thus morphs represent variation within individual populations, regardless of geographical locality.

Consequently, they should not be confused with subspecies. For these represent variation between collections of populations occurring in specified geographical localities. A subspecies can be defined as a collection of morphologically similar populations of a species, inhabiting a geographical subdivision of that species' total distribution range, and differ taxonomically from other populations of that species.[12] Subspecies, therefore, do have taxonomic significance and so receive formal scientific names. Thus the leopard's pale Sinai-located subspecies is called *Panthera pardus jarvisi*, its very diminutive Somali-located subspecies is *P. p. nanopardus*, its rare Barbary subspecies is *P. p. panthera* etc.

As we shall see, some mystery cats may be undiscovered subspecies (of known species). Equally, certain other mystery cats may actually be undocumented morphs (of known species); various abnormal (mutant) forms of the six principal genes[13] responsible for felid coat colouration (see Table 3) have already yielded many unusual known felid morphs (e.g. orange leopards, blue lynxes, white tigers) – which brings us to the subject of coat-colour genetics in felids.

In most cases, each of a cat's genes is represented per cell nucleus by two copies, one on each member of the specific pair of chromosomes possessing that gene. However, these two copies are not always identical, i.e. a given gene can have more than one form (allele). This can have notable consequences regarding an animal's external appearance, as demonstrated with the following examples using leopards and the agouti gene.

The pelage of a leopard possessing two copies of the agouti gene's normal (wild-type) allele exhibits the typical yellow-brown background colouration, serving to enhance its contrasting black

Table 3: Genetics of Cat Colouration

As described in full by felid geneticist Roy Robinson,[13] genetically induced mutant colour forms (morphs) in felids involve the mutant alleles of six major genes. These genes, their normal (wild-type) and mutant alleles, and the appearance of felids expressing these alleles, are as follows:

Gene	Allele	Appearance of Felid Expressing Allele
Agouti	1. wild-type	Hairs of fur each banded with yellow and black stripes, yielding grey- or gold-coloured fur – locally or widely distributed over animal.
	2. *non-agouti* (melanistic) mutant	Yellow stripes on fur hairs absent – entire animal black.
	3. *black-and-tan* mutant	Dorsal body regions black, ventral body regions pale.
Black pigmentation	1. wild-type	Animal possesses various black body regions.
	2. *brown* mutant	In combination with *non-agouti*, these body regions are brown instead of black.
Full colour	1. wild-type	Animal possesses black (eumelanin) and yellow (phaeomelanin) pigments.
	2. *chinchilla* mutant	Eumelanin present, phaeomelanin absent – animal's background body colour pale, body markings still present, eyes often blue.
	3. *acromelanic* mutant	Phaeomelanin absent, eumelanin limited to body extremities – animal very pale all over except at extremities, eyes often pink.
	4. *complete albino* mutant	Phaeomelanin and eumelanin both absent – animal totally white, eyes pink.
Dense pigmentation	1. wild-type	Normal degree of coat colour density for species concerned.
	2. *dilute* mutant	Coat colour pale – appears blue (*blue dilute*) when in combination with *non-agouti*.
Extension of black	1. wild-type	Black pigment distributed to normal degree in hairs, yielding normal fur colour for species.
	2. *non-extension of black* mutant	Black pigment's distribution restricted in hairs – fur appears red or yellow.
	3. *supra-extension of black* mutant	Black pigment excessively distributed in hairs – fur predominantly/entirely black.
Dark-eye	1. wild-type	Eye colour dark, coat colour normal.
	2. *pink-eye* mutant	Eye colour pink/red, coat colour variable but generally pale.

Other genes exist whose mutant alleles also affect felid coat colour – responsible for silvering, piebald spotting, roan colouration etc.

rosettes. Conversely, the pelage of a leopard possessing two copies of the agouti gene's mutant non-agouti allele is jet black or very dark brown, because the non-agouti allele stimulates overproduction of the black pigment eumelanin. Consequently, a black leopard's rosettes are virtually hidden amidst its pelage's abnormally dark background colouration, so that the felid initially appears to be totally black; such individuals are termed 'melanistic'. Nonetheless, their cryptic rosettes can often be discerned if observed closely and at certain angles. Melanistic leopards are popularly called black panthers.[14]

Of great interest is the fact that the pelage of a leopard possessing *one* copy of the wild-type allele plus *one* copy of the non-agouti allele exhibits wild-type (normal) colouration. This is because the wild-type allele masks the effect of the mutant non-agouti allele – the former is thus termed 'dominant' and the latter 'recessive'.

Felids with two copies of the same allele for a given gene are termed 'homozygous' for that allele; while felids with one copy of one allele and one copy of another for a given gene are termed 'heterozygous' for both alleles.

Thus, a leopard homozygous or heterozygous for the agouti gene's wild-type will be spotted, while only leopards homozygous for its non-agouti allele will be black (i.e. no leopard heterozygous for non-agouti can be black).[14]

Moreover, spotted leopards homozygous for the agouti gene's wild-type allele bred with other spotted leopards homozygous for this same allele will always produce spotted cubs. Similarly, black leopards (i.e. always homozygous for non-agouti) bred amongst themselves will (excluding further mutation) always produce black cubs.[14]

However, spotted leopards heterozygous for the agouti gene's wild-type will, when bred amongst themselves, produce some spotted cubs and some black cubs (in an approximate 3:1 ratio). The black cubs are those which have inherited a non-agouti allele from both parents, thereby lacking any wild-type allele for this gene.[14]

Certainly, cat genetics is of considerable importance relative to mystery cat identification, though, before we put too much store in this, we could do well to recall the following lines from Patrick Chalmers's poem 'The Tortoiseshell Cat':

> Every cat in the twilight's grey,
> Every possible cat.

Cryptozoological cats are certainly no exception to this!

On this and all other reference pages, locations are given except in the case of British publications.

1 Corbet, G.B., and Hill, J.E., *A World List of Mammalian Species*, second edition (Brit. Mus. Nat. Hist., 1986)

2 Denis, A., *Cats of the World* (Constable, 1964); Walker, W.F., *A Study of the Cat* (W.B. Saunders, 1967); Boorer, M., *Wild Cats* (Hamlyn, 1969); *Grzimek*, B. (ed.), *Grzimek's Animal Life Encyclopaedia*, Vol. 12 (Van Nostrand Reinhold, 1975); Ricciuti, E., *The Wild Cats* (Windward, 1979); Macdonald, D. (ed.), *The Encyclopaedia of Mammals*, Volume 1 (Allen & Unwin, 1984)

3 Savage, R.J.G., *Palaeontology*, Vol. 20, pp. 237-71 (1977)

4 Guggisberg, C.A.W., *Wild Cats of the World* (David & Charles, 1975)

5 Leyhausen, P., *Cat Behavior* (Garland, New York, 1979).

6 Lawrence, M.J., and Brown, R.W., *Mammals of Britain: Their Tracks, Trails and Signs*, revised edition (Blandford, 1973); Bang, P., and Dahlstrom, P., *Collins Guide to Animal Tracks and Signs* (Collins, 1974); Nelson, E.W., *Wild Animals of North America*, revised edition (National Geographic Society, Washington, 1930); Seton, E.T., *Animal Tracks and Hunter Signs* (Edmund Ward, 1959); Smithers, R.H.N., *Land Mammals of Southern Africa* (Macmillan, Johannesburg, 1986)

7 Tabor, R., *The Wildlife of the Domestic Cat* (Arrow Books, 1983); Gonyea, W., and Ashworth, R., *Journal of Morphology*, Vol. 145, pp. 229-38 (1975)

8 Romer, A.S., *Vertebrate Paleontology*, third edition (University of Chicago Press, Chicago, 1966); Steel, R. and Harvey, A.P., (eds.), *The Encyclopaedia of Prehistoric Life* (Mitchell Beazley, 1979)

9 Savage, R.J.G., and Long, M.R., *Mammal Evolution: An Illustrated Guide* (Brit. Mus. Nat. Hist., 1986)

10 Bryant, H.N. and Churcher, C.S., *Nature*, Vol. 325, p. 488 (5 February 1987)

11 Kurten, B., *Pleistocene Mammals of Europe* (Weidenfeld & Nicolson, 1968); Kurten, B. and Anderson, E., *Pleistocene Mammals of North America* (Columbia University Press, New York, 1980)

12 Mayr, E., *Populations, Species, and Evolution* (Belknap Press, Massachusetts, 1970); Mayr, E., *Principles of Systematic Zoology* (Tata McGraw-Hill, New Delhi, 1971)

13 Robinson, R., *Genetica*, Vol. 46, pp. 1-31 (1976); Robinson, R., *Carnivore*, Vol. 1, pp. 68-71 (1978)

14 Robinson, R., *Journal of the Bombay Natural History Society*, Vol. 66, pp. 423-9 (1970); O'Grady, R.J.P., *Proceedings of the 4th Symposium of the Association of British Wild Animal Keepers*, Vol. 4, pp. 32-41 (1979)

1 Surrey Pumas and Exmoor Beasts

Great Britain

But cats to me are strange, so strange
I never sleep if one is near;
And though I'm sure I see those eyes,
I'm not so sure a body's there.

W.H. Davies, *The Cat*

During the Pleistocene epoch, Great Britain possessed a notably diverse felid fauna. This included the cave lion *Panthera leo spelaea*,[1,2] leopard *P. pardus*,[1,2] Owen's panther *P. pardoides*,[2] European jaguar *P. gombaszögensis*,[3] Martelli's wildcat *Felis lunensis*,[1,2] common wildcat *F. silvestris*,[1,2] and northern lynx *F. lynx*,[1,2], plus the greater and lesser scimitar cats *Homotherium sainzelli* and *H. latidens* respectively.[1,2] Furthermore, remains of a leopard-like felid provisionally labelled *Panthera aff. pardus* have recently been discovered at Pontnewydd Cave, North Wales.[4] Out of all of these species, however, only one survived into historic times here – the common wildcat, nowadays confined to Scotland. In addition, populations of feral (run-wild) domestic cats *F. catus* exist throughout the UK.

This is the *official* history of Britain's felids. The *unofficial* version is rather different.

Many descriptions and sightings have been reported from all parts of the UK concerning a wide variety (judging at least from the diversity of eyewitness accounts) of felids alive and well in its countryside but allegedly much larger than any wildcat. Since the beginning of the 1960s, Britain's multitude of mystery cats has attracted ever-increasing attention from the media and from cryptozoological researchers, but we should begin our examination of this subject by looking at various accounts which pre-date (sometimes very considerably) the 1960s.

Pre-1960s Evidence

Though a Pleistocene inhabitant of England and Wales, the cave lion did not appear to reach Scotland, and in any event it died out entirely in the UK some 40,000-50,000 years ago, according to fossil evidence. Hence it must be somewhat disconcerting to palaeontologists to learn that the sixteenth-century chronicler Ralph Holinshed wrote: 'Lions we have had many in the north parts of Scotland, and those with manes of no less force than those of Mauretania; but how and when they were destroyed as yet I do not read.'[5]

As recognized by writers Anthony Dent and Michael Goss, worthy of mention in connection with British mystery cats is the eighteenth-century poem 'Black Annis'. Its mythical subject – an ill-defined witch-like creature – possessed notable talons and a tendency to leap down from the overhanging branches of an oak tree onto victims passing beneath, and suck their blood. As Dent and Goss suggest, this could perhaps be taken as an anthropomorphic description of some felid form; worth noting is that in later legends 'Black Annis' became known as 'Cat Annis'.[6,7]

Though superficially dubious, that item acquires greater potential as a result of this next example. During the spring of 1810, flocks of sheep all over Ennerdale Water in Cumberland were being slaughtered by an elusive but ferocious beast which became known as the Ennerdale or Girt Dog; rather surprisingly (in view of this name), it was never heard to bark.[8] Moreover, it exhibited the rather macabre, non-canid behaviour of biting into its prey's jugular vein and sucking the blood (comparable with another mystery sanguivore reported from Cavan, Ireland, in 1784[9]). The Girt 'Dog' was sighted many times throughout the spring and summer of 1810 and hunted frequently but without success, until a dog supposedly identified as this bizarre beast was cornered and shot dead on 12 September. Its body was preserved and displayed for a time at a museum in Keswick but has since been lost.[8] Though it was generally classed as a dog, eyewitness Will Rotherby – who was actually knocked over by the creature whilst it was escaping from a hunting party, and who therefore probably saw it at closer range than anyone else – remained convinced that the animal which he observed was not a dog, but a lion-like cat.[10]

In *Rural Rides* (Volume 1),[11] William Cobbett described a visit which he made with his son on 27 October 1825 or thereabouts to Waverley Abbey. Whilst there, Cobbett showed his son: '... a very old elm tree, which was hollow even then, into which I, when a very little boy [he was born in 1762] once saw a cat go that was as big as a middle-sized spaniel dog, for relating which I got a great scolding, for standing to which I at last got a beating; but stand to which I still did. ... When in New Brunswick I saw the great wild grey cat which is there called a Lucifee; and it seemed to me to be just such a cat as I had seen at Waverley.'[11]

Waverley being in the very centre of Surrey, it would be very tempting to presume that the lucifee is, in fact, the puma, which in Cobbett's day was indeed well established in New Brunswick, Nova Scotia. In truth, however, 'lucifee' is apparently a corruption of 'Loup Cervier', a term used throughout Nova Scotia and also New England from the late eighteenth century onwards for the North American lynx *F. lynx canadensis*.[7] Nevertheless, if Cobbett's identification was correct, a *lynx* sighted in Surrey 200 years ago is still very worthy of note!

One of the most remarkable pre-1960s mystery cat episodes from the UK took place in 1927 and was featured in a detailed account published by the *Daily Express* on 14 January of that year.[12] On account of a series of sheep kills in Inverness, Scotland, plus sightings made there of an animal 'like a leopard, but without spots on its coat' and the discovery of 'tracks like those of a gigantic cat', a steel trap had been set by one alarmed farmer. Upon checking it the next morning, he was stunned to discover that it had snared a 'large fierce yellow animal', which he promptly shot and sent to London Zoo for identification. It was found to be a lynx! Moreover, according to the newspaper report, two other lynxes had been shot in this same area during this same period. No clue was given as to the whereabouts of these specimens, whilst, with regard to their equally perplexing origin, the report could only offer the opinion that '... they must have escaped from some travelling menagerie.'[12] The final twist to this tantalizing tale is that, according to London Zoo's senior veterinary officer, Dr James Kirkwood, the zoo has no record of ever having received such a creature at that time (Kirkwood, pers. comm.).

On 19 March 1938 *The Field* published a letter from Irene Roberts of Lightwater, Surrey, in which she related that she had frequently heard some very strange cries that she was unable to associate with any known form of animal in the area. She described them, when heard at 2 a.m. in July 1937, as being '... of peculiar intensity, expressing, it seemed, mortal fear and physical pain', continuing for about ten minutes and '... punctuated by a queer half-snoring, half-purring sound, produced by something probably considerably larger than a cat'. On a later occasion, this time at 1.30 a.m., '... they seemed to be something between a bark and a scream, and did not appear to be produced from anything of the shape of a beak. They seemed to begin with a B. B'yow!

B'yow! long drawn-out, and penetrating. ...' It lasted for about five minutes, periodically yielding a crescendo.[13]

Irene Roberts' letter stimulated much ensuing correspondence in *The Field*, with suggested identities as diverse as badgers, foxes, otters, owls, domestic cats and even lovestruck hedgehogs! Little did anyone realize, of course, that this very location would soon become the centre of a hunt for a certain felid whose screaming cries fit Irene Roberts's above-noted description very closely indeed. Namely the puma. Just a coincidence? Equally interesting is the fact that puma sightings were being reported from Surrey during the 1940s but received little notice, due to the weightier events of World War II. Yet by the end of the 1960s the Surrey puma saga had become one of the most famous mystery animal cases of all.

In all the following accounts from the 1960s onwards of so-called 'pumas', 'cheetahs', 'panthers', 'lionesses', 'lynxes' etc, quotation marks should be understood, as in most cases no conclusive evidence to confirm the taxonomic status of these animals has yet been obtained. In addition, so many mystery cat cases have emerged from Great Britain during this period that it would be quite impossible to provide anything approaching a comprehensive coverage within a single chapter. Instead, I have sought to provide a selected coverage which concentrates upon those episodes that have proved to be of greatest importance and interest and which have offered the most significant clues relative to the identities of the animals featured in them. To supplement this, I heartily recommend *Alien Animals* by Janet and Colin Bord,[14] *Mystery Animals of Britain and Ireland* by Graham McEwan[15] and the excellent series of mystery cat updates by Robert Rickard and others which appear regularly in *Fortean Times*.

The Shooters Hill Cheetah and Surrey Puma

The first British mystery cat to attract widespread media attention in the early 1960s was a long-limbed, cheetah-like cat with a lengthy, upward-curling tail, sighted on the roadside in the area of Shooters Hill, Woolwich, by lorry-driver David Back at 1 a.m. on 18 July 1963. It moved off into the nearby woods as he approached and, despite a well-manned police search of the area following later sightings, evaded all attempts to capture it – though it made its presence felt very effectively, by audaciously leaping over the bonnet of one of the police cars. In addition, tracks were discovered in the soft mud leading down the path of a dried-up woodland stream; they measured several inches across and were recognizably different from those of the police alsatians. Moreover, they bore the clear impression of claws.[16] Cheetahs *habitually* leave clawed prints, which would therefore support the cheetah identity for this mystery cat – except for the fact that clawed prints are also associated with many other UK mystery cat cases involving felids which do not look anything like cheetahs.

Following the unsuccessful cheetah hunt, some snarls and sightings were reported during the next few days, but by August Shooters Hill's strange visitor had apparently moved on, as it was not reported again (though sightings of shorter-legged, puma-like beasts would be documented from various Kentish localities in future years).[16]

Moreover, on the media front, the Shooters Hill cheetah's disappearance was itself eclipsed by a puma of sorts – an unidentified felid destined to become known worldwide as 'the Surrey puma'.

At about 7.45 a.m. on 16 July 1962, whilst Mid-Wessex Water Board official Ernest Jellett was cycling down a wooded path leading to Heathy Park Reservoir, he observed a rabbit being stalked by a most unusual animal, one which he felt certain was neither fox nor dog. Instead, he considered it to be not unlike a young lion, with a flat face, large paws, pale-brown pelage and a height of 18-24 in/45-60 cm. As he watched, it pounced at the rabbit but missed, and then bounded up towards Jellett himself, who, understandably apprehensive, shouted at it and succeeded in scaring it away.[15]

During the winter of 1962-3, a variety of odd cat-like beasts of predominantly nocturnal nature made several visits to Bushylease Farm, between Crondall and Ewshot. According to manager Edward Blanks, such visits were usually accompanied by a strong ammonia-like smell and yowling cries, and left the farm dogs terrified. He described one such felid as being alsatian-sized and sandy-brown in colour, with a cat's head and long tail. Eighteen months later, events here took a more sinister turn. On 30 August 1964, a 4 cwt/203 kg Friesian bullock on the farm was discovered badly mauled, though still alive, bearing severe lacerations on its flanks, shoulders and neck. Ministry of Agriculture officials who later examined this animal claimed that the wounds had been made by barbed wire, and identified strange red pellet-like objects found in the vicinity of the bullock as clots of congealed blood. Conversely, a vet called in to see the bullock favoured an animal assailant as the originator of the wounds, but not one of any species native to Britain. Furthermore, whilst lying in wait for the mystery animal on subsequent nights, Blanks found more 'blood clots' on the ground – and this time there was no victim from which they could have originated. The elusive predator itself, meanwhile, maintained its low profile.[14,15]

During the remainder of 1964, puma pandemonium not only filled Surrey but also spilled over into neighbouring counties, with dozens of reports emerging during the last months. Notable amongst these were: a short-legged beast with a cat-like face, dirty-brown or golden pelage, large paws, a height of 3 ft/90 cm and a total length exceeding 5ft/150 cm, sighted by blackberry-picker George Wisdom near Munstead's water tower, Surrey (4 September); a large unidentified creature that left behind gigantic clawed spoor measuring 5¼ in/13 cm in diameter near some riding-stables at Munstead (7 September); a dead roe deer with broken neck and wounds compatible with a felid killing discovered at Cranleigh, Surrey (23 September); a puma-like cat sighted by two policemen at the Thomas Grey memorial at Stoke Poges, Bucks (12 November); and a similar cat sighted at Nettlebed in Oxfordshire (20 November) and at Ewhurst in Surrey (15 December). And frequent reports of spine-chilling screams and growls were recorded from Surrey and its environs during periods of puma activity.[17-20] By then, using Godalming's station as headquarters, the Surrey police were compiling a puma-sightings book, carrying out frequent searches and consulting numerous wildlife experts in an all-out attempt to solve the mystery of Surrey's cryptic cougar. Victor Manton, curator of Whipsnade Zoo, made several forays into Surrey puma country armed with a tranquillizer-bearing rifle, and although he never cornered his quarry, he did come across a roe deer whose neck had been broken (an act requiring a very sizeable predator). He also collected hairs from a barbed-wire fence through which a puma-like animal had allegedly passed; the hairs were later found to compare closely with those from the tail-tip of a puma.[21]

Little happened during 1965, but sightings returned with a vengeance in 1966, of which the following were especially significant. 4 July saw a classic encounter at Worplesdon, Surrey, when a puma-like cat stalked and killed a rabbit in full view of police and villager witnesses watching from 100 yards/91 m away and for a full 20 minutes.[22] It was described as being ginger-brown in colour, and the size of a labrador, with a cat-like face. Curiously, its tail was tipped with white – a puma's is normally black-tipped, like the hairs discovered two years earlier by Victor Manton. Worth noting, however, is that black hairs can sometimes be replaced by white ones following an injury (such as a tail-tip being trapped on barbed wire?). In early August 1966 ex-police photographer Ian Pert actually succeeded in taking a photograph of a strange cat at a distance of only 35 yards/32 m – again sighted at Worplesdon. This animal had a small feline head, a muscular body (especially the hindquarters), a rather thick tail measuring 13 in/32.5 cm, a sandy-coloured pelage, and a total length of about 3 ft/90 cm.[23] Two months later, another photograph was taken of a mystery cat – this time at Upper Hale, but it appears to have been lost, with no details concerning it having been recorded.[15]

Encouraged by these recent sightings, providing positive proof of the existence of at least one strange Surrey felid (E.J. Rogers had noted earlier that puma sightings had actually been reported on both sides of the Thames at much the same time, thereby suggesting the existence of at least *two* such animals,[24] but one was more than enough for most investigators), further police searches were mounted at the end of August and October, but once again all in vain.[17] Moreover, though it was apparently fond of deer and rabbits, no evidence had been collected to indicate that it posed any threat to humans – quite the reverse in fact, judging from its evident desire and ability to elude them.

Consequently, in mid-August 1967 the Surrey police formally terminated their investigations. The great Surrey Puma Hunt – which had given rise between September 1964 and August 1966 alone to 362 formally listed sightings and many more claimed but not officially declared[20] – was over, which in turn has since led to a fall in this mystery beast's public profile. Indeed, this may well have fuelled the rumour prevalent at the close of the 1960s that the Surrey puma had been shot by a farmer and then buried without publicity on his lands because he did not have a license for his gun.[15] Similarly, a fox shot in daylight near one of the mystery cat's known haunts in Surrey's Ash Ranges in February 1970 was 'identified' as the puma.[17] The recurrence of puma sightings in this and other localities within (and beyond) Surrey's county border soon afterwards, however, quelled both of the above attempts to end the mystery.

Indeed, sightings have continued right up to the present day. A significant footnote: While compiling an impressive dossier of records concerning a tawny puma-like beast frequently reported from various Cornish localities during the 1980s, Exeter based zoologist Dr Frank Turk learned of a strange feline animal sighted in August 1984 near the Surrey village of Peaslake. Hair samples had been collected and were passed on to him. After subjecting them to exhaustive microscopical analyses to discover their owner's identity, Dr Turk announced to the media in January 1985 that they were from a puma. He also stated that he was '… absolutely certain these animals are living wild in Britain', and his find was considered by the British Museum to be 'very exciting'.[25] Respectability at last for the Surrey puma?

Its disappearance from national headlines in 1967 created a mystery cat hiatus which was to last for almost a decade. By this, I do not mean that mystery cat sightings were not being made. Far from it. Hertfordshire and Hampshire, for example, played host to many reports of such animals between 1971 and 1973, including a dog-sized, long-tailed creature with large paws, grey-brown pelage and (according to one eyewitness) 'an ugly cat-like face', that leapt out of a tree to chase a dog (Farnborough, 25 May 1971); a grey cat roughly 2ft/60 cm high described as puma-like by its police eyewitnesses (near St Albans, 15 July 1971); a sturdy brown cat lacking markings, standing 2ft/60 cm high, with large paws and a long tail curving upwards at its tip (Aldershot's Fleet Station, August-September 1972 – amazingly, this felid was ultimately 'explained' as a pet Siamese cat); a tawny brown cat larger than an alsatian, with sizeable head and pricked ears, compared with a puma illustration by its boy eyewitnesses (New Forest, September 1972); and an animal described by its police observers at less than 30 yards/30 m away as being 'the same size and colour as a puma', with pointed ears and long tail (Farnborough, 19 June 1973).[14,17,26]

Breaking the monopoly (and monotony) of puma sightings, a large *black* feline beast was sighted one evening in late April 1971 near Surrey's Road Research Laboratory at Crowthorne; the tail of a huge but similarly pantheresque cat (with short head and long but low-slung body) was hit by a car whilst it was running in front of the vehicle along the A35 from Christchurch to Lyndhurst, Hants (January 1973); and a large black felid also ran in front of a car on the Rake-Harting Combe road, Hants, on 3 November 1973.[26] Yet, although the stories were of local interest, the national media were not impressed – until the coming of the Nottingham lioness in 1976. It is noteworthy that that year saw the beginning of a marked increase in the number, diversity and geographical distribution of British mystery cat reports – a trend maintained in all subsequent years.

Nottingham Lioness, Glenfarg Lynx and Others

In late July 1976 two milkmen were rather taken aback to see a large beast that they unhesitatingly identified as a lioness (they specifically recalled that the tip of its tail was tufted, a diagnostic feature of *Panthera leo*) walking round the edge of a field at Tollerton, Nottingham. Other sightings followed, large pawprints were reportedly spied in various local inhabitants' gardens, and on 31 July the mysterious felid visited the garden of Nottingham's deputy coroner, Dr John Chisholm, of Normanton-on-the-Wold. Like the milkmen, he noted in particular that its tail was identical to that of a lioness. The police were called at once, but as their cars drew near, Dr Chisholm's wife saw the animal move away, probably frightened by the vehicles' headlights. By 6 August the number of sightings had risen to sixty-five but still unaccompanied by any clue regarding the creature's origin or current location. Animals which *were* tracked down turned out to be large dogs – and in one incident a particularly large, dark-coloured carrier-bag! Finally the police made a formal statement to the effect that the Nottingham lioness was truly nothing more than a large dog, and the case was officially closed. The fact that no large dog (and certainly no large carrier-bag!) resembles a lioness did not appear to attract much attention.[27]

Let us move from England to Scotland and from the leonine to the lynx-like. On the evening of 9 August 1976, an inhabitant of Glenfarg, Perthshire, walked into her garden to find out why her terrier was barking – and discovered a 3ft/90 cm-high feline beast crouching on top of her garden wall, spitting and snarling at her. The two features which caught her attention most of all were its 'burning orange' eyes and its ears – which were long and pointed, with tufts at their tips. As she cautiously retraced her steps, with terrier carried aloft, towards her open door, her unexpected visitor leapt down onto the ground beyond her garden and made its exit through the bordering fields.[14,28]

Mystery cats sighted elsewhere in Britain that year included a lioness-like beast at Skegness,[10] a puma-like creature at Nuneaton[7] and an elusive felid at Blantyre.[7] Intermittently reported through 1976 and 1977 were the Bettyhill/Skerray beast and the North Berwick puma,[7,29] supplanted during 1978 by the Conon Bridge lioness (so called because eyewitness Helen Fitch of Bishop Kinkell considered it to be very similar to animals she had seen whilst living in Africa).[29]

In 1979 a photograph was taken of a black panther-like felid seen in Ayrshire, but Glasgow Zoo officials felt that it was merely a large domestic cat.[15]

Pumas were rife throughout 1979 and 1980 and provided some significant reports. In a letter to Graham McEwan, J.M. Jenkins recalled that in the summer of 1979 he had observed a felid in Midlothian at a range of 6ft/1.8 m, which had a black bar crossing its face and pelage the colour of a golden labrador, and which appeared to be pregnant. Yet it was not aggressive – in contrast, it seemed rather curious about Jenkins' activities (he was using a metal-detector at the time). Jenkins affirmed that it was identical in appearance to the pumas at Edinburgh Zoo.[15]

In the summer of 1980, Wolverhampton became the unlikely venue for a puma-hunt. A number of closely corresponding eyewitness descriptions confirmed that the mystery cat in question was a brown, unspotted felid the size of a large dog, with a round head, pricked ears, long tail and shortish limbs, most closely resembling a puma. Yet, despite repeated searches by police and Dudley Zoo curator Mike Williams, who had caught sight of it himself by 25 July, the beast of the Black Country remained uncaptured and, in the best mystery cat traditions, eventually vanished without trace.[30]

The Cannich Puma and Wonders from Wales

On 27 October 1979 farmer Edward Noble saw a lioness-like animal stalking ponies on his farm, near Cannich, Inverness-shire. He reported it to the police, also mentioning that livestock had been disappearing inexplicably from his farm for more than a year. The police organized a search of the area but found nothing. Over the next twelve months, Noble continued to see large cat-like beasts and to lose livestock – especially sheep, but, even though other locals by now were reporting strange beasts too, he failed to engender sufficient interest for another search. So in desperation he decided to solve the mystery himself – by erecting a specially constructed steel cage near his farm and baiting it each day with fresh meat. When he inspected it with his son on 29 October 1980, he discovered that he had at last obtained the evidence which he had sought for so long – 5ft/150 cm of furry evidence that snarled and spat at him. For his cage contained an adult female puma.[31] Mr Noble's claims had been vindicated – or had they?

When the puma was examined by wildlife experts (including Highland Wildlife Park director Edward Orbell and vet George Rafferty), she was found to be aged, arthritic and atrociously tame, even allowing her visitors to tickle her ears. Hardly the ferocious sheep-slaughterer that everyone had envisaged! More like a pet recently released into the wild – the opinion, in fact, of a number of wildlife authorities.[31] Had Noble been the victim of a hoax, perhaps of deliberate intent to make him appear foolish, or simply through some opportunist's using his cage and reports of strange cats in the area as a perfect cover for letting loose an unwanted exotic pet? In favour of Noble's belief that the puma had genuinely been in the wild for some considerable time, however, was Dr Hans Kruuk of Banchory's Institute of Terrestrial Ecology, basing his belief upon analyses that he had carried out on two of the puma's faecal droppings within hours of her capture. For one of these was composed almost entirely of deer remains, the other of sheep – exactly what one would have expected from a puma in such surroundings for an extensive period.[31]

Nevertheless, some authorities remained – and remain – sceptical. As for the puma herself – soon named Felicity, she spent the remainder of her life comfortably at the Highland Wildlife Park, dying peacefully of old age in February 1985 and leaving behind the riddle of her origin still unsolved.[32]

Curiously, sightings of a puma on the loose in the Cannich area continued to be reported long after Felicity's capture. (There are even claims that a puma colony exists in the remote Guisachan Forest![33]) Perhaps more than one mystery cat had been responsible for the farmstock disappearances (at one stage, the police were actually investigating a rumour that a prisoner at Winchester had released two pumas into the Highlands before being gaoled in 1979, but nothing substantial emerged from this[34]). Alternatively, as Felicity's critics would aver, perhaps the *real* feline culprit has yet to be captured.

While Scotland was being confused by the Cannich puma, Wales was being perplexed by 'the Powys beast'. On 23 October 1980 – just a month after a lynx-like beast had been sighted near Churchstone, Powys, by a district nurse[35] – farmer Michael Nash of Llangurig, Powys, heard strange snoring sounds emanating from some bales of straw in his barn. Being mindful of the fact that four of his sheep had recently been killed in a manner unlike earlier dog kills, and having observed a large spoor just outside the barn, he contacted the police. They surrounded the barn and kept watch all night, but when they entered the barn the next morning, they found nothing. Nonetheless, even though the beast seemed to have dematerialized, the spoor had not. Almost 5 in/12.5 cm long, it possessed a relatively small plantar pad and four elongate toe pads (each of which terminated in a claw), yielding in overall shape a long, rather than rounded footprint – totally unlike that of a lynx or indeed any other felid.[35]

Also in Wales, November 1981 saw considerable activity on the felid front in the small village of Tonmawr, as documented in Di Francis' *Cat Country*.[36] A large grey cat was seen by various villagers and was photographed at long distance by Steven Joyce – the resulting picture sadly revealing little detail, however, except for a white throat contrasting with the animal's otherwise darker pelage.[36] Conversely, by setting up bait in his garden, Joyce succeeded in photographing at close range one of two smaller cats (referred to as 'cubs' in Francis' book) seen earlier by local councillor Howell Britton in company with the larger felid.[36]

The photos depicted the 'cub' standing on its hindlegs and stretching upwards as it retained its grip on the suspended bait with its forepaws, thereby accentuating its long, slender outline. Judging from a photo published alongside this one in *Cat Country*, depicting a black domestic cat in the same position at the same location, the Tonmawr cat seemed slightly larger in absolute size but of comparable relative body proportions. Moreover, its combination of silver-grey pelage marked laterally with blotches of varying size and transverse stripes, its striped limbs, ringed tail, white chest and lower jaw, plus pale paws[36] corresponded very closely to the morphology of blotched domestic tabbies. During this period, Francis visited Tonmawr herself and photographed a large all-black beast measuring about 4ft/120 cm in length, judging from a scale given in her book.[36] Regrettably, as noted by Graham McEwan, the great distance between cat and camera does not permit any positive identification of the animal to be made.[15] Blood-curdling screams frequently emanated from the surrounding mountains during this spate of sightings, and as a final twist to the Tonmawr tale, in spring 1982 Francis took a cast of a print almost 5 in/12.5 cm long and wide, found in mud there and seemingly left behind by a black panther-like cat. A photograph reveals that it contained four clear claw-marks and a pair of toe pads (the back pair) whose two members differed in size from one another.[36]

Other mystery cat reports during 1981-2 included a puma at Fobbing, a cheetah at Brighton and another puma at Ilkeston;[7] and 1983 saw the début of the Isle of Wight on the mystery cat front, offering eyewitness accounts of panthers, pumas and even an occasional lynx.[37,38]

The Beasts of Exmoor

Apparently incorporating quite a variety of different carnivore types, the saga of the Exmoor Beast(s) is without doubt the most complex and significant of all British mystery cat cases. And since the end of 1986 very important new evidence from several different sources has been obtained regarding Beast identities. Yet much of this has never been included in any cryptozoological book. Consequently, in order to document it below, while concomitantly preventing this section from becoming disproportionately long, the earlier exploits of the Beasts (already extensively documented in a number of previous publications) are represented here via a concise summary of those most integral incidents. For further details concerning early Beast history, I strongly recommend the accounts provided by Graham McEwan,[15] Robert Rickard[38,39] and, especially, Trevor Beer (the leading Exmoor Beast investigator and author of the invaluable booklet *The Beast of Exmoor: Fact or Legend?*[40]).

Sightings of jet-black panther-like animals on Dartmoor and at Tedburn St Mary (between Dartmoor and Exmoor) have been occurring for some considerable time and have been reported spasmodically by the media since the beginning of the 1980s.[41] Conversely, the unexplained losses of several lambs during spring 1982 from Drewstone Farm, owned by Eric Ley of South Molton, Exmoor, and rumours of a similarly pantheresque creature having been seen in the area, somehow attracted little attention. And so, when news broke regarding dramatic events taking place in the very same location, but this time during April 1983, as far as the media were concerned the Exmoor Beast saga appeared to have sprung into existence Athena-style – fully formed and fully armed.

Local and national newspapers revealed that, between the beginning of the 1983 lambing season and 15 April of that year, Eric Ley had lost no fewer than thirty lambs (one almost every evening) to some unknown predator, and that other farmers had also suffered losses. Searches by the police and locals failed to discover the culprit; several dogs suspected of the killings were shot, but the killings continued. The method which Exmoor's mysterious slaughterer – soon nicknamed 'the Beast' – adopted was to crush the skull of its lamb victim between its jaws or to break the neck and then eviscerate the victim from the neck downwards, leaving its skeleton virtually untouched.[39,42]

By May, the situation had become so serious that Royal Marines stationed at Lympstone were called in, bringing along their infra-red searching-equipment and digging camouflage trenches for all-night monitoring of the South Molton region. At 5.35 a.m. on 4 May, Marine sniper John Holden saw a very large and powerful all-black creature cross a railway line some distance away. Holden declined to shoot, as a farmhouse was sited directly behind it; also, the Marines' primary instruction was to capture the Beast alive if at all possible.[39,43]

Throughout the Marines' stay on Exmoor, an interesting paradox prevailed: while Beast sightings made by local inhabitants generally suggested a large felid (supported by the frequent sounding out of high-pitched cat-like screams in the area at night), the Marines and police pursued the belief that it was a dog – and offered dog fur found at kills plus spoor identified as canid in support of this. So who was right? Quite possibly everyone, for Major John Watkins, in charge of the Marines' endeavours, ultimately stated that there might be *two* animals at large and commented that he had been informed of rumours concerning a possible puma in the area.[39,44]

A reward of £1,000, offered on 7 May by the *Daily Express* for the first unpublished photo of the Beast,[45] was criticized by police and the Marines as a potential danger (encouraging people to enter an area already besieged by gun-toting officials and locals) and ultimately resulted in the Marines formally withdrawing[39] – though by popular demand they secretly returned on 17 May for a second surveillance period.[46]

The police continued to popularize a canid identity for the Beast, even holding a canine identity parade to illustrate the kind of dog (a dark-coloured lurcher type[47]) that they felt was involved – but locals continued to see dogs *and* panthers.[39,48]

In early July the Marines pulled out again, confessing defeat and utter bewilderment at the uncanny cunning which their quarry had shown, eluding their every move with calculated ease;[49] such extreme elusiveness seemed to favour a feline rather than a canine identity. During the remainder of July, reports of sheep killings seemed to be on the wane – and on 29 July the police announced that the Beast was dead, a proclamation hastily forgotten when killings bearing the hallmarks of its mode of operation began again in August![50] And by now, ideas concerning its identity had greatly proliferated – from a rogue dog, wolf or puma to a panther, an eagle or even a laboratory-created escapee.[51] A radio listener known only as 'Bob' even claimed that the Beast was a black bear which he had killed three weeks earlier and had buried on Molland Common near South Molton! The police were reported to be following up this story, but it was ultimately denounced as a hoax.[52]

Two local naturalists who have been investigating the Exmoor Beast case from its very beginning have their own hypotheses. Nigel Brierley favours a mutant race of feral domestics of abnormally large size. In contrast, Trevor Beer believes that, although large-sized cats of some type *are* being sighted, they are not responsible for the actual killings, suggesting instead that these are the work of big dogs.[40] Though differing on the subject of the Beast's identity, Beer and Brierley are united in their conviction that more than one individual of large cat is present, both men having filed eyewitness accounts of such beasts that were made far apart in location but at virtually the same time. Moreover, during 1984 Trevor Beer had revealed that not *all* mystery cat sightings on Exmoor were of black animals; as many as twenty per cent of the reports which he had gathered described fawn-coated felids resembling pumas.[53] During this same year, he announced that he had learnt of the existence of a cache of a number of deer carcases within a broadleaved wood on Exmoor; one carcase which he examined and which had not fully decomposed had a gaping hole at the neck base but bore no other sign of wounding. What had killed these deer? Poachers would not have left venison to rot, and water samples taken for analysis were shown not to contain toxins. Trevor Beer revisited the site several times and was intrigued to note that his dog was always agitated there.[40] On his sixth visit, he came face to face with what may well have been the answer to both of these anomalies.

Whilst crossing a stream, he observed the head and shoulders of a large jet-black animal emerge out of some bushes nearby. The head seemed almost otter-like – sleek and broad with small ears, raised above a thickset neck, deep chest and powerful forelegs. Suddenly it turned away and moved swiftly through the trees; its gait reminded Beer of a greyhound's, its forelimbs pushing through the hindlimbs. Seen in its entirety, it resembled a large black panther, long in the body and tail. Beer estimated its body length at 4½ ft/135 cm, its shoulder height at about 2 ft/60 cm, and its weight at 80-120 lb/36-54 kg.[40,54]

Also noteworthy from Exmoor in 1984 were sightings of wildcat-like felids during the spring at Holcombe near Dawlish, estimated by eyewitnesses to be twice the size of normal domestic cats.[38] And in July, whilst conducting an ornithological field-trip at Cloutsham on Exmoor, Trevor Beer and seven members of his tour watched a family of very large tabby-like cats (two adults, two juveniles) at Stoke Ridge; Beer noted that their markings were all vertical and that their tails were bushier than those of normal domestics. The family eventually moved off into the edge of Horner Woods.[55]

1985 saw more panther and puma reports, and in November Nigel Brierley announced that fur identical to that of feral domestic cats had been found at a sheep kill from 1983 and again on barbed wire through which a possible sheep-assailant had passed just prior to another killing. He had also noted the presence at some killings of a very strong odour reminiscent of brussels sprouts.[40,56] November was also the month in which the Exmoor Beast doubled its media exposure, with newspapers recording the fact that sightings were now being made of two black cat-like beasts prowling the east moor *together*, leaving behind two sets of tracks.[57] And December saw the Beast gain – and lose – a new identity. 'Experts' identified a large spoor discovered near an Exmoor out-house as that of a bear-like non-British relative of weasels called the wolverine – until Trevor Beer pointed out that, whereas a wolverine's spoor always possessed five distinct toe prints, the out-house example exhibited only four.[58] Exit the wolverine.

Puma and panther sightings continued to emerge all through 1986 (together with some sheep kills reputedly similar to those of the nefarious 1983 outbreak), but this year was most notable for reports of yet another felid form on Exmoor – the lynx. In January the Mugleston family spotted a creature near Muddiford whose pointed ears reminded them of a lynx; at the same time, their description of its tail as 'bushy' is not suggestive of the short, slim tail characterizing these felids.[59] More substantial was the announcement in November by Nigel Brierley that hairs found at a sheep kill had been formally identified as those of a lynx,[60] and in an article published by the *West Briton* in December, Dr Frank Turk openly favoured the likelihood of this species' existence in Britain.[61] Also noteworthy is that a brown spaniel-sized cat with a short tail and notably tufted, pointed ears was sighted at close range by fourteen-year-old Marcus Matthews and his mother whilst driving through the Mendips; sadly, a photo taken of the creature (which had reminded them of a North American bobcat) as it bounded away captured only a small portion of its back (Matthews, pers. comm.).

In January 1987 nine pawprints (each about 3 in/7 cm in diameter and also in length) discovered by Trevor Beer at Muddiford were considered by zoologist Dr Steven Harris to be definitely feline and consistent with those of a wildcat or lynx.[62,63] This was soon followed by an equally significant revelation – the positive identification of a puma hair from Exmoor.[64] After four years of anecdotal evidence, the much-needed physical proof for the existence of large cats here was finally surfacing! The lynx form continued to stay in the news too – a sighting of one such beast was reported by two eyewitnesses at Tarr Steps in late January, with further observations coming from Cloutsham and from Malmsmead on the River Oare during late spring. In one of these latter incidents, the spaniel-sized felid in question was actually sighted carrying a rabbit in its jaws.[55]

1987 also saw its fair share of puma and (especially) panther reports. Notable amongst the latter were sightings of a huge black felid near Muddiford in mid-March and a similar (or the same?) creature in the Dunster deer park area (later implicated in sheep kills within this region and hunted by a search-party – though not discovered).[55,65] But at the August Bank Holiday the panther saga entered a new and most significant phase, for one such animal was not only seen by Trevor Beer and three other witnesses but actually photographed. Beer estimated that it was about 100 yards/91 m away when he took his nine photos, using a hand-held 300 mm Pentacon lens on a Praktica MTL50. They show a large black beast with rather small head and powerful limbs; Beer estimated its length to be 4-4½ ft/120-135 cm, and its shoulder height at 2 ft/60 cm. Though it is not possible to identify the creature positively from the photos themselves, Trevor Beer and his companions were able to observe the creature in detail as it stalked and caught a rabbit, and had no doubts that it was a large panther-like cat and not a dog.[55,66] One of the photos was published in a *BBC Wildlife* report;[66] another one appears in this book. Trevor Beer has so far not released publicly any details of the precise locality of his sightings; hence, in deference to his wishes, I shall refrain from doing so here.

For several years Trevor Beer has been compiling a detailed map of black mystery cat sightings from Exmoor, recording all of those which were made in good viewing-conditions over a decent period of observation and in which the eyewitness concerned was certain that the creature itself was a cat and not a dog. In addition, he has marked most of these sightings with the month and year in which they have occurred.[55] As I discovered when Trevor Beer very kindly lent it to me for inspection, the scatter of sighting-points in relation to the months in which they had taken place clearly demonstrated that the cats underwent a seasonal migratory passage across Exmoor, which began and ended in the same location each year and which appeared to follow the movements across the moors of the deer; statistical analyses which I carried out on the scatter of the points in relation to their months confirmed a marked migratory pattern. This is the first time that a British mystery cat's movements have been plotted in such detail as this, providing a very significant insight into the creatures' behavioural patterns – for which Trevor Beer should be highly commended. He will release full details concerning his map in a future report.

1988 opened spectacularly with a close-up photo of a large black creature claimed by the person who took it – a mysterious, unidentified figure known only as 'the Jungle Man' – to be the infamous Exmoor Beast. The photo was published on the front page of the *Mid Devon Star* on 1 January, having been brought to the newspaper's attention by recent Beast eyewitness Peter Bailey of Colliepriest Farm Bungalow.[67] It depicted a sturdy, all-black animal the size of a large dog, with quite narrow (but not long) limbs and a relatively large head bearing pricked, pointed ears. The head's precise shape could not be discerned, as it merged into the equally dark pelage of the animal's shoulders and back. Thus it was not possible conclusively to identify the animal. A panther identity cannot be ruled out but the prominent muzzle provided the head with a strongly canine mien (though this might be due simply to the angle at which the photo was taken – the total blackness of the animal greatly hinders visual analysis). Another problem with this photo is its complete absence of background – making any attempt at placing its location quite impossssible.[68]

By the end of January, police were investigating a series of Shetland lamb killings at Ovis Farm, near Bratton Fleming; thirty lambs had been killed over the past two months – and all to the same pattern. One night the predator responsible would kill and eat half of the carcase; on the next night it would return and consume the remainder (leaving behind only the fleece). Automatically, the Beast was blamed, but Trevor Beer felt that a large dog rather than a large felid was most likely to be the culprit.[69,70] And certainly, it is only too easy to blame a mysterious, unidentified animal for such events rather than look for a more commonplace answer.

This was demonstrated well by a later incident. At the end of January, a day-old-foal was discovered with its throat torn out in a Muddiford field.[71] As usual, the Beast was immediately suspected (and indeed it *is* known that pumas have a great liking for foals[20]). The Ministry of Agriculture took the corpse for formal analysis and discovered that the foal had died of hypothermia, after which its carcase had been preyed upon by a fox (fox scats had been found nearby that contained foal hairs) and also by crows.[70] Trevor Beer visited the site soon after the foal had been found, and he noted a number of dog prints there too, but no cat spoor.[55]

In late January teenagers Simon Hopwood and Sebastian Carmell spied a 6-7 in/15-17.5 cm-long skull possessing very long canines, lying at the side of a hedge near the Dartmoor village of Lustleigh. In various newspaper accounts it has been described as puma-like,[72] but judging from photographic evidence available (all depicting its left-hand profile[72]), a leopard identity is equally likely – though naturally I would hesitate to offer a definite specific identity for it without having first examined the skull directly.[68,73] Nonetheless, it *is* unequivocally from some large-sized cat species, so how can its occurrence be explained? Pumas and black leopards (panthers) *are* being reported from this region (and local rumour relates that a sizeable cat was released onto the moors two years ago[72]). Alternatively, it may have been placed there deliberately by a hoaxer, in the hope that someone would indeed come along and find it.

Worthy of note is that, a while later, a supposed lynx skeleton was discovered at Ilfracombe (north-west of Exmoor); it proved to be that of a large domestic cat.[55]

In mid-April, an Asian leopard cat *Felis bengalensis* was shot by a farmer on Dartmoor.[74] Little larger than a domestic cat, that felid is clearly not responsible for the sheep-killings attributed to the Beasts of Dartmoor and Exmoor. Nonetheless, its unexpected presence here still constitutes a significant occurrence, for it provides unequivocal support for the possibility not only that exotic cat species are indeed being kept in captivity (probably as pets) in this region but also that some are indeed escaping (and/or being deliberately released?) onto the moors.[68,75] By a remarkable coincidence, during the same period an escapee pet leopard cat was reported from Scotland, but that was recaptured alive (Andrew Kitchener, pers. comm.).

A final point worth mentioning about the Exmoor and Dartmoor Beasts is that, in addition to high-pitched screams comparable with those made by pumas (see Chapter 5), deeper, roaring sounds (some ending in a cough-like grunt) have been heard there;[55] these are more suggestive of leopards.

Clearly the moors of Somerset and North Devon contain large felids belonging to more than one species. Whether or not they will ever receive formal scientific recognition, and whether or not they are the animals responsible for the farmstock killings, however, are other matters entirely.

Identifying Britain's Large-Sized Mystery Cats: The Composite-Identity Theory

The thought of London's housing flocks of exotic ring-necked parakeets (which it does) or of wallabies bounding across the Peak District's heather moorlands (which they do) is hardly likely to incite trepidation. The same cannot perhaps be said in relation to images of sizeable cat forms prowling the countryside (despite the incontrovertible fact that these animals are going out of their way to avoid man at all cost). It is probably for this reason more than any other that it is proving so difficult to convince non-eyewitnesses that such animals *are* doing so. Moreover, although some people are willing to admit to the likelihood that large felids of *one* given species may exist here, the possibility that a number of *different* species may in fact be doing so is for the great majority of people a rather unpalatable notion. Yet, in view of the notable diversity of sightings reported in this book and elsewhere, this latter solution to Britain's mystery cat phenomenon is the only logical one – attempts to identify *all* sightings as pumas, or panthers, or lynxes, or simply feral domestic cats, fail miserably to accomplish this goal.

Having studied the British mystery cat saga for many years, I now wish to offer my own theory concerning the likely taxonomic status of these animals. I have named it 'the Composite-Identity Theory', for it comprises a series of identities that *collectively* account for the various forms being reported, i.e. it propounds that no *single* species is responsible for all such forms. There are four identity categories.

1) Feral Domestic Cats

Scientific studies carried out with feral domestics at a number of British localities have revealed that, contrary to popular belief, they are on average no larger or heavier than their tame counterparts[76] (over-size specimens are occasionally reported but very rarely submitted for formal scientific verification). Yet, despite their small size, it seems likely that certain mystery cat incidents have feral domestics at their foundation.

On Exmoor, for example, Nigel Brierley has found positively identified feral cat hairs at certain sheep-kills and has noted a strong odour reminiscent of brussels sprouts. Zoologist Dr Maurice Burton reports that this odour is commonly associated with ferals and also foxes (but not with larger felids[20] such as pumas). Yet ferals are neither large nor powerful enough to kill sheep, so how can the presence of their fur and odour at such kills be explained? The most plausible answer is that they have scavenged meat from kills already made by some much larger predator. In contrast, Nigel Brierley has suggested that such larger predators are themselves feral domestics but of a mutant strain which has attained puma-sized proportions. Yet the world's largest domestic cat on record weighed only 42 lb/19 kg (by comparison, a puma on average weighs 200 lb/91 kg), and this specimen was tremendously obese.[77] Even though feral domestics have established themselves throughout the world, no evidence has been obtained to suggest that *F. catus* can and does attain a body size commensurate with sheep- or deer-killing. And with Exmoor already providing a wide range of prey sizes suitable for feral cat predation, it seems most unlikely that natural selection would act upon such cats here in a manner necessary to engender the dramatic evolutionary changes required for the escalation in size from normal feral to puma-sized feral.

Despite the Worplesdon cat being sighted in the heart of Surrey puma country during the peak of Surrey puma sightings, even the comparison of the photo of it by Ian Pert with any photo of a puma (adult or juvenile) is sufficient to demonstrate at once that the two felid forms bear little or no resemblance to one another. It is quite hopeless to reconcile as one and the same species the sharp-faced, thick-tailed, short-bodied Worplesdon cat with the much larger and rangier, flatter-faced, thin-tailed, long-bodied puma. Conversely, I have seen several taxiderm specimens of domestic cats which compare very closely with the Worplesdon cat – one in particular (a Victorian specimen) was a near-perfect match.

In a review of *Cat Country*, wildcat expert Dr Nigel Easterbee from the Nature Conservancy Council stated that the 'cub' photographed at Tonmawr appeared to be 'an unusual but none-the-less adult domestic cat',[78] one identity which I also favour. Its colouration and markings are certainly consistent with this, as are its relative body proportions. In *Cat Country*, a particular point is made of comparing this cat's paws (seen stretching for the bait) with a hand and fingers;[36] in fact, there is nothing unusual about such an appearance – quite the reverse, for when any domestic cat extends its claws, '... the paw digits [toes] are normally spread "hand-like" at the same time', to quote Roger Tabor.[76] Similarly, when describing a photo of a domestic cat pulling at some meat, Dr Steven Harris noted that: '... the toes of this animal are stretching up and scratching at the meat, stretched out almost like fingers.'[62] In short, the Tonmawr cat's actions reveal just how very *like* a domestic cat it is. In fact, the oddest feature about this animal is its relatively large size, though if, as Dr Easterbee suggests, it is an adult rather than a cub, this becomes less significant. An adult identity is also suggested by its confident poise, as pointed out by king cheetah expert Lena Bottriell; she also notes that, if this cat were a cub, its mother would not have allowed it to test the bait.[79] And as for the much larger cat seen together with this and another 'cub', it was more likely to have been a puma (pumas have been reported from Wales in recent years) than any relation of them. Indeed, in the wild state, large felids frequently pursue smaller ones to attack and/or to take from them any prey which they may have obtained, which would explain the situation at Tonmawr.

Finally, it is certainly true that large creatures can be 'created' out of smaller ones via optical trickery if seen at a distance and/or in poor lighting conditions. Consequently it is by no means unlikely that some British mystery cats may indeed be nothing more than poorly spied feral domestics. Coupled with this is the frequent occurrence in mystery cat episodes (in Britain and abroad) of such excitement and interest (not to mention apprehension) that after a time almost *any* animal seen is automatically 'identified' as the mystery cat concerned. The conversion of a feral domestic cat into a much more formidable felid in the eyes of an observer 'tuned in' to reports of mysterious 'big cats' in his/her vicinity may have happened many times; indeed, Dr Maurice Burton has suggested that feral cat sightings are the explanation for most (if not all) of the 1964-6 Surrey puma sightings.[20]

2) Wildcat

Despite the wildcat being distributed widely across the British mainland (for the Irish situation, see Chapter 2) in earlier times, today, due to relentless persecution prior to World War I by gamekeepers and hunters, it is officially present only in parts of Scotland. Nonetheless, since the 1920s its distribution within

Scotland has re-expanded considerably.[80] In addition, certain mystery cat reports suggest that its range may even have re-extended beyond Scotland.

But first, a short description of the wildcat. The background colour of a pure-bred British specimen's pelage is buff-grey (paler ventrally, and white on the throat), marked with several vertical stripes running down from the dark dorsal stripe to the belly. The limbs are also transversely striped, and the black-tipped tail is encircled by a number of rings (of which at least the last two or three are complete). Its forehead bears four or five longitudinal stripes running down to the neck's nape, where they converge to form the dorsal line. The wildcat can be distinguished from most (but not all) domestic tabbies by its absence of blotched markings. Unfortunately, however, feral domestics tend to revert to a striped pelage pattern which is deceptively similar to a true wildcat's, and to make matters worse, wildcats will mate with such ferals to yield hybrids that are equally similar to pure-bred wildcats.[80,81] Consequently it is exceedingly difficult to decide, from pelage morphology alone, whether a given tabby-like cat sighted within the wildcat's known range is truly a wildcat or simply a hybrid or feral domestic.[81] Generally, however, a wildcat is about a third larger in overall size than a domestic, its head broader, its teeth larger (in some cases the upper canines protrude even when the jaws are closed), its body stouter, its limbs longer and its tail shorter (and ending bluntly rather than tapering at the tip).[80,81]

From the photographic evidence recorded for the striped Tonmawr 'cub', Lena Bottriell feels sure that this is without question a wildcat – 'from the ears and white throat right through to the tip of the tail'.[79] And certainly there are similarities in overall size and pelage morphology. Even so, in view of the Tonmawr cat's having a notably long, many-ringed tail, plus spotting on its body, a wildcat × domestic cat (i.e. a hybrid) is favoured over a pure-bred wildcat identity. This adds weight to the opinion of Colin Matheson from Cardiff's National Museum of Wales that a 'wildcat strain' may have survived among feral domestics in some areas of Wales.[82] In short, any re-expansion of its range into former haunts is only one side of the wildcat distribution coin; the obverse comprises the possibility that in some of the more secluded regions of England and Wales the wildcat never died out in the first place. Perhaps the Tonmawr cats are descendants of a reclusive remnant of the original Welsh wildcat contingent rather than recent emigrants from Scotland.

This suggestion can also be applied to the English situation. Some wildcat-like felids were sighted by Trevor Beer and others in 1984 on Exmoor[55] – which makes the following account of particular interest. In her book *Living on Exmoor*,[83] Hope Bourne recorded that Room Hill was home for a very long time to some very sizeable cats, reported right up to World War I. Their ferocity was renowned throughout the area – apparently not even the farm dogs would dare to attack them, and the cats would unhesitatingly kill any farm cats they encountered. Fred Milton, past president of the Exmoor Pony Society, recalled to Bourne one of his own sightings, when he observed one of these cats slinking down a nearby lane. He described it as being about the size of a male fox, with a grey or tawny-grey pelage marked all over with dark stripes. Its head seemed very large in comparison with that of a domestic cat, its fangs protruded below its lip, its limbs appeared to be rather long (especially the hind pair), it walked with a slouching gait, and its tail was blunt.[83] Could one ask for a better description of a pure-bred wildcat? Reports of these remarkable felids dried up after the war; hence it was assumed that they had died out. Perhaps instead they simply moved on to a new location, with their descendants being responsible for thc 1984 sightings.

Also worthy of mention here is that during 1922 two very large cats which had been sighted on several previous occasions on the Westmorland-Lancashire border near Carnforth were shot in two separate incidents. The male was shot by a poacher and presumably died of its wounds shortly afterwards, as it was not seen again. In November the female was also shot, this time by Dr Frederick Hogarth, who fortunately had the specimen preserved; it was displayed for many years thereafter in his Morecambe surgery.[84] Upon his death, it was donated to Lancaster's City Museum, where it was subsequently measured by Ron Freethy. Following comparison of its measurements with those available for known wildcats, Freethy was unable to rule out the possibility that Hogarth's exhibit was a genuine English wildcat.[85]

3) Escaped Exotics

One of the most popular theories put forward by sceptics of many reports concerning mystery creatures is that sightings of such beasts simply involve specimens of various foreign/exotic species which have somehow escaped (accidentally or with assistance) from captivity (e.g. zoos, parks, private collections, homes). In some instances this theory has failed dismally to explain satisfactorily a given mystery animal sighting, but in relation to certain other incidents it is quite plainly the most logical answer. The latter would seem to be particularly true of many mystery cat cases both in Britain and abroad (the reason for covering this theory here in particular detail) and can offer a very convincing identity for no fewer than four of the major felid forms reported from the UK.

The puma *Felis concolor* is the largest of the Small Cats, averaging 5 ft/150 cm in head-and-body-length, with an extra 28 in/70 cm of tail and a similar figure for shoulder height. Its head is small, its face (bearing a black bar on each side that connects nose with jaws) and ears are short and rounded. Its neck is relatively long, leading to a noticeably elongate, narrow body borne on strong, muscular, large-pawed limbs and terminating in a cylindrical and proportionately long, well-furred tail with black tip. The puma has two colour morphs – red and grey. The former ranges from tawny to rufous, the latter from silver-grey to slate. In both forms, colouration is lighter on the flanks and shoulders, and almost white ventrally. The above description corresponds very closely with some of those given from Surrey, Midlothian, the New Forest, the Isle of Wight and Exmoor, to name just a few localities from which puma-like cats have been reported. There are also the puma hairs positively identified from Surrey and Exmoor, plus the capture of Felicity in Cannich.

Though variable in colour, only a single *black* puma has ever been officially documented – from South America (see Chapters 5 and 6). Hence it is highly unlikely that melanistic pumas could be the large all-black cats being sighted in Great Britain. Far more likely is the possibility that these are black panthers, the melanistic morph of the leopard *Panthera pardus*. They average 6½ ft/195 cm in total length, of which about 32 in/80 cm comprises the tail. The panther's body is very elongate and muscular and is borne upon massive, broad-pawed limbs that are slightly longer than those of the puma. Its tail is also proportionately longer, and its head somewhat more elongate, but its ears are once again small and rounded. At anything but the shortest of viewing distances, the panther appears uniformly black. This description clearly matches very closely those of the black beasts on Exmoor and Dartmoor, plus felids from the Isle of Wight, Farnborough, Durham etc. (In Scotland, some panther reports may be due to a recently discovered black wildcat-like felid called the Kellas cat, discussed in the next chapter.)

On average, the northern lynx *F. lynx* weighs 63 lb/29 kg and has a shoulder height of 27 in/67.5 cm and a head-and-body length of 40 in/100 cm. Its tail length ranges from 4½-10 in/11-25 cm,[86] thus demonstrating that, contrary to popular belief, some lynxes possess quite notable tails. Other than its tail, its most striking features are its sturdy but lengthy limbs, its long black-tufted ears and its piercing golden eyes (the iris of most other felids tends to be greenish in colour[87]). Its pelage varies from yellowish-grey to reddish-brown, with spots of differing degrees of distinctness. This description is consistent with those of certain felids from Exmoor,

Powys, Glenfarg, the Isle of Wight, etc; we must also remember Cobbett's Surrey lucifee, the lynxes supposedly shot in Scotland during 1927, and the positively identified lynx hairs from Exmoor.

And the noticeable black tuft at the tip of the Nottingham mystery cat's tail suggests that this was quite probably an escaped lioness.

On morphological grounds, it can be seen that the existence of some escapee pumas, panthers and lynxes within the British countryside would go a very long way towards explaining the majority of large-sized mystery felids being reported here. But there is more than mere morphology in support of this suggested solution.

Once in range of its intended prey, the puma rapidly sprints towards it and, at the moment of contact, generally sinks its claws into the victim's head or hindquarters (rather than the flanks). Prey of ungulate size are additionally bitten in the back of the neck (sometimes the throat), and if this is not sufficient to kill the victim, the puma increases its jaws' grip in order to break the animal's neck, though in many cases the force of impact between puma and victim is enough to do this.[88] The carcases of uneaten puma victims are not usually wounded to any extent externally.[86] Panthers and other large felids follow the same principal killing mode, differing mostly only in specific details. Animals killed in this way have been reported on many occasions from various locations across Britain, as testified in some instances by veterinary officers and zoologists called in to examine them. Notable consumption of the victim's abdominal organs, lack of damage to its bones, and location of its carcase in a secluded spot (remember the Exmoor deer cache?) are typical features of felid feeding behaviour and have also been described from various British kills.

Though large felids' preferred prey species are the larger ungulates, they are certainly not incapable of surviving for considerable periods on much smaller prey species if conditions necessitate – especially rodents and rabbits (which in any case constitute the preferred prey of lynxes). Consequently, it would be unwise to suggest that the British countryside could not provide sufficient prey for long-term survival of the larger felids; in any event, roe deer are extremely plentiful, for example, in a number of British regions – including Exmoor and Surrey.

And, of course, if prey becomes scarce in one area, such cats will extend their hunting-territory considerably to seek out new prey sources, often trekking hundreds of miles in times of food shortages.[88] Indeed, one wide-ranging individual could actually be responsible, over a period of time, for mystery cat sightings in a number of different localities (remember the migratory Exmoor cats?). Hence the number of cats on the loose may well be a lot smaller than that implied by report counts. Coupled with this is the extreme elusiveness of these cats. As discussed in this book's Introduction, this is to be expected when dealing with felids. The puma's ability to remain unseen in its native America, for example, is renowned.[89] Deserving of mention is an anecdote recorded by Guggisberg, in which a hunter confessed that although he had shot no fewer than seventy pumas in Montana, he had never once caught sight of any of them until they had been treed by his dogs![86]

As also discussed in the Introduction, the finding of clawed spoor in relation to supposed mystery cats should not lead the discoverer automatically to discount a feline identity for their owner. The lynx in particular is a case in point here, for, as noted by Bjärvall and Ulström,[90] whenever the claws of a lynx are extended to give a better grip whilst walking, they leave behind very clear impressions; moreover, when extended in this way, the toes themselves are also extended, greatly increasing the overall size of the spoor. And when one adds to this the fact that lynxes sometimes display graded pads (i.e. the two members of a given pad pair differ in size),[90] the spoor displaying claws and graded pads discovered at Tonmawr suddenly become less odd. A good example of a lynx trail showing claw marks was documented by Kare Elgmork.[91]

Critics of the escapee theory in relation to sightings of exotic species in Britain frequently argue that such animals would be unable to survive in conditions and habitats so alien from those of their native lands. A scan through any of Sir Christopher Lever's definitive volumes on naturalized animals[92] will very swiftly disprove this. In any case, the native ranges of the puma and lynx already contain habitats and climatic conditions corresponding very closely with those found in the UK.

As far as tropical felids are concerned, we need only examine the case of the clouded leopards. This species is a highly specialized arboreal felid indigenous to the humid tropical forests of South-East Asia. Hence, when one escaped from Howletts Zoo in 1975, it was not expected to survive for more than a few days in the British countryside. It was eventually shot by a farmer *nine months* after its escape, and in very good health, having fed upon rabbits and lambs.[93] Consequently, the possibility of the much hardier and more adaptable black panther surviving here is indeed good. At the same time, of course, a lot depends upon individual disposition. In 1987 two clouded leopards escaped from Howletts Zoo during very severe hurricane conditions. One was captured almost immediately; the other, named Xiang, virtually gave himself up, by walking into a baited cage and curling up inside to go to sleep, awaiting collection by his keeper, whom he greeted with evident delight (see Plate 15).[94]

Many known examples of naturalized animals are descendants of original escapees from small private collections or escaped exotic pets, rather than from large public zoos or parks. The reasons for this trend are numerous and varied, ranging from the difficulties faced by private individuals of meeting the high level (and cost!) of security required for ensuring retention of their animals, to the equally awesome (and again costly) legal problems to be faced if such animals do escape. Consequently it would seem reasonable to suppose that in general the private sources of captive animals are those most likely to lose animals and those least likely to report such losses.

An event having great bearing upon this and upon felid escapees in particular was the passing in 1976 of the Dangerous Wild Animals Act in the UK. This banned the keeping of various species, including the larger cats, on any premises other than those licensed to do so (and the licenses in question were extremely expensive). Is it just coincidence that the last few months of 1976 were marked by a dramatic increase in mystery cat sightings, and from all over Britain? Is it unreasonable to suppose that license requirements proved too expensive for many private owners of large cats and that the secret release of their pets into the countryside proved too tempting a solution to avoid? And more legislation brought into force during 1981 under the Wildlife and Countryside Act in relation to exotic pets adds further food for thought in this direction.

Exotic pets may provide the answer to the mystery of why so many black panthers (i.e. melanistic leopards) are being reported in the wild compared with a very much smaller number of felids reminiscent of the normal spotted form. If someone is intent upon buying a large-sized exotic felid as a pet, the more exotic the form the better. And we only have to take note of television and glossy magazine adverts, films and pop videos to discover that the black panther is by far the most popular choice of felid for introducing an exotic image. Coupling panther popularity as privately owned pets with earlier remarks concerning the greater chances of such animals escaping from and remaining unreported by private ownership, the prevalence of panther sightings is now less of a puzzle. The keeping of large cats as pets in the UK can offer other pertinent links with the British mystery cat phenomenon too. Roderick Moore of the Nature Conservancy Council has commented that most of the first major sightings, in the early

1960s, occurred in affluent areas of southern Britain (e.g. Surrey, Hampshire), where one would expect to find more people who could afford to maintain exotic pets such as large cats.[95] Linking this with the inevitable escapes which must have occurred provides a very plausible solution to the Surrey puma saga. Worthy of mention at this point is an article published in *Wide World*, titled 'A Puma Hunt in Surrey'.[96] Nothing special, you may think, in view of the many puma searches occurring during the 1960s here. Very true – except that this particular hunt occurred prior to 1903! The puma in question was a pet which had escaped; it was finally recaptured and sold to a zoo. This demonstrates well that pumas were actually being kept as pets in Surrey more than fifty years before the Surrey puma episode – providing important support for Moore's comments.

One final facet of the exotic escapee identity to be considered here is its temporal aspect. The captivity of animals (even the most ferocious ones) within the menageries and 'collections of living curiosities' of earlier days (some dating back to medieval times) was certainly not attended by the laws and security measures operative in relation to today's zoos and parks. The potential for felid (and all manner of other) escapees must therefore have been much greater – a most interesting and thought-provoking concept, researched by mystery cat investigator Phil Bennett of Wolverhampton. Certainly it provides a plausible explanation for early British cases – Cobbett's lucifee, for example, and the Girt 'Dog'. In the same vein, Michael Goss noted that during the nineteenth century a Clent inhabitant writing under the pseudonym 'Vigorn' commented upon 'the prevalence of stories concerning wild beasts that have escaped from menageries' and noted a rumour that '... at Broadwas, a village in the Teme Valley, a lion is roaming at large ...'.[7] Moving back a few centuries, a panther supposedly escaped from the park at Chillington Hall, West Midlands, in the early 1500s and was about to attack a woman and baby when it was shot through the head with an arrow by the Hall's owner, Sir John Gifford; today a monument known as Gifford's Cross marks the spot where the panther was killed.[97]

Unknown Species?

This is an appropriate point at which to review an identity not incorporated within my Composite-Identity Theory but which has attracted some publicity and therefore requires examination here before moving on to my theory's non-felid section.

In *Cat Country*[36] and also in a *Fortean Times* article,[98] Di Francis has proposed that many sightings of large-sized mystery cats in Britain are due to the existence here of a native felid species currently unknown to science (at least in the living state), which she refers to as 'the British Big Cat'.

So far, this possibility has won little support from scientists. In their respective reviews of *Cat Country*, Dr Nigel Easterbee called it '... a contender for the most implausible book of the year. That or an elaborate hoax!',[78] whilst in reply to Francis' claim in *Cat Country* that she had written it to try to prove such an animal's existence, Lena Bottriell felt that Francis '... has singularly failed to do so'.[79] Even Dr Frank Turk, whilst in support of the existence of pumas and lynxes in Britain's countryside, remarked that, 'Miss Francis believes most of such [British mystery cats] may be survivals of some prehistoric race but very few zoologists, including myself, would agree with this interpretation.'[61]

For myself, although I would be only too delighted and thrilled if a totally new species of large felid were to be discovered in Britain, as a zoologist surveying the possibility realistically my personal opinion of this is that its chances of success are gravely hampered by basic problems within the original proposition.

To begin with, the British Big Cat would need to be nothing short of a shapeshifter to account for the immense variety of felids reported – cats which are black, grey, every shade of brown, striped, spotted, with long legs, with short legs, with long tails, with short tails, with ear-tufts, without ear-tufts, which roar, which scream, which are of small dog size, which equal the size of the largest dog breeds etc etc. Certainly no single non-domestic species of felid (indeed no wild mammal of *any* single species, known or unknown) could possibly exhibit so many markedly different forms – for the above-listed variations do not merely cut across pelage colouration, they also involve basic anatomy (e.g. limb skeleture, throat structure – see p.26).

Then we have its mode of existence to contend with. Francis argues that her British Big Cat has survived its meeting with man in post-Pleistocene times by becoming arboreal.[36] However, as Lena Bottriell points out, though that in itself is a reasonable enough proposal, it suffers a severe setback as a result of the three cast-prints laid out in *Cat Country* as important evidence for an unknown native species' existence, all very clearly showing the impression of claws.[79] I have noted earlier that, in addition to the cheetah's permanently extruded claws, the claws of other felids *can* be extended to facilitate movement and balance if ground conditions require this. But any felid which *habitually* moves with extended claws – and it is emphasized in *Cat Country* that in at least one of the three casts the claws actually exhibited road wear[36] (thereby demonstrating beyond doubt that they were frequently if not permanently extended) – would *not* have tree-climbing tendencies; for the whole purpose of predominantly extended claws in felids is to provide thrust and propulsion to the animal whilst sprinting, as in the cheetah and serval. And as for the graded pads in some cast-prints, these are sometimes displayed by a variety of felids, including leopards, lynxes and lions (as an excellent example of this, see the spoor diagram for the lion contained in Dr Reay Smithers' *Land Mammals of Southern Africa*[99]), thereby adding further support for the exotic escapee identity instead. Injuries and genetic defects can also produce abnormal pads.

Equally anomalous is that not one single specimen of a British Big Cat has ever been brought to the attention of science, despite Britain's being one of the most well-explored regions on Earth. Again as noted by Lena Bottriell,[79] the much smaller (and hence less conspicuous) wildcat was hunted to near-extinction within a century once gamekeepers and farmers began believing that it was killing livestock. Yet to support the British Big Cat theory we must assume that a much larger felid (and hence surely a much greater threat to livestock in the eyes of man) has escaped this scourge to the extent that it is not represented by a single skin or skeleton in any museum, retaining its hundred-per-cent record of elusiveness even during the taxidermy craze of the Victorian era. For a naturalized exotic species to be on the loose for twenty years or so before dying without capture, is one thing; the total avoidance of man for hundreds of years by an endemic *breeding* felid of puma stature is quite another! Similarly, local folklore, artistic depictions, medieval songs and writings – all valuable sources of information concerning the native fauna of any country – are equally barren in relation to such an animal.

By meticulous analysis of numerous reports via a punchcard system, Dr Bernard Heuvelmans has convincingly demonstrated that certain mystery beasts which seemed to be impossibly diverse in terms of morphology are clearly non-existent composites rather than real entities. That is to say, they have been 'created' by the erroneous lumping together of reports and descriptions that actually refer to several totally different animal types rather than just a single one. The mysterious East African Nandi bear is a good example of this, for Dr Heuvelmans has advocated that this creature is actually a composite based upon reports of hyaenas, ratels (honey badgers), large baboons, aardvarks, witch-doctor activities and perhaps even a surviving chalicothere (a horse-like ungulate with claws, supposedly extinct since the Pleistocene epoch), all amalgamated together rather than being segregated and identified as the separate entities which they are.[100] It is very likely that the British Big Cat comprises another of these cryptozoological composites, in reality divisible into a number of different species of felid and also most likely certain non-felids – as I have demonstrated with my own Composite-Identity Theory for Britain's mystery cats.

Finally, although in relation to the possibility of an unknown British Big Cat's existence Heuvelmans has commented that '... this, of course, is quite unacceptable to most zoologists',[101] he does suggest that the lynx may have lingered undetected here into the present-day[101] (instead of having died out about 10,000 years ago, as officially believed[2,102]). Though more probable, relatively speaking, than the prospect of an *unknown* form of large native felid existing in Britain, this lynx hypothesis still falls foul of some of the same objections raised with regard to the latter, e.g. lack of specimens (unless the three from Inverness and Cobbett's lucifee are examples).

4) Non-Felids

As will be seen throughout this book, it is highly likely that some mystery felid sightings, plus various examples of spoor and kills attributed to such animals, involve dogs rather than cats. Certainly, if seen at a distance and perhaps for only a short time, some dogs (especially those breeds with relatively small heads, short faces, rounded ears and/or shortish limbs) can appear surprisingly cat-like. And with respect to farmstock kills, the very real menace of stray dogs is only too familiar to farmers throughout Britain. On Exmoor and Dartmoor, in particular, farmers are becoming increasingly convinced that the savaging of sheep is the work of hunting-dogs being deliberately set loose, and many dogs have been shot in the act of killing sheep there;[40,103] Trevor Beer's belief is gaining ground all the time. Additionally, he has seen various kills *known* to have been caused by dogs which appear identical to some of the South Molton examples.[40] Another very pertinent point made by Trevor Beer is that, although the panther-like felids have been sighted chasing deer and killing rabbits, no record currently exists of anyone's having seen such a felid actually killing a sheep or even devouring the flesh from an already-dead specimen – in stark contrast to dogs.[55] Moreover, packs of stray dogs could easily leave a sheep carcase almost devoid of flesh and viscera after a single session, a feat likely to be matched only by the most voracious of solitary felids.

As already discussed, absence or presence of claw marks within paw-prints should not be looked upon as a foolproof indication of whether their owner was feline or canine. In some cases, a far more reliable guide to its identity is the overall size of the prints. Take, for example, the set of spoor discovered near some stables at Munstead in 1964 and attributed at that time to the Surrey puma. The fact that they were clawed does not automatically eliminate a felid identity for their owner: far more significant in this respect is their size, for each measured a massive 5¼ in/13 cm in diameter. Any felid capable of producing such enormous spoor would need to be either a simply colossal cat notably larger than an alsatian, *if* its paws were in proportion to the rest of its body, or a smaller cat but with outlandishly large paws totally out of proportion to the rest of its body. As neither of these types has been reported (as yet) in Britain, it seems safe to assume that these prints' owner was a dog – also suggested by the large size and elongate shape of the toe pads relative to the plantar pad. As a postscript to this episode, it later transpired that a lady frequently took her pet mastiff for walks in this very area – the diameter of a mastiff's print is 5-5½ in/12.5-13.75 cm. Equally likely to be of canine rather than feline origin are the 5 in/12.5 cm prints noted at Llangurig, Powys, in 1980 (possessing a notably canine shape too), and the comparably outsized spoor with abnormal pads from Tonmawr in 1981 (a canine identity for this latter is also suggested by the claws' possessing road wear).

After having discussed whether certain mystery cat sightings are actually based upon dogs, we should now consider whether alleged sightings of a certain dog type are actually based upon mystery cats! The canids involved here are the phantasmal Black Dogs, those preternatural creatures supposedly sighted many times in earlier days and even occasionally in the present day. According to tradition, they bring death to anyone who touches them and disappear into thin air in full view of their observer, but in external appearance they usually resemble an ordinary large-sized, black-coloured dog such as a labrador or hound (except for their glowing red eyes).[104] It has sometimes been suggested that sightings of these were really observations of large black panther-like cats – if correct, Britain's mystery panthers would gain a centuries-old history.

In truth, however, it is a theory beset with problems, for, as pointed out by Andy Roberts, accounts of Black Dogs and black panthers share only a superficial similarity. Black Dogs differ markedly from these felids in their frequent possession of long shaggy or woolly coats, their willingness to follow or brush against humans, their ability to pass through solid objects, their unpleasant breath (sometimes sulphurous) and the sounds of water splashing or even chains rattling which often accompany their appearances.[10] In addition, Black Dog legends are very common and widespread in Ireland – whilst reports of black panthers from that island are virtually unknown.[10] In any event, in

Strange cat photographed by Ian Pert at Worplesdon, Surrey, in August 1966

Felicity, the puma captured at Cannich in 1980, now a preserved specimen exhibited at Inverness

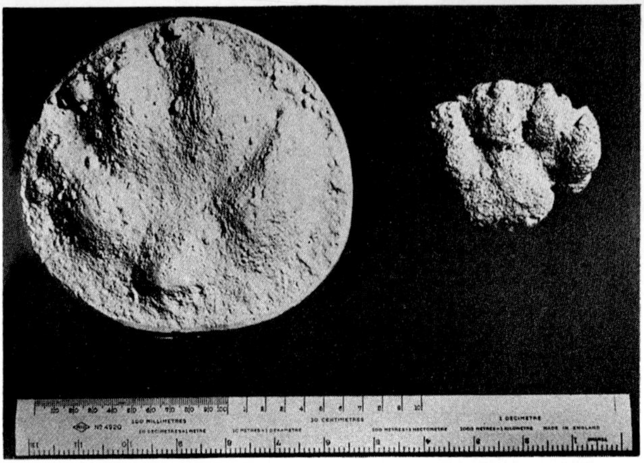

Cast of large spoor (left) discovered near stables at Munstead, Surrey, on 7 September 1964 – compared with cast of puma spoor (right)

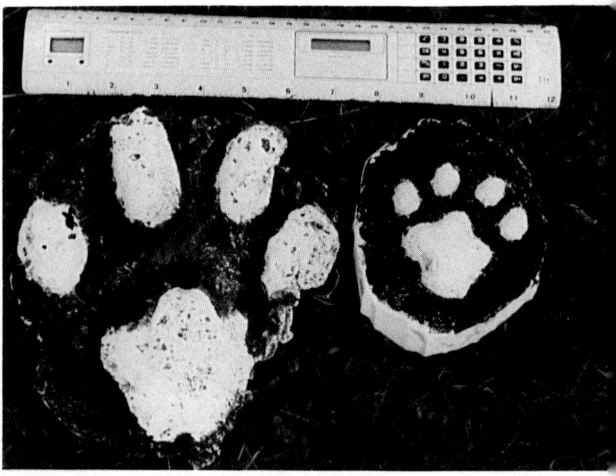

Casts of two spoor (the larger dog-like, the smaller lynx-like) discovered on Exmoor by Trevor Beer. The ruler measures 12 in/ 30 cm

Spoor observed outside Michael Nash's barn in Powys, Wales, on 23 October 1980

Swamp cat killed by a car in July 1988 at Hayling Island, Hampshire

The northern lynx; are naturalized specimens inhabiting Exmoor, northern Scotland, the Isle of Wight and other British localities?

Trevor Beer's photograph of the large black creature sighted by him on Exmoor during August 1987

Skull of large felid (puma or leopard) discovered on Dartmoor during January 1988

The black panther (melanistic leopard); are naturalized specimens inhabiting parts of Britain, continental Europe, North America and Australia?

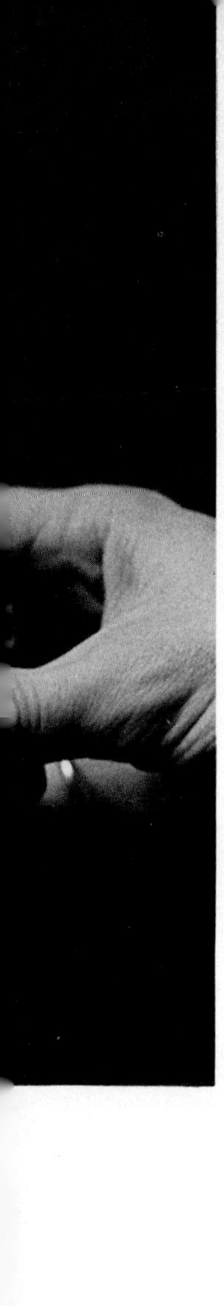

Pencil sketch of the black animal observed by Trevor Beer at close range on Exmoor during summer 1984

Scottish wildcat – are wildcats alive not only in Scotland but also in Wales and on Exmoor?

Young Kellas cat shot in October 1985 near to Kellas – note the pronounced gracility characterizing this mystery cat form

Head of mounted adult Kellas cat displaying striking canine teeth

Xiang, the clouded leopard and escapee from Howletts Zoo, clearly happy to be back with his keeper

Pure white (*complete albino* mutant) tiger, as exhibited in London during the 1820s

Normal cheetah cubs in background, and king cheetah cubs in foreground with backs to the camera, revealing their striking longitudinal dorsal stripes

Adult king cheetah in the Kruger National Park

view of the fact that Black Dogs make a habit of approaching their observers very closely, it is most unlikely that they would be mistaken for any form of cat. In exactly the same way, in those many sightings of mystery cats that have been made at very close range and often for decent periods of time (and sometimes actually by vets, zoologists and other eyewitnesses with detailed knowledge of wildlife), it is again very difficult to believe that confusion with dogs could have occurred. Whatever phenomenon they represent, it is clear that Black Dogs have little or no connection with mystery cats; similarly, it is evident that some but by no means all reports of such cats are the result of misidentification of normal dogs.

Finally, it is worth noting that some mystery felid cases have involved neither cat nor dog. For example, a 'cat seven feet in length' discovered in July 1929 by Preston poultry farmer Tom Cartmell within one of his hen cotes proved to be a binturong (a huge relative of civets and genets) which had recently escaped from a Blackpool zoo.[105] In 1970 a creature described as being like a puma but coloured tan and black with yellow streaks attacked a dog in Sussex's Ashdown Forest. Hair samples and spoor casts were positively identified at the British Museum (Natural History) as spotted hyaena. The animal was later shot but eluded capture and disappeared.[106] And on 7 February 1983 the body of a supposed mystery 'big cat' (exhumed earlier from a Berkshire garden) was passed on by Di Francis to Ian Linn, Senior Lecturer in Biological Sciences at Exeter University, for formal identification.[107] He examined the skull first and on 8 February announced that it was 'definitely that of a badger'.[107]

To date, there is no indication that Britain's long-running mystery cat saga is drawing to a close. On the contrary, new characters continue to make their début. Other notable examples include the Durham Beast,[108] the Cornish puma[25,61] and the panther-like Black Beast of Moray[109] (not to be confused – though unfortunately it frequently is – with the much smaller, gracile Kellas cat described in Chapter 2), and even a lynx-like creature reported from Ballyvourney in the Irish Republic's County Cork.[110]

Most recently of all, a long-limbed mystery felid was killed by a car on 26 July 1988 at Hayling Island, Hampshire, and was tentatively identified by Marwell Zoo director John Knowles as a swamp (jungle) cat *Felis chaus*,[111] an identity with which I fully agree. Although similar in some ways to the caracal *Felis caracal*, the swamp cat is readily differentiated by several noticeable features, including shorter ear tufts, more rounded ears, wildcat-like stripes on head, vaguely striped limbs, and white upper lip (all readily discerned in a good news-report photo of the Hampshire felid). As the swamp cat is native to the Middle East and Asia and uncommon in British zoos, the Hampshire specimen is most likely an escapee pet.

The existence within Great Britain of a variety of out-of-place felids – which for the most part unquestionably comprise escapees from captivity in the form of black panthers, pumas and lynxes – can no longer be doubted. It is time for science to abandon its futile attempts to dispute the indisputable, and instead to use every means at its command to demonstrate their existence conclusively, so that this significant subject can finally receive the serious scientific attention and interest which it so richly deserves.

In *Proper Studies*, Aldous Huxley stated: 'Facts do not cease to exist because they are ignored.' Neither do mystery cats.

1 Kurten, B., *Pleistocene Mammals of Europe* (Weidenfeld & Nicolson, 1968)
2 Sutcliffe, A., *On the Track of Ice Age Mammals* (Brit. Mus. Nat. Hist., 1985); Stuart, A.J., *Pleistocene Vertebrates in the British Isles* (Longman, 1982)
3 Bishop, M.J., *Special Papers in Palaeontology*, No. 28, pp. 1-108 (1984)
4 Green, H.S., *National Museum of Wales Quaternary Studies Monographs*, No. 1, pp. 171-80 (1984)
5 Clair, C., *Unnatural History* (Abelard-Schuman, 1967)
6 Dent, A., *Lost Beasts of Britain* (Harrap, 1974)
7 Goss, M., *The Unknown*, No. 13, pp. 5-10 (July 1986); No. 14, pp. 16-21 (August 1986); No. 15, pp. 70-75 (September 1986); No. 16, pp. 62-7 (October 1986); No. 17, pp. 11-17 (November 1986)
8 *Chambers's Journal*, Series 6, Vol. 7, pp. 470-72 (1904)
9 Fort, C., *The Books of Charles Fort* (Henry Holt, New York, 1941)
10 Roberts, A., *Cat Flaps!* (Brigantia Books, 1986)
11 Cobbett, W., *Rural Rides*, Vol. 1 (J.M. Dent, 1912; first published 1830)
12 *Daily Express*, 14 January 1927
13 Roberts, I., *The Field*, Vol. 171, p. 677 (19 March 1938)
14 Bord, J., and Bord, C., *Alien Animals*, revised edition (Panther Books, 1985)
15 McEwan, G., *Mystery Animals of Britain and Ireland* (Robert Hale, 1986)
16 *Kentish Mercury*, 19 and 26 July 1963
17 Rickard, R.J.M., *INFO Journal*, No. 13, pp. 3-18 (May 1974)
18 Clark, E., *The Observer*, 11 October 1964
19 Head, V., *The Field*, Vol. 225, p. 627 (8 April 1965)
20 Burton, M., *Animals*, Vol. 9, pp. 458-61 (December 1966)
21 Middleton, C., *Radio Times*, Vol. 249, pp. 100-101 (17 May 1986)
22 *The Times*, 5 July 1966
23 *Sunday People*, 14 August 1966
24 Rogers, E.J., *The Field*, Vol. 225, p. 770 (29 April 1965)
25 *Western Morning News*, 14 January 1985
26 Rickard, R.J.M., *The News*, No. 14, pp. 3-8, 17, 24 (January 1976)
27 *Nottingham Evening Post*, 29, 30 and 31 July, 2, 3, 4, 5 and 6 August 1976; *Fortean Times*, No. 18, pp. 25-6 (1976)
28 *Fortean Times*, No. 20, pp. 18-19 (February 1977)
29 Ibid., No. 26, pp. 43-4 (summer 1978)
30 *Express and Star* (Wolverhampton), 23, 24, 25, 26, 28 and 31 July 1980;

Rickard, R.J.M., *Fortean Times*, No. 34, pp. 21-2 (winter 1980)
31 Dow, A., Airs, G., et al, *Daily Record* (Glasgow) 30 and 31 October, 6 and 11 November 1980; Rickard, R.J.M., *Fortean Times*, No. 34, pp. 24-5, 36 (winter 1980)
32 *The Scotsman*, 7 February 1985
33 McGovern, B., *Sunday Express*, 27 January 1985
34 Mowat, B., *Daily Record* (Glasgow), 10 November 1980
35 Bord, J., and Bord, C., *Fortean Times*, No. 34, pp. 18-20 (winter 1980); Bord, J., and Bord, C., *Pursuit*, Vol. 14, pp. 54-5 (summer 1981)
36 Francis, D., *Cat Country. The Quest For the British Big Cat* (David & Charles, 1983)
37 Coppell, D., et al., *The News* (Portsmouth), 20 August, 12 and 15 September, 13 and 20 October 1983; 15 March, 20 December 1984; 17 June, 22 July 1985; *Fortean Times*, No. 42, pp. 40-2 (autumn 1984); Elsdon-Dew, M., *Sunday Express*, 29 April 1984
38 Rickard, R.J.M., *Fortean Times*, No. 44, pp. 28-31 (summer 1985)
39 Rickard, R.J.M., ibid, No. 40, pp. 52-61 (summer 1983)
40 Beer, T., *The Beast of Exmoor: Fact or Legend?* (Countryside Productions, 1984)
41 Rickard, R.J.M., *Fortean Times*, No. 35, p. 45 (summer 1981)
42 Howe, R., *Western Morning News*, 22 April 1983
43 Ibid., 5 May 1983
44 Hart-Davis, D., *Sunday Telegraph*, 10 July 1983
45 *Daily Express*, 7 May 1983
46 *Western Morning News*, 19 May 1983
47 *The Times*, 6 and 7 June 1983; *Daily Express*, 7 June 1983
48 *Western Morning News*, 31 May 1983; *The Times*, 31 May 1983
49 Charleston, M., *Daily Express*, 9 July 1983
50 Coates, J., and Taft, A., *Sunday Times*, 31 July 1983; Seton, C., *The Times*, 1 August 1983; *Western Morning News*, 16 August 1983
51 Fletcher, K., *Sunday Times*, 10 July 1983
52 *Western Morning News*, 17 September 1983
53 Henderson, D., *North Devon Journal-Herald*, 1 November 1984
54 Ibid., 4 October 1984
55 Beer, T., personal communications (1987-8)
56 Simpson, D., *Western Morning News*, 13 November 1985
57 *Sunday Times*, 1 December 1985; *The Mail on Sunday*, 1 December 1985
58 Metcalfe, T., *Western Morning News*, 10 December 1985
59 Clough, M., ibid., 17 January 1986
60 *The Sun*, 6 November 1986
61 Turk, F.A., *West-Briton*, 31 December 1986
62 Jewell, L. (producer), *The Natural History Programme* (BBC Radio Bristol, first broadcast on 22 January 1987)
63 Staddon, G., *North Devon Gazette*, 30 January 1987
64 Thomas, A.C., personal communication (1987)
65 *Daily Telegraph*, 7 May 1987
66 *BBC Wildlife*, Vol. 5, p. 610 (November 1987)
67 Richey, C., *Mid Devon Star*, 1 January 1988
68 Shuker, K.P.N., *Fortean Times*, No. 52 1989)
69 *Western Morning News*, 23 January 1988
70 Staddon, G., *North Devon Gazette*, 5 February 1988
71 *Express and Star*, 30 January 1988
72 *Sunday Independent* (Plymouth), 31 January 1988; Sage, A., *Western Morning News*, 31 January 1988
73 Reynolds, D., *Sunday Independent* (Plymouth), 21 February 1988

74 Bradley, C., *Western Morning News*, 21 April 1988; *The Times*, 22 April 1988; *Express and Star* (Wolverhampton), 22 April 1988
75 Shuker, K.P.N., *Western Morning News*, 3 May 1988
76 Tabor, R., *The Wildlife of the Domestic Cat* (Arrow Books, 1983)
77 Wood, G.L., *The Guinness Book of Pet Records* (Guinness Superlatives, 1984)
78 Easterbee, N., *Wildlife*, Vol. 25, p. 264 (July 1983)
79 Bottriell, L.G., *Cryptozoology*, Vol. 4, pp. 80-83 (1985)
80 Tomkies, M., *My Wilderness Wildcats* (Macdonald & Jane's, 1977); Corbet, G.B., and Southern, H.N. (eds.), *The Handbook of British Mammals*, second edition, (Blackwell, 1977)
81 French, D.D., Corbett, L.K. and Easterbee, N., *Journal of Zoology*, Vol. 214, pp. 235-59 (1988); Robinson, R., *Carnivore Genetics Newsletter*, Vol. 2, pp. 93-4 (1972)
82 Denis, A., *Cats of the World* (Constable, 1964)
83 Bourne, H.L., *Living on Exmoor* (Galley Press, 1963)
84 Robinson, H.W., *The Naturalist*, No. 849, p. 292 (1927)
85 Freethy, R., *Man and Beast. The Natural and Unnatural History of British Mammals* (Blandford, 1983)
86 Guggisberg, C.A.W., *Wild Cats of the World* (David & Charles, 1975)
87 Weigel, I., in Grzimek, B. (ed.), *Grzimek's Animal Life Encyclopedia*, Vol. 12 (Van Nostrand Reinhold, 1975), pp. 312-32
88 Ricciuti, E.R., *The Wild Cats* (Windward, 1979)
89 Young, S.P. and Goldman, E.A., *The Puma: Mysterious American Cat* (American Wildlife Institute, 1946)
90 Bjärvall, A., and Ullström, S., *The Mammals of Britain and Europe* (Croom Helm, 1986)
91 Elgmork, K., *Fauna*, Vol. 25, pp. 258-64 (1972)
92 Lever, C., *The Naturalised Animals of the British Isles* (Hutchinson, 1977); Lever, C., *Naturalized Mammals of the World* (Longman, 1985); Lever, C., *Naturalized Birds of the World* (Longman, 1987)
93 Rickard, R.J.M., *Fortean Times*, No. 20, p. 20 (February 1977)
94 *Daily Mail*, 17 and 30 October 1987.
95 Moore, R., *Cryptozoology*, Vol. 5, p. 146 (1986)
96 Stephenson, C., *Wide World*, Vol. 11, pp. 511-15 (1903)
97 Oswald, A., *Country Life*, Vol. 103, pp. 378-81 (20 February 1948)
98 Francis, D., *Fortean Times*, No. 39, pp. 34, 42 (spring 1983)
99 Smithers, R., *Land Mammals of Southern Africa* (Macmillan, Johannesburg, 1986)
100 Heuvelmans, B., *On the Track of Unknown Animals* (Rupert Hart-Davis, 1958)
101 Heuvelmans, B., *Cryptozoology*, Vol. 5, pp. 1-26 (1986)
102 Jenkinson, R.D.S., in Gilbertson, D.D., and Jenkinson, R.D.S. (eds.), *In the Shadow of Extinction: A Quaternary Archaeology and Palaeoecology of the Lake, Fissures and Smaller Caves at Creswell Crags SSSI* (Department of Prehistory & Archaeology, University of Sheffield, 1984)
103 *Mid Devon Star*, 1 January 1988; Powell, J., et al., *Western Morning News*, 5 January, 1 June 1988
104 Innes, S., *The Unexplained*, No. 86, pp. 1710-13, and No. 87, pp. 1730-33 (1983)
105 *Reynolds's Illustrated Newspaper*, 7 July 1929
106 Rickard, R.J.M., *Fortean Times*, No. 19, pp. 9-10 (December 1976)
107 Doyle, P., et al., *Express & Echo* (Exeter) 7 and 8 February 1983
108 Screeton, P., *Folklore Frontiers*, No. 4, pp. 19-25 (January 1987); Bell, E., ibid., No. 7, pp. 11-14 (1988)

109 *Forres Gazette*, 14 March 1984, 10 April 1985, 20 January 1988
110 Shiels, A., *Fortean Times*, No. 34, pp. 39-41 (winter 1980/81) and No. 37, pp. 28-30 (spring 1982)
111 *The News* (Portsmouth), 28 and 29 July, 7 September 1988; *Daily Post* (Liverpool), 29 July 1988

2 Kellas Cats and Scimitar Cats

Great Britain (Concluded) and Continental Europe

The Naming of Cats is a difficult matter;
It isn't just one of your holiday games ....
T.S. Eliot, *Old Possum's Book of Practical Cats*

One would surely imagine that a mystery cat ceases to be a mystery once at least one specimen is finally obtained and submitted to science for detailed examination. Remarkably, however, this is not the case with the Kellas cat from northern Scotland. Four years after its official discovery – and despite being represented by a series of preserved specimens – this enigmatic and controversial felid form still awaits a conclusive scientific identification.

It may seem a little strange to discover not only the Kellas cat but also the Irish wildcat ensconced within a chapter concentrating upon mystery cats from mainland Europe. The reason for my inclusion of these two felids here rather than in Chapter 1 is to maintain intact a notable link between each of these animals and various mystery cats which *are* found in continental Europe. Like Great Britain, modern-day Europe's official contingent of cat species is a pallid reflection of its Pleistocene plethora. Yet judging from the variety of unofficial felids being reported in more recent times, Europe may not be quite so devoid of catlife after all.

The Kellas Cat

The history of the Kellas cat began publicly on 19 September 1984, when a Moray newspaper, the *Forres Gazette*, devoted its entire front page to a detailed world-exclusive report written by its editor David Morgan.[1] Its subject was the hitherto little-publicized capture within the Scottish Highlands three months earlier of a large and most striking cat – one which did not resemble any felid known to science.

'Mystery "Big Cat" Could Shake World!' read the eyecatching

headlines. 'Does West Moray shelter a species unknown to man ...?'[1] The photograph immediately beneath these imposing lines was no less startling and certainly lent them its full support, for it depicted a quite extraordinary cat. Its pelage was dark and bristly, predominantly black in colour but flecked all over with very long, gleaming white primary guard hairs. Its broad head tapered to a narrow muzzle, with jaws that contained spectacularly prominent upper and lower canines (the upper pair actually projecting from the mouth even when the jaws were closed).

A second photograph showed the specimen laid down upon its right flank beside a measuring-ruler, whose scale revealed that the cat, an adult male, was approximately 3½ ft/105 cm in total length. This photograph also depicted the remarkable gracility of the cat – its slender body and notably lengthy limbs.[1]

It had been trapped in a fox snare in June 1984 within the grounds of Revack Lodge. The Lodge's gamekeeper, Ronald Douglas, had subsequently discovered the dead body and brought it back, whereupon, as a result of its very noteworthy appearance, Edward Orbell and local veterinary surgeon John Robertson were invited to view it, and photographs were taken.[1,2]

News of this singular find rapidly travelled throughout Great Britain and, recognizing its potential scientific worth, Ronald Douglas sent the specimen to an unnamed taxidermist in Kirkmichael, Perthshire, for preparation.[3] It was never seen again! Whether this specimen *has* been prepared or was simply neglected until its condition deteriorated to the point at which it became necessary to dispose of the remains, is unknown.[4] The ultimate tragedy is that this example was never subjected to a detailed, formal scientific examination.

However, on 3 October 1984 the *Forres Gazette* was once again dominated by news and accompanying photos of a large, black, ferocious-looking cat.[5] As I discovered when I examined this specimen myself, it was clearly of the same felid type as the Revack cat – a second adult male, complete with sparkling white guard hairs (plus two small white spots, one on the middle of the chest, the other inguinal), massive canines and gracile build. It measured 26 in/65 cm in head-and-body-length, with a further 12 in/30 cm comprising the tail.[6]

Apparently it had been one of a pair of such cats observed in January 1983 by local laird Tomas Christie, near the River Lossie in the vicinity of the tiny village of Kellas in West Moray. He shot one, the other escaped unharmed. Christie had seen and shot other cats of this form in the past, and decided to have this latest example preserved as a permanent exhibit.[5] Thus it was mounted for display purposes by a local taxidermist, who placed it upon a robust pine branch in a somewhat menacing pose. Having read the *Forres Gazette* account of the Revack cat, Christie realized that his own specimen was evidently closely related to it; he therefore contacted editor David Morgan to inform him of its existence.[5]

Within a fortnight of this new specimen's media début, the Revack cat had vanished. Suddenly Tomas Christie's exhibit was the sole preserved representative of this newly discovered felid form known to be in existence. Needless to say, it therefore received considerable publicity – so much so, in fact, that the entire cat form itself began to be referred to as 'the Kellas cat', after this Kellas-derived example. Moreover, this name was both descriptive (alluding to a locality within the cat's known distribution range) and specific (no other type of cat was referred to by this name). Consequently, when I instigated my own researches relating to this felid, culminating in my production of the first scientific paper to document it and to discuss zoologically its most likely taxonomic status,[6] I formally adopted the name 'Kellas cat' for this new felid form within the latter work – a name which has since been popularly used and acknowledged as its official British name.

When the Revack specimen first attracted public attention, it was assumed by some to be an immature individual of the black pantheresque mystery cat reported from Exmoor and elsewhere in Britain. However, it soon became clear that it represented a completely separate felid form. By then, Di Francis had announced her interest in the Kellas cat,[1] and with Tomas Christie's permission she submitted his mounted specimen to the British Museum (Natural History),[7] after which the scientific world and general public alike sat back to await its experts' pronouncement.

Although a most significant (and at that time unique) animal, this Kellas-derived example was not ideally suited to precise and painstaking taxonomy. For example, certain cranial bones were missing, including the nasals – crucial in cat classification. In addition, by being a mounted exhibit, its internal structure could not be readily studied. Fortunately, however, the museum was able to counter this latter problem to a certain extent, by employing X-ray analysis to obtain an indirect view of those components of its skeleton preserved within its mounted form.[8]

In the late spring of 1985, a short, currently unpublished report was issued by small-mammal expert Daphne Hills, in which the museum's opinion concerning Tomas Christie's Kellas cat was summarized. It stated that, although the possibility of the specimen's being either a domestic cat × wildcat hybrid or a feral domestic cat could not be totally ruled out, available evidence suggested that it was most probably a melanistic wildcat – and as such the first ever documented in the UK.[8]

This identity had also been put forward independently by certain other zoologists, including Dr Frank Turk.[9]

In April 1985 gamekeeper Leslie Mallinson bagged a young male Kellas cat (about twelve months old) on the Aberlour road, near Advie, a small village roughly 10 miles/16 km north of Revack Lodge. Its body was sent to Di Francis, who noted that it was in excellent condition[10] and formally presented it to the British Museum (Natural History) for permanent retention there (its official registration number is BMNH 85.815).[11] Significantly, being a perfectly preserved, complete specimen, the Advie cat presented itself as a prime candidate for detailed external and internal scientific examination, which in turn should reinforce and enhance the determination of these mysterious felids' status begun earlier with Tomas Christie's exhibit.

Like the latter animal, the Advie specimen was examined at the museum by Daphne Hills, who subsequently prepared a corresponding report (again currently unpublished).[11] This revealed that in external appearance it was virtually identical (ignoring certain age-related size differences) to Tomas Christie's cat, except for a very restricted degree of cryptic striping, i.e. faint bands encircling the Advie cat's tail and marking its upper limbs but visible only when viewed at certain angles (comparable with the rosettes of black panthers).[11] But what of its scientific status?

Contrary to everyone's expectations that it would proffer an unequivocal answer to the Kellas cat's identity, the Advie specimen provided a notable surprise, for, as a result of precise direct skeletal and cranial analysis not possible with the mounted specimen from Kellas, it was found to exhibit certain domestic cat similarities. Consequently, and with understandable caution, the museum's account concluded that this latest Kellas cat was probably a wildcat × domestic cat hybrid, though one most closely allied to its supposed wildcat progenitors.[11]

On 14 October 1985 an immature male Kellas cat was observed by a gamekeeper protecting a pheasantry near Kellas and the neighbouring village of Dallas, and was promptly shot. David Morgan was contacted immediately and came to the site at once to view the body.[12] A superb photograph (Plate 13) of this specimen taken by Sandy Brander clearly reveals the characteristically gracile body, powerful hind limbs and small, squat head possessed by the previous three Kellas cats. Within two hours of the cat's demise, a sample of blood had been taken directly from its heart by a local vet and was forwarded promptly by the *Forres Gazette* to the University of Aberdeen for chromosomal analysis to ascertain definitely the Kellas cat's status at last.[12] Frustratingly, however, the vital blood sample was apparently contaminated – and therefore useless.[4]

Since this young Kellas cat's procurement, four further specimens have been obtained from Aberlour and Darnaway, thereby extending very considerably the Kellas cat's known distribution range.[13] It has also received a recent resurgence of public interest, plus international media coverage,[13-15] for at the Sixth Annual Members Meeting of the ISC, held at Edinburgh's Royal Museum of Scotland in July 1987, I presented a paper[16] covering my researches and professional opinion concerning the Kellas cat's taxonomy and origin, together with that of the British Museum. In addition, as part of her own presentation concerning UK mystery cats, Di Francis displayed a mounted Kellas cat.

It is important to note that a BBC television documentary devoted to British mystery cats, entitled *On the Trail of the Big Cat* (first screened on 22 May 1986) featured a memorable climax – the capture within a specially baited cage (sited two months earlier in the Highlands) of a sizeable felid which appeared to be a Kellas cat, totally unharmed and very much alive! Moreover, blood samples taken from this cat and subjected to chromosomal analysis by Dr Fox of the University of Aberdeen's Zoology Department to investigate its scientific status revealed unequivocally that it was a wildcat × domestic cat hybrid.[17] The programme thereby seemed sensationally to have solved the three-year-old riddle of the enigmatic Kellas cat's identity.

If only it could have been that simple! For, according to the opinions of various observers with first-hand experience of Kellas cats, the living specimen was not a Kellas cat at all. For example, Edward Orbell (at whose Highland Wildlife Park the animal in question has been maintained since its capture) asserted that it differed significantly from the Revack cat (which was virtually identical to all the other Kellas cat specimens).[18] The living cat was also given short shrift by observers from the Nature Conservancy Council, describing it as resembling 'a moggy gone wild'.[18]

The reasons for this dismissal of the living cat were based upon a number of morphological discrepancies (clearly visible even on the programme itself) between the series of preserved Kellas cats and this new living specimen. Certainly the latter creature was notably large and exhibited a glossy, bristly black pelage, sprinkled with white primary guard hairs. Relative to the Kellas cats, however, the living felid's body was stouter, its limbs shorter, its head somewhat larger and its teeth much smaller. Hence *in toto* it did indeed merely resemble a large black domestic cat, with a fierce temperament befitting either a feral domestic or a genuine wildcat.

Consequently, it is quite different from the preserved Kellas cat specimens. Nonetheless, it remains an extremely important specimen relative to this riddle – as will be discussed a little later.

On 28 February 1988 another wildcat-sized black cat was caught alive and unharmed in northern Scotland, this time in a home-made cage set by Tony Sill of Redcastle, whose Aylesbury ducks had been disappearing from his home for some time.[19] This felid measured 3 ft/90 cm in total length and weighed 13lb/6 kg. Its pelage was jet black, except for a scattering of very long white primary guard hairs, plus a small white spot on its chest and between its eyes. It has since been transferred to the Highland Wildlife Park; Edward Orbell considers that this cat does closely resemble the Revack specimen (Orbell, pers. comm.).

Recently, genetic tests utilizing tissue samples taken from some of the more recent, preserved Kellas cat specimens have been instigated at London's University College, under the supervision of Professor Robert Berry.[15,20] These will most probably include DNA hybridization trials, for such techniques should be able to reveal whether the Kellas cat is a separate taxonomic form or merely of domestic, wildcat or hybrid origin. As genetic investigations of this type are both comprehensive and complex, it is unlikely that conclusive results will be obtained and publicly recorded for some time to come. In the meantime, however, a lucidly defined insight into the most (and least) likely identities of the Kellas cat can still be obtained – by scrutinizing concisely in turn each identity contender in terms of morphological, behavioural, ecological and historical attributes. This has constituted a primary component of my personal Kellas cat researches, and a condensed version of my full analysis of the Kellas cat's identity in my scientific paper[6] is now provided here.

1) A Feral Domestic Cat?

It is certainly possible that a population of feral domestics, isolated from all other Highland felids by some topographical factor, could ultimately give rise to a strain of morphologically uniform but highly distinctive cats which, depending upon survival requirements, could possess features such as long limbs, extra-large teeth and jet-black pelage.[6,16,21] Also, one of the genes responsible for black coat colouration in felids is pleiotropic, i.e. it has a number of other effects too, one of which is to increase the organism's overall body size. This could therefore account for the Kellas cat's large size (of wildcat stature),[6,16,21] in comparison with the generally smaller British ferals.[22]

Nonetheless, for the Kellas cat to have originated from an isolated population of feral domestics and yet for it nowadays to be distributed widely across the Highlands (as suggested by the widely separated provenances of the various near-identical specimens so far obtained), we must assume that the ancestral population eventually expanded its range very considerably – but without its members' unique combination of morphological features becoming diluted by interbreeding with normal domestics. This is all rather unlikely, unless evolution within the original population was so extensive that a totally new species ultimately developed, incapable of producing fertile offspring from matings with domestic cats. In short, the only scenario offering a domestic cat origin for the Kellas cat is also one which requires the latter to have since become a separate species.[6,16,21]

Also arguing against a pure domestic cat identity for the Kellas cat are its many non-domestic features. These include: various cranial characteristics (shape of nasal bones' junction, certain lower jaw projections' prominence), body shape, non-tapering tail, short gut length, very large teeth, extremely long primary guard hairs. Taken together, these yield a much more extensive deviation from the typical domestic cat state than can be readily explained solely by insular evolution, especially when these differences from the domestic cat are actually similarities with the wildcat![6,16,21] Consequently, this points towards the Kellas cat's second possible identity – a hybrid.

2) Domestic Cat × Wildcat Hybrid?

Hybrids of these species are known both from captivity and from the wild.[6,23-25] Nevertheless, in some ways this identity is not as promising as it may at first seem for, in contrast to the morphologically diverse offspring that sometimes result from a given mating between two separate felid species (i.e. each offspring usually possessing an interspecific combination of features different from that of its siblings), the Kellas cats so far obtained all share considerable morphological uniformity. Moreover, they also possess certain features – notable gracility, extremely prominent canines, small head, shortish tail – not exhibited by either proposed parent species. Conversely, *known* domestic cat × wildcat hybrids frequently display an overall resemblance to wildcats, though with rather longer tails.[23,24] Indeed, although all-black and from the same locality as some of the Kellas cats, even the morphology of the BBC's black hybrid can be readily seen to constitute nothing more than a combination of wildcat and domestic features, with none unique to itself.[6,16,21] So is the hybrid identity totally untenable for the Kellas cat? Actually, no.

I have always considered that the existence of an all-black

wildcat hybrid in the very same area as the Kellas cats was a rather formidable coincidence, even allowing for its differing morphology. At that time nothing suggested a more significant explanation – until the capture of the Redcastle cat in spring 1988. Here was a felid much more reminiscent of the Kellas cats, yet still not entirely comparable. Indeed, it seemed somewhat intermediate between these and the BBC's cat. Then there was the Advie specimen of Kellas cat, which itself possessed certain features (cryptic striping, brown eyebrows) that contrasted with typical Kellas cat morphology.[6,16,21] And most recently, Dr Nigel Easterbee and his colleagues, in their detailed wildcat hybridization paper, reported a basically black Scottish felid which they assumed to be a domestic – until comprehensive morphometrical analysis revealed that it was actually a domestic cat × wildcat hybrid.[25] This therefore expanded the morphological range of mysterious Scottish black cats even further.

Consequently, to my mind it now seems very plausible that a morphologically graded, near-continuous 'chain' of black hybrids exists in the Highlands – a chain whose 'links' range from felids which seem pure domestic in all but skeletal and chromosomal identity through a series of felids in which domestic cat features gradually diminish in favour of wildcat ones, and ultimately to distinctive felids not only possessing an abundance of wildcat features but also exhibiting some unique to themselves. In short, at one extreme of this chain is Easterbee's domestic-lookalike specimen, which links to the BBC's cat, which in turn connects to the Redcastle cat. This latter felid at the same time has morphological ties with the Advie-derived Kellas cat, which is itself linked to the remaining Kellas cats, these latter thereby comprising the chain's opposite extreme.

Such a situation could have arisen from introgressive crossbreeding, involving the mating of hybrids with pure-bred wildcats and/or domestics. Such back-crossing can yield progeny which are very different morphologically not only from their hybrid parents but also from their original pure-bred progenitor species, thereby offering an explanation for the Kellas cat's distinctive appearance.[6]

3) A Melanistic Wildcat?

No scientific study of Kellas cat behaviour has been carried out so far, but various facets have been reported by eyewitnesses and, intriguingly, these suggest that Kellas cat behaviour differs notably from that of wildcats. According to such sources, Kellas cats seem to hunt in pairs and in daylight (wildcats usually hunt alone and crepuscularly, i.e. at dawn and dusk). Moreover, they do not appear to be arboreal (wildcats, conversely, are adept climbers), and they run with a singularly graceful loping gait, taking long, easy strides (wildcats display a stealthy, compact gait). Apparently they tend to prey upon relatively small prey, such as rabbits and birds, not taking such larger mammals as lambs and young deer which could be killed by the bulkier wildcat.[17,26,27] Curiously, Kellas cats have even been reported swimming and catching fish in the River Lossie,[26] but this is surely an idiosyncrasy on the part of certain individuals rather than a trait of the felid form as a whole – certainly the Kellas cat does not possess any specific adaptations for an aquatic lifestyle.[6]

Assuming that the Kellas cat is merely a melanistic morph of the wildcat, are such marked behavioural differences to be expected? In fact, although admittedly not widely known, a number of different mammals (notably rats and various canid species) possess intraspecific colour morphs which do differ from one another in terms of both colour and behaviour.[28]

Equally favourable to a melanistic wildcat identity for the Kellas cat is the latter's predominance of wildcat morphological features. Even its white throat patch lends support – as far back as the sixteenth century, Conrad Gesner recognized this as a wildcat characteristic.[9] Similarly, the Advie specimen's cryptic stripes are eminently compatible with a wildcat identity, nor does the lack of such markings in the other Kellas cats disprove this, for, even amongst well-known melanistic morphs such as black panthers, certain individuals lack any vestige of markings.[6,16,21]

Nonetheless, the melanistic wildcat identity still poses at least one major problem. Although melanistic individuals of a given species differ from normal intraspecific individuals in terms of colour, sometimes behaviour, and sometimes overall body size, they do not differ from them in actual body outline, i.e. relative body proportions. Yet, in comparison with the wildcat, the Kellas cat has a smaller head, longer limbs, more slender body, shorter tail and larger teeth. Even a pleiotropic gene increases an animal's size only in an absolute (isometric) manner – conversely, the size differences listed above for the Kellas cat against the wildcat are relative (allometric).[6,16,21] One would not expect this from a simple melanistic wildcat.

Consequently, in order to remain with a pure-bred wildcat identity for the Kellas cat, it is necessary to consider the possibility that the Kellas cat originated as a melanistic wildcat but has since diverged morphologically as well as behaviourally from the normal form via evolution to yield a different felid.[6,16,21] But how different? Just a distinctive morph or perhaps a separate taxonomic form?

4) Separate Taxonomic Form?

Hybridization between domestics and wildcats in the Highlands has engendered much taxonomic turmoil and confusion – so much so, in fact, that it seems likely that only genetic analyses will determine conclusively whether or not the Kellas cat really is a separate taxonomic form (i.e. a subspecies or a species). If these should prove that it is, its distinctive morphology has evolved to fill a specific ecological niche – but what could that be?

Many long-limbed, gracile animals exhibit a predominantly cursorial (running) lifestyle. Could the Kellas cat be developing into a cursorial cat form?[6,16,21] Among felids, the species most specialized for such an existence is, of course, the cheetah, which makes the following statement by felid specialist Reginald Pocock concerning its cursorial activity well worth recalling: 'As is well known the cheetah does not, at all events as a rule, adopt the true cat's method of pouncing on its prey from a point of vantage at comparatively close quarters, but runs down antelope in the open by sheer speed of foot. All its more obvious external features – its small light head, narrow chest and body, thin, sinewy legs, and powerful hind quarters – are obviously adapted to that end.'[29] It hardly need be said that Pocock's last sentence comprises a most precise morphological description not only of the cheetah but also of the Kellas cat!

In addition, carnivore authority Professor Robert Savage defines long-legged carnivores as those whose hind limb length is eighty per cent or more of the vertebral column, and notes that all these species are cursorial (and mostly high-speed runners);[30] the measurements available for the Advie cat[11] (the only Kellas cat to have been measured in detail so far) reveal that its hind limb length is approximately eighty-three per cent of the vertebral column. If the Kellas cat is indeed of separate taxonomic status, clearly there are sound morphological grounds for considering it to be of cursorial persuasion.[6]

Even the eyewitness accounts of its behaviour – a diurnal, terrestrial hunter moving via a graceful, loping gait – agree with such a lifestyle.[6,16,21] Of course, unlike those of the cheetah and also the gracile serval, the Kellas cat's claws are fully retractile. Yet this feature should not be used to dismiss a cursorial lifestyle for this felid. Relative to body size, the world's fastest felid is the caracal – and its claws are fully retractile too.[31] In any case, there is no reason why the Kellas cat should not extend its claws when running, if to do so enhances its stability and cursorial capability.[6,16,21] Further cursorial considerations have been given in my paper.[6]

Celtic Place-Names and Cait Sith

It is clear that, until the findings of the genetic tests are made public, controversy regarding the Kellas cat's identity will continue. Yet whichever identity is shown to be correct, this felid will remain a most valuable, significant scientific find; for if such studies determine conclusively that it is indeed of separate taxonomic status, this will profoundly affect current ideas concerning felid evolution and ecology. Similarly, if instead one of the other identities is confirmed, the fact that the Kellas cat is so different from known examples of each such form will demonstrate the need for a reappraisal of present views relating to the mechanisms controlling the production of such forms.[6,16,21]

Whatever its identity, one point seems well founded: the Kellas cat is not of very recent origin – at least, not if we take note of two very intriguing items of information (in addition, of course, to generations of local sightings of Kellas cats).

Firstly, as I learnt from Professor Charles Thomas, director of the University of Exeter's Institute for Cornish Studies and a leading archaeologist specializing in prehistoric and protohistoric Britain, evidence from early place-names in northern Scotland indicates that one of the native animals incorporated into this region's tribal nomenclature of early Roman/post-Roman times may have been a fairly large black form of cat.[6,16,21,33]

Secondly, whilst researching Scottish mythology in relation to the Kellas cat, I discovered that Highland folklore includes a legendary cat form called the *cait sith*, fairy cat, a sizeable creature which comes complete with black bristly pelage, white throat patch and sparks over its fur.[6,16,21,34] If these 'sparks' refer to gleaming white primary guard hairs (and one could hardly ask for a more accurate description of these than 'sparks'), the *cait sith* bears an almost exact resemblance to the Kellas cat.[6,16,21] Thus, if the Kellas cat is only of very recent origin, it is truly a most remarkable coincidence that the only region of Great Britain from which specimens or sightings of Kellas cats have emerged is also the very same region which possesses in its folklore a creature bearing an uncanny similarity to the Kellas cat.[6,16,21]

No less surprising is the existence of a felid which at least on first sight seems to be an Eastern European counterpart to the Kellas cat, yet just such an animal was scientifically documented as long ago as 1904.

The Transcaucasian Black Cat

Shortly after I first began researching the Kellas cat, I was surprised to uncover a scientific paper from the Zoological Society of London's 1904 *Proceedings* concerning a black cat which appeared very reminiscent of the Kellas cat but which inhabited Transcaucasia (a region of the USSR to the south of the Caucasus mountains). In the latter paper,[35] this cat had been formally described and named – *Felis daemon* by the noted Russian zoologist Professor C. Satunin, basing his description upon two mounted specimens, three skins and three skulls, all housed in what is now the Leningrad Academy of Sciences.[35]

Other scientists, however, did not share Satunin's view that this felid warranted separate taxonomic status. When S. Ognev later documented these specimens, he demoted them to the level of feral domestic cat, even though he did concede that a melanistic morph might exist with the Caucasian wildcat population.[36] Felid taxonomist Reginald Pocock also classed *F. daemon* as a feral domestic in 1951,[37] and it has remained thus ever since. Yet is this a truly accurate assessment of its status? And how (if at all) is *F. daemon* related to the Kellas cat?

Feral domestic or not, *F. daemon* certainly displays some marked morphological similarities to the Kellas cat, as the following description of this Transcaucasian mystery cat demonstrates. Its length from nose to tail-base ranged between 22½ and 30 in/56 and 75 cm, tail length between 13½ and 15 in/34 and 38 cm. Fur colour varied from black with slight reddish tinge to reddish-brown, slightly paler on underparts, inner surface of extremities and distal under-surface of tail. Held at certain angles, black transverse stripes were visible on flanks on the body's foreparts, more conspicuous on faded skins. Very long white hairs were scattered scantily all over body. Vibrissae and eyebrows were brown; claws, white. With respect to cranial features, Satunin noted that *F. daemon* differed from the wildcat both in the possession of a somewhat narrower frontal region and in the extension of the upper jaw-bones further back than the nasals (the reverse condition to that exhibited by the wildcat).[35]

Clearly, the dark pelage flecked with long white hairs exhibited by *F. daemon* compares with that of the Kellas cat – and especially with the Advie specimen, which additionally shares its cryptic striping and even its brown eyebrows and vibrissae. But how closely do their relative body proportions compare?

With the exclusion of one oversized skin (probably stretched during preparation), the *F. daemon* specimens examined by Satunin do compare favourably in head-and-body length with the Scottish wildcat and the two Kellas cats measured in detail (those examined by the British Museum). Conversely, the tail lengths recorded from the *F. daemon* specimens are rather longer than those documented for the Scottish wildcat and Kellas cat. Worth recalling here is that an increased tail length is one condition proposed by Mike Tomkies and others as evidence for wildcat × domestic cat hybridization within the Scottish Highlands.[24]

Possibly *Felis daemon* is a simple melanistic hybrid, i.e. more comparable with the BBC's specimen than with the Kellas cats – though, as with these latter felids, only genetic tests can offer a conclusive answer.

Mediterranean Wildcats

The taxonomy of the wildcat *Felis sylvestris* has been at the centre of much chaos, confusion and controversy over the years. To begin with, it was once referred to scientifically as *F. catus* (the name by which the domestic cat is known today), but in the early part of this century Reginald Pocock renamed it *F. sylvestris*, by which it has been known ever since. Furthermore, at one stage several different species of wildcat were recognized. Nowadays, however, all these have been amalgamated within *F. sylvestris*, of which twenty-one subspecies are generally recognized.[31] These in turn are clumped together into three groups – namely, the European group, containing the European wildcat *F. sylvestris sylvestris* and related subspecies (including the Scottish *F. s. grampia*); the African group, containing the African wildcat *F. s. lybica* (the ancestor of the domestic cat) and relatives; and the Asian group, containing the Asian wildcat *F. s. ornata* and three others.[31]

Although, as would be expected, most wildcats in Europe belong to the European group, not all of them do, for, though not widely known and frequently omitted from the more general, popular-format cat books, the wildcats existing upon certain Mediterranean islands are not of the European group at all but are in fact African-related subspecies. The felids in question are those wildcats inhabiting the Balearic Isles, Crete, Sicily, Sardinia and Corsica. In view of this zoogeographically significant situation, it is therefore very surprising to discover that hardly any detailed studies dealing with these unexpected residents of Europe have ever been carried out, making them amongst the most neglected and mysterious of all officially recognized felids. Even more disturbing is the stark fact that in the very near future some of these intriguing insular wildcats may well be extinct.

For example, the Majorcan wildcat (formally described from Santa Margarita in 1930, and named *F. s. jordansi*[38]) may now be extinct, having been hunted relentlessly by man due to its liking for his chickens. According to James Parrack in *The Naturalist in Majorca* (published in 1973),[39] no recent record of trapped wildcats exists, and sight records are always rather ambiguous due to the plentiful supply of feral domestics on the island.[39] However, a few descriptions of clearly observed, unusually large cats do hold some promise for its continuing survival, and Parrack himself saw one felid of characteristic wildcat build and tail near Punto de Pollensa.[39]

Also gravely endangered is the Cretan wildcat *F. s. agrius* – though not through hunting this time but instead through genetic dilution, due to interbreeding with feral domestic cats.[40] If measures are not taken to preserve the pure-bred form (first described in 1905[41]) in the very near future, it is inevitable that this wildcat will soon be replaced totally by hybrids.

The wildcats of Sicily and Sardinia belong to the subspecies *F. s. sarda*, and of all the Mediterranean forms, these compare closest with those from Africa itself.[31] Much more mysterious, however, is their Corsican counterpart *F. s. reyi*, for this island wildcat is known only from a handful of specimens, all obtained within a few months.

The Corsican Wildcat

December 1929 saw the publication of a paper by L. Lavauden,[42] in which he noted that, although several previous articles had referred to the supposed existence on Corsica of a lynx, none had apparently mentioned the presence here of a wildcat form. While undertaking some research concerning this alleged lynx, however, Lavauden had received the skull and skin of a female wildcat, sent to him by a Mr Rey-Jouvin (a teacher at the Lycée de Bastia), who had obtained it in February 1929 at the Forêt d'Aunes, south of Bastia.[42]

The Corsican lynx was never discovered, for Lavauden recognized that the wildcat before him constituted a hitherto unknown form, and concentrated his attention thereafter on this instead, resulting in his scientific paper. In honour of its discoverer, he named the new wildcat *Felis reyi* (since demoted to *F. s. reyi*). Lavauden saw that it differed from the Sardinian wildcat by way of its very short tail, lack of russet shading on the backs of its ears, and very dark pelage, and from the continental European wildcats by way of its dark coat once again, its slender body and a black mark on the sole of each hind foot which extended between the toes.[42]

This latter mark was especially significant, for this is a morphological characteristic of African wildcats, and Lavauden suggested that the Corsican form was indeed most closely related to these, despite its European locality.[42]

Some time after having sent the first skin and skull to Lavauden, Rey-Jouvin obtained two further Corsican wildcat skins, which he passed on to the Musée de Grenoble at Isère. No subsequent specimen of this subspecies has ever been documented scientifically.[42] Yet, according to Rey-Jouvin and also Mr Rotgès (warden of the lakes and forests at Ajaccio at that time), the Corsican wildcat was not rare and could be encountered not only in the mountains and forests but also in hilly scrub and the thickets of the open country. In his paper, Lavauden suggested that the reason for this felid form's not having been reported earlier was that it must be very shy of man, and also that its pelage was in any case not of sufficient worth to warrant any active hunting.[42] Whatever the validity of this second suggestion, if the statements of Rey-Jouvin and Rotgès are accepted, we must certainly endorse the validity of his first, for, despite almost sixty years having passed since the publication of his paper, we are still awaiting a fourth specimen of the Corsican wildcat. Either this felid is indeed exceedingly elusive (even for a cat), or, sadly, it is now extinct.

The Ile du Levant Wildcat

Even more mysterious is the wildcat form inhabiting the Ile du Levant, one of the Iles d'Hyères, located off the coast of the Var, France, for, although there is no question that it exists, no specimen has ever been submitted for scientific examination, hence it continues to evade formal recognition.

Nonetheless, one fact is well established concerning this elusive felid: it attains a considerable size. Dr Bernard Heuvelmans records that in 1932 one specimen seemed to the local inhabitants who observed it to be so large in size that they named it 'the lynx of Paille'.[40] Moreover, during World War II, several specimens were actually snared in rabbit-traps; some allegedly weighed more than 22 lb/10 kg.[40] If only they could have been sent to a museum! Dr Heuvelmans spied one specimen several times himself in 1958, observed whilst savagely attacking some feral domestic cats.[40]

As no specimen has so far been examined, the precise taxonomy of the Ile du Levant wildcat is unknown. In addition, as this island lies much closer to the European mainland than do the other wildcat-inhabited Mediterranean islands noted here, it is particularly difficult to speculate whether this too is most closely allied to the African wildcat or whether it is instead a relative of the continental European subspecies. Yet, regardless of which group lays the greater claim to its taxonomic allegience, the Ile du Levant wildcat is almost certainly a distinct subspecies, and Heuvelmans has proposed '*F. s. levantina*' as a suitable name for it.[40]

The Irish Wildcat

Unlike the British mainland, few reports emerge from Ireland concerning unexpected cats of the Exmoor Beast or Surrey puma variety. Nevertheless, this island is far from bereft of feline mystery – on account of the Irish wildcat. For this officially non-existent felid is anomalous not just as a result of the European wildcat group remaining totally unknown in Ireland both in the living and in the fossil state (despite having once existed not only in Scotland but also in England and Wales). Even more remarkable than this is that reports of alleged wildcats have suggested a closer relationship to the *African* wildcat group than to the European one.

Some of the material in support of Irish wildcats stretches back centuries, interwoven with ancient Celtic mythology. For example, an archaic poem believed to date from the ninth century (translated by Eugene O'Curry and published by Sir William Wilde) tells of the Irish hero Fin mac Cumhaill being held captive by the king of Erinn, Cormac mac Art, who pledged to free him only if a male and female of every species of wild animal inhabiting Ireland were brought to him at the ancient city of Tara. The poem subsequently lists many different animal forms, including a pair of cats brought from the cave of Cruachain.[43]

While on the subject of Irish mythology, Patrick Chalmers argued that, despite the wildcat supposedly being unknown in both Ireland and the Western Islands, the warrior King Cairbar of Connacht was surely called 'Cinn Chait' on account of the pelt of wildcat which he bore on his casque.[44]

This leads us to another aspect of the Irish wildcat mystery. Chalmers's comments drew a response in letter form from A. MacDermott, who maintained that this cat form has never existed in Ireland and that in his own boyhood the name 'wildcat' was actually applied not to any felid but to the pine marten – an arboreal relative of the weasel.[45] Compare this with information obtained nearly fifty years earlier by William Andrews, for he had discovered that the inhabitants of the remote glens of Kerry's western reaches knew of the pine marten *and* of a genuine wildcat form. They even had separate names for the two creatures – calling the marten 'tree cat' and the wildcat 'hunting cat'[46] – thereby destroying MacDermott's notion that the Irish wildcat was nothing more than the result of an etymological ambiguity.

The usage of 'hunting cat' in Ireland relative to supposed wildcats was also noted within the mammalian tome of the Reverend J.G. Wood's series entitled *Illustrated Natural History*,[47] together with an anecdotal account taken from *Notes on the Irish Mammalia* by the well-known Irish naturalist William Thompson. After having noted on several occasions grouse feathers strewn near a water-break in his Irish beat, as well as a number of grouse corpses beheaded but otherwise undamaged, the gamekeeper responsible for that area set a trap and caught two specimens of what appeared to be genuine wildcats, one adult and one juvenile.[47]

Thompson had taken a particular interest in reports of alleged wildcat sightings in Ireland, notably in the mountains of Erris in the county of Mayo. He had himself seen a very large cat, weighing 10 lb 9 oz/4.75 kg, which had been shot in the wild at Shane's Castle park, County Antrim. Apparently this specimen resembled the European wildcat in every way except for its tail (which was not bushy at its tip) and its fur (which was of a finer texture).[48] Consequently, when the *Larne Journal* reported in February 1839 that the wildcat occurred in Tullamore Park and also used to be found along the shores of Ballintrae, Thompson naturally sought out further details. He questioned Lord Roden's gamekeeper, who informed him that he had never seen wildcats in Ireland. All through his researches, Thompson encountered similar conflicts of opinion on this subject, and even his own ultimate conclusion is somewhat paradoxical; for, whilst never becoming entirely convinced (at least not in print) of the wildcat's occurrence here, after comparing the Shane's Castle specimen with two Scottish wildcats he nonetheless offered the opinion that it was probably a wildcat × domestic cat hybrid[48] – needless to say, for a wildcat hybrid to be produced in Ireland, there must be pure-bred wildcats there in the first place.

In his own volume, Wood mentioned that Maxwell's *Wild Sports of the West* contained several accounts concerning a fierce, wild-living felid form in Ireland which was depopulating the rabbit warrens. Apparently one of these cats was killed after a severe battle, and was, according to Wood, '... of a dirty-grey color, double the size of the common house Cat, and its teeth and claws more than proportionately larger. This specimen was a female, which had been traced to a burrow under the rock, and caught in a rabbit-net. With her powerful teeth and claws she tore her way through the net, but was gallantly seized by the lad who set the toils. Upon him she turned her energies, and bit and scratched in a most savage style until she was despatched by a blow from a spade.'[47]

As noted earlier in relation to the Kellas cat, though certainly fierce, feral domestics do not normally attain sizes larger than their tame counterparts. Similarly, in his own wildcat write-up, Wood did not attempt to ally ferals with the much larger and mysterious cat form typified by the beast in the above incident.[47] In any case, both in Wood's time and in the present day, feral domestics are very familiar animals in Ireland, not likely to be mistaken for anything else.[49]

In or around 1883, whilst shooting rabbits near County Galway's Annaghdown, F.C. Wallace sighted an animal which in his opinion seemed to be a magnificent specimen of a bona fide wildcat, but as no physical evidence was obtained, no formal identification could be made.[43]

If the Irish wildcat controversy were ever to be resolved, it was evident that a specimen would have to be procured and submitted for official scientific examination. Such an event appeared, at least initially, to have finally taken place in 1885. For on 28 January of that year, W.B. Tegetmeier exhibited the skin of an alleged wildcat from Donegal at a meeting of the Zoological Society of London[50] and subsequently permitted Dr E. Hamilton to examine it thoroughly. In the Society's *Proceedings* for 3 March, Dr Hamilton's report on this specimen was published – in which he unhesitatingly classified it as nothing more than a feral domestic cat, and included excerpts from letters by earlier researchers interested in the Irish wildcat saga which all supported his own belief that the latter felid did not exist.[48]

Irish wildcat R.I.P.? Not quite – for a most unexpected and pertinent discovery was made a few years later which added a completely new dimension to the mystery. In the report of the Irish Cave Committee sent to the British Association meeting in 1904, Dr R.F. Scharff announced that he had discovered amongst a collection of felid subfossil remains obtained from the Edendale and Newhall Caves near County Clare's Ennis, a number which comprised two distinct series, one small in size, the other larger – and that he considered the larger to be of wildcat identity. Moreover, in a short report published by the *Irish Naturalist* in April 1905, Dr Scharff dramatically reopened the case for the modern Irish wildcat by stating that the position and nature of the bones found suggested that the felid was not long extinct in Ireland, and that it was even possible that a few specimens may still survive in the western regions' more remote mountainous areas.[51] Scharff then went on to comment that until then, it had always been assumed that if a wildcat did actually exist in Ireland it would naturally belong to the Scottish form. However, as a startling climax in his report, Scharff disclosed that the County Clare cave remains were comparable not with the Scottish but with the African wildcat, and that its tail was not bushy at its tip but pointed[51] – just like that of the sizeable cat observed by William Thompson, in fact.

This complete turnabout in the tale of the Irish wildcat resulted in a series of letters on the subject by other interested parties appearing in subsequent months within the *Irish Naturalist*. Some received Scharff's findings favourably and contributed further news regarding the Irish wildcat; others were more critical and remained sceptical. For example, R. Welch related an old fisherman's account originally given to William de Vismes Kane, concerning the wildcat's supposed existence in some numbers on the banks of Lackagh.[52] Conversely, Robert Warren poured cold water on this report, arguing that if such cats were indeed so common within this wild and little-traversed region, then some representatives should still be there today.[53] Yet as noted later by Scharff, in view of the above-mentioned similarity between feral domestic cats and African wildcats (both having tapering tails), perhaps they are.[54] Warren also attested that the finding of sub-fossil bones of a wildcat in Ireland did not prove that the wildcat *was* a native of Ireland – a quite paradoxical statement which the editors of the *Irish Naturalist* were prompt to point out in a footnote at the end of his letter of June 1905.[53]

Scharff published his findings in a formal scientific paper[43] the following year, describing fully the unearthed remains. Meticulous comparisons made by Scharff between these and specimens of Scottish and African wildcats were also included, and which demonstrated conclusively in Scharff's opinion that the Clare cave remains were indeed most closely related to the latter wildcat.[43]

Similarly, G.E.H. Barrett Hamilton had planned to include historical evidence favouring this felid's existence in a forthcoming book on British mammals, but his untimely death prevented this information from being published.[55]

Nevertheless, one would have expected Scharff's researches to have been of sufficient importance in themselves to have initiated a new surge of interest and investigation regarding the Irish wildcat enigma. Instead, the possible existence of living and fossil wildcats in Ireland is nowadays totally dismissed – but why? In a paper published in July 1965, A.W. Stelfox re-examined Scharff's findings, and offered a very different explanation for them. First of all, he considered that Scharff was too willing unconditionally to accept anecdotal evidence of Irish wildcats, and gave the Tegetmeier specimen as an example, which Scharf used in support of their existence (even though it had been denounced as a feral domestic by Hamilton). And as far as the cave remains were concerned, Stelfox was convinced that a much simpler explanation than Scharff's was available for these. Namely, that instead of the smaller ones being domestic cats and the larger ones being wildcats, both sets were of domestic identity – the smaller being females and the larger being males (especially as the two sets were found at the same geological level and in the same mineralized condition). Stelfox also noted that although one would expect remains of fossil wildcats to be associated with those of other wild fossil species of mammal in Ireland if it did indeed possess wildcats at one time, no such find has been discovered; instead, all cat remains known from Ireland have occurred only at levels where the bones of domesticated mammals have been found, and Stelfox reported that he has not uncovered any evidence of cat remains in Ireland that date back further than the Bronze Age.[56] All of which argues very much against a genuine Irish wildcat.

Nonetheless, sightings of large felids not readily explained away as feral domestics continue to emerge from Ireland. In 1968, for example, while seeking out lake monsters in western Ireland, Captain Lionel Leslie and his team were taken aback when a very sizeable felid suddenly appeared on the opposite side of Connemara's Lough Nahooin (i.e. only about 100 yards/91 m away) to where they were standing. According to team member F.W. Holiday, Captain Leslie stated afterwards that he had never seen anything like it before. Dublin zoologists later contacted by Leslie concerning this were equally bemused – a suggestion that it might simply have been a fox was flatly rejected by the team.[57] With leprechaun-like elusiveness, the Irish wildcat continues to evade explanation.

Cave Lions and Scimitar Cats

Unlike its wildcats and lynxes, Europe's larger Pleistocene felids have long since vanished. Even so, various theories and discoveries suggest that some such extinctions may have occurred far more recently than previously supposed.

From fossil remains, palaeontologists know that the European cave lion *Panthera leo spelaea* was still alive at the time of the Palaeolithic artists (about 40,000 years ago), becoming extinct some time after that date. Though not commonly portrayed in their cave paintings, some pictures of this felid are known, including the four painted and engraved frontal views in the Cave de Trois Frères, France, and also a splendid frieze of lions (again engraved) from the Cave de la Vache at Ariège.[58] One of the lions shown in this latter depiction possesses a well-defined tail tuft, thereby eliminating any possibility that it represents a tiger;[58] at one time, some palaeontologists considered that the cave lion may really have been a cave tiger.[59]

The frieze at the Cave de la Vache is approximately 11,000 years old. However, it has been postulated that not only the lions still existing in Greece in 480 BC (some of which attacked the baggage train of Xerxes during his march through Macedonia) but also some of the Assyrian lions of the ancient monuments may actually have been cave lions, rather than a modern subspecies.[60]

Equally, there is a most captivating piece of evidence to support the claim that another of Europe's larger Pleistocene felids may also have survived several millennia longer than many palaeontologists once thought. During the Upper Palaeolithic age, our ancestor Cro-Magnon Man attained a level of culture known as the Aurignacien (34,000-30,000 years ago), from which date the earliest of man's artistic creations, including not only cave paintings but also sculptures. In 1896, an Aurignacien stone statuette measuring about 6½ in/16 cm in length was discovered in a Pyrenean grotto at Isturitz. Though slightly damaged (the limbs' lower portions were missing), it was still recognizable as a sculpture of some form of felid. A photograph was taken of this intriguing item – very fortunately as it turned out, for shortly afterwards the statuette itself was lost, and it has never been recorded since.[61]

The creature which it portrayed had a very large heavy head, a rather short body, long, powerful limbs and a short tail. The most noticeable feature, however, was its lower jaw, which was very powerful, heavy and exceedingly deep.[61]

For a long time after the statuette's discovery, palaeontologists simply assumed it to be a representation of the cave lion, but Czechoslovakian scientist Dr Vratislav Mazak was not at all satisfied with this classification. The felid's curiously shaped lower jaw, as well as its short tail (which appeared to have been deliberately created as such by the Palaeolithic sculpturer concerned, rather than being the result of damage to an originally longer sculptured tail) did not agree with a cave lion identity. The more Mazak studied the photo of the statuette, the more he came to realize that, instead of a cave lion, it most closely resembled another, very different Pleistocene felid, namely the lesser scimitar cat *Homotherium latidens*.[61] This was a species of sabre-tooth (machairodontid) which existed until the late Pleistocene epoch in Great Britain but died out rather earlier on the European mainland (as did its larger relative *H. sainzelli*).[62]

It was a most peculiar animal. Based upon palaeontological evidence, in life it would have borne a superficial resemblance to a giant lynx but was instantly distinguishable from this felid and even from mainstream sabre-tooths by its teeth. The upper canines of scimitar cats were not enlarged to such a notable extent as those of other sabre-tooths. Instead, they were very curved, extremely flattened and razor-sharp, as they were used not for stabbing but for slashing and slicing. In order to house these most unusual upper teeth, the lower jaw was deep in shape and curved down anteriorly on each side to serve as a pair of sheaths for these. This latter modification was peculiar to the machairodontids; none of the true felids (e.g. lion, leopard, tiger, lynx etc) display this, as they have no need of such – their upper canines are much smaller.[62]

Thus, the appearance of the lesser scimitar cat's lower jaw as verified from fossil evidence very closely matches that depicted by the Isturitz statuette and, in combination with the other morphological similarities of the latter with this felid, supports Mazak's exciting theory. Moreover, if this is indeed correct, it provides evidence for believing that on mainland Europe the lesser scimitar cat did not die out (as hitherto believed) about 200,000 years ago but instead lingered for at least a further 165,000 years.

Mazak's paper, published in 1970, attracted the interest of French scientist Dr Michel Rousseau, who published his own account and views on the Isturitz statuette the following year.[63] In this he came out in favour of Mazak's belief but felt that the subject warranted a more detailed investigation – which he himself supplied at the end of 1971, by way of a formal scientific paper published in *Mammalia*.[64] In this, Rousseau not only re-explored in depth the degree of morphological correspondence apparent between the statuette and the lesser scimitar cat but also documented details of various other Palaeolithic works of art that could possibly represent this felid species.[64] One of these consists of an engraving on a fragment of stone, again from Isturitz, which depicts the shoulders and head of a felid with a chin even deeper than the jaw of the statuette's cat. An engraving on limestone at Badegoule portrays three partly superimposed profiles of animal heads – they share the eye and ears but the muzzles, of which two have deep chins, are separate. And an engraving at the Cave de Trois Frères displays the profile of what appears to be the head of a lion, but possessing a fairly deep lower jaw, though less prominent than the previous examples.[64]

The problem to be faced when attempting to categorize these as scimitar cat representations, however, transcends mere morphology, for they all belong to time periods even more recent than that of the Isturitz statuette and during which (as far as Rousseau is concerned) the survival of the scimitar cat would therefore have been quite impossible. After all, there is still no stratigraphical evidence to support its existence during the period when the Isturitz statuette was made, let alone during even more recent times.

And here the tale, unfinished, has remained. Were the above works of Palaeolithic art nothing more than inaccurate or idealized depictions of cave lions, or do they comprise genuine proof that the extraordinary scimitar cat was a contemporary of our ancestors for a far longer period of time than hitherto believed?

An intriguing footnote on this subject of sabre-tooth

iconography is supplied by Charles Berlitz,[65] noting that on an ancient piece of Scythian goldwork (thus dating from approximately 12,000 years ago) a struggle is portrayed between hunters and a beast that markedly resembles a sabre-tooth. Yet the most recent species of mainstream sabre-tooth in Eurasia – *Megantereon inexpectatus* – died out at least 500,000 years ago (and the related *M. megantereon* even earlier), according to current belief.[62] Evidently the artistic creations of ancient man are worthy of close attention not only from the archaeologist and palaeontologist but also from the cryptozoologist.

Pumas, Lions, Panthers and Other Out-of-Place Oddities

Just like Great Britain, continental Europe continues to file reports on a wide range of mystery felids strongly reminiscent of exotic species such as pumas, lions and panthers. So closely, in fact, do these European enigmas correspond with their British counterpart in terms of both appearance and behaviour, and so comparably do the explanations offered in Chapter 1 for the origins and identities of the British cats apply to their European equivalents too, that there seems little point in devoting too much space here to Continental examples, as this would simply involve repetition.

Nonetheless, certain cases are worthy of brief mention. For example, 1927 saw reports of the discovery of a non-fossilised (i.e. modern) leopard skull within a cave in Ariège, France.[66] Its origin was unknown. Two decades later, an outbreak of mystery cat accounts and farmstock killings hit the headlines in central France. Not only was a 'lion' killing sheep, but wolf-like, lioness-like and even leopard-like beasts were also being reported during the later 1940s,[67] all from this same region. All of these were frequently lumped together to yield a protean-like mystery creature dubbed 'the beast of Cezallier'.[67] In 1951 a genuine wolf *was* killed – near to Grandrieu, Upper Loire – and the Cezallier Beast episode came to an end.[67]

Nevertheless, it is rather difficult to believe that a wolf could be responsible for the mystery cat sightings too – more likely is that it served as a convenient 'official' solution to them.

A similar French episode occurred in 1978, involving a pair of panther-like beasts sighted in the Vosges area,[68] while the equally elusive 'beast of Valescure' (also nicknamed 'the beast of Estérel' and classed as a lioness, wolf, puma and various other carnivores) occupied newspaper headlines during February 1983 but was never caught, and eventually disappeared.[68,69] At much the same time, West German zoologists were examining the tracks of a puma-like animal sighted in Hanover;[70] sightings surfaced again briefly in

1985, but the mystery was never resolved.[68] (1982 had seen a similar outbreak of German puma reports, but centred instead on Hamburg.[68]) Italy's contribution to continental Europe's cryptic cats includes a pair of pumas reported in 1983 at Bari,[68] whilst Switzerland's Graubünden was the scene in 1974 for the observation by two hunters of a supposed tiger![68] The history and sociological implications behind various other recent continental cases, such as the Pornic panther and especially 'the beast of Noth', are dealt with succinctly by Jean-Louis Brodu and Michel Meurger in *Les Félins-Mystère*.[71]

Not all recent accounts of out-of-place Continental felids involve non-European species – some refer to species reappearing in localities from which they supposedly died out many decades before. In the Jura, for example, where the wildcat has officially been extinct for many years, cats continue to appear which, when scientifically examined, prove to be not feral domestics but genuine wildcats. Dr Peter Lüps of the Berne Natural History Museum has documented several recent examples;[72] it is likely that they are migrants from bordering France.[31] Similarly, the last reliable report of a lynx in the Italian Alps dated from 1915[31] – until 1983, that is, when a new record of a lynx was made, from Belzano in the eastern Alps.[73] And in Switzerland, where the last formally documented lynx was officially taken in 1872 (a few unconfirmed later reports also exist), continuing reports of doe deer and small stock kills by mysterious predators since World War II suggest that the lynx may be re-establishing itself here too[31] – always assuming, of course, that it had ever died out.

The Russian Mystery Beast

During the 1980s, Britain's most publicized mystery felids have been the Kellas cat and the Exmoor Beast. In the Soviet Union, comparable creatures were active many years earlier. We met *Felis daemon*, a Russian counterpart of sorts to the Kellas cat, towards the beginning of this chapter. Now let us bring it to a close with an examination of an Eastern European equivalent of the Exmoor Beast – the unaccountable carnivore of Orel Province.

The saga reached Britain quite inauspiciously, via a brief note contained in *The Field* for 12 August 1893, which read: 'For some days past a panther, which escaped from the grounds of a landed proprietor who had a fancy for keeping wild animals, has been at large in the province of Orel, Russia, to the terror of the villagers. The panther has already killed six persons; and although repeated *battues* have been organised by various sportsmen of the district, they have not succeeded in slaying the beast.'[74] A very unpleasant but nonetheless unremarkable incident. In the months to come, however, it was to transform into a thoroughly bewildering affair. Whole pages were soon devoted to this business, yet few real developments occurred. Sightings of the creature and attacks upon people and animals continued, but repeated searches by soldiers following instructions from the province's governor, together with interested sportsmen from near and far (plus contingents of the local populace), all failed totally in their attempts to shoot or snare it. By the end of the year, however, the sightings had petered out, and nothing further was heard of Orel's mystery assailant. Apparently the creature ate two poisoned sheep and disappeared, its tracks leading into the forest beyond the River Vetebet.[75,76]

And so it was never caught – which is a great tragedy, because by far the most extraordinary aspect of this whole incident is the thorough confusion concerning the creature's supposed appearance. Despite many sightings having been reported, no one seemed at all sure of its identity – a fact underlined by the shooting of animals as diverse as dogs, hens and even a striped pig by soldiers who began to see savage carnivores everywhere.[75,76]

For example, the panther identity soon gave way to a lynx, a wolf and (helped along by a sighting made by the commander of a massive thousand-man beat) a tiger.[75,76] As it happens, tigers are not unknown in Russia, sometimes driven by starvation during harsh winters to prowling villages and towns (especially in the Soviet Far East[31] – as recently as January 1987 two Amur tigers were shot dead on snow-covered streets in Vladivostok[77].) And 100 years ago, tigers did exist not all that far south of the Orel region. Nevertheless, what makes the tiger identity particularly bizarre in the case of the Orel beast is that none of the eyewitnesses on record could actually recall seeing stripes on the animal.[75]

In view of this, it is hardly surprising that not everyone believed the tiger theory. The Moscow sportsman Prince Sherincki-Shakhmatoff was invited to seek the creature, which he and his companions did, but without success. Nonetheless, he did observe spoor allegedly left behind by it; and based upon this, together with the manner of its attacks and the types of wounds which it inflicted upon its victims, he judged the animal to be a panther[76] – an opinion shared by R.G. Burton, who prepared a detailed history of the Orel Beast that appeared in *The Field* on 9 December 1893.[76] Conversely, another sportsman who had also been pursuing it closely considered it to be nothing more than a large dog. Combining these schools of thought were the opinions of various other hunters, who felt that there were two totally different beasts involved – one large and one small. Worth noting is that in this area at that time dogs were often kept together with panthers in menageries. Perhaps this gave rise to a further belief – that a dog and a panther had escaped together.[76]

Certainly, little can be ascertained from the descriptions documented of the Orel Beast. In a report published by *The Field* on 19 August 1893, it was described as being, '... the height of a wolf, of a yellow colour, with a blunt muzzle. His tracks are round, like a wolf's, about 3½ in [8.75 cm] in diameter, but the claws imprint pointed tracks'.[75] In Burton's later account, he adds that its ears were round and pricked, and its tail was long, smooth and hanging, while in overall size the beast appeared not to have been very large or remarkably powerful, no more so than a dog.[76] It is quite likely that the original creature was indeed an escaped felid but that it later became confused with sightings of large dogs (perhaps even wolves[78]) and ultimately disappeared out of the district, and that its presence was replaced thereafter by canids. Unfortunately, as no scientific investigation was put into operation, there is little hope that this baffling case will ever be solved.

In 1939 Sir Winston Churchill described the action of the Soviet Union in relation to World War II as being 'a riddle wrapped in a mystery inside an enigma'. The same could also be said of its mystery beast from Orel Province.

Abbreviation: *PZSL* = *Proceedings of the Zoological Society of London*

1 Morgan, D., *Forres Gazette*, 19 September 1984
2 Ibid., 13 June 1984
3 Ibid., 26 September 1984
4 *Fortean Times*, No. 45, pp. 10-12 (winter 1985)
5 *Forres Gazette*, 3 October 1984
6 Shuker, K.P.N., Scientific paper awaiting publication in *Cryptozoology* (written in 1986)
7 Boyne, I., *Daily Telegraph*, 15 December 1984
8 Hills, D., Unpublished report (compiled in 1985)
9 Goss, M., *BBC Wildlife*, Vol. 3, p. 100 (March 1985)
10 *Forres Gazette*, 29 May 1985
11 Hills, D., Unpublished report (compiled in 1986)
12 Morgan, D., *Forres Gazette*, 16 October 1985; *Daily Telegraph*, 17 October 1985
13 *Press & Journal* (Aberdeen), 27 July 1987
14 Dash, M., *Fortean Times*, No. 49, pp. 36-9 (winter 1987); Greenwell, J.R., (ed.), *ISC Newsletter*, Vol. 6, p. 4 (winter 1987)
15 Bailey, M., *The Observer*, 26 July 1987 – and syndicated abroad in: *Cincinnati Post*, 3 August 1987; *Mesa Tribune*, 3 August 1987; *Rocky Mountain News*, 3 August 1987; *San Francisco Examiner*, 3 August 1987; *Vindicator* (Youngstown, Ohio), 10 August 1987; *Press* (New Zealand), 11 August 1987; *Beaumont Enterprise* (Texas) 19 August 1987
16 Shuker, K.P.N., Paper presented at the ISC Annual Members Meeting, Royal Museum of Scotland, 26 July 1987

17 Hughes-Games, M. (producer), *On the Trail of the Big Cat* (BBC television, first broadcast 22 May 1986)
18 Morgan, D., *Forres Gazette*, 30 April 1986
19 Jacks, H., *Press & Journal* (Aberdeen), 1 March 1988
20 Douglas, D., *Glasgow Herald*, 27 July 1987
21 Shuker, K.P.N., Communications (unpublished) containing personal researches and opinions concerning Kellas cat origin and identity, sent to Di Francis (1984-7)
22 Tabor, R., *The Wildlife of the Domestic Cat* (Arrow Books, 1983)
23 Robinson, R., *Carnivore Genetics Newsletter*, Vol. 2, pp. 93-4 (1972); Pitt, F., *The Field*, Vol. 163, p. 1,528 (23 June 1934)
24 Tomkies, M., *My Wilderness Wildcats* (Macdonald & Jane's, 1977)
25 French, D.D., Corbett, L.K., and Easterbee, N., *Journal of Zoology*, Vol, 214, pp. 235-59 (1988)
26 *Forres Gazette*, 25 June 1986
27 Corbet, G.B., and Southern, H.N., *The Handbook of British Mammals*, (second edition) (Blackwell, 1977)
28 Keeler, C.E., *Journal of Heredity*, Vol. 33, pp. 371-84 (1942); Keeler, C.E., ibid., Vol. 38, pp. 271-7 (1947); Keeler, C.E., in Fox, M.W., (ed.), *The Wild Canids. Their Systematics, Behavioral Ecology and Evolution* (Van Nostrand Reinhold, 1975), pp. 399-413
29 Pocock, R.I., *Annals and Magazine of Natural History*, Series 8, Vol. 18, pp. 419-29 (1916)
30 Savage, R.J.G., *Palaeontology*, Vol. 20, pp. 237-71 (1977)
31 Guggisberg, C.A.W., *Wild Cats of the World* (David & Charles, 1975)
32 Weigel, I., in Grzimek, B. (ed.), *Grzimek's Animal Life Encyclopedia*, Vol. 12 (Van Nostrand Reinhold, 1975), pp. 312-32.
33 Thomas, A.C., Personal communication -- a detailed account describing the linguistic connection of names of native (known or unrecognized) Scottish fauna with early tribal history (unpublished, 1984)
34 Campbell, J.G., *Superstitions of the Highlands and Islands of Scotland* (J. MacLehose, 1900); Briggs, K., *A Dictionary of Fairies* (Allen Lane, 1976).
35 Satunin, C., *PZSL*, pp. 162-3 (1904)
36 Smirnov, N., *Bulletin du Musée de Caucase* Vol. 11, pp. 84-6 (1917); Ognev, S.I., *Mammals of the USSR and Adjacent Countries. Vol. III: Carnivora* (Israel Program for Scientific Translations: Jerusalem, 1962)
37 Pocock, R.I., *Catalogue of the Genus Felis* (Brit. Mus. Nat. Hist., 1951)
38 Schwarz, E., *Zoologischer Anzeiger*, Vol. 91, pp. 223-4 (1930)
39 Parrack, J.D., *The Naturalist in Majorca* (David & Charles, 1973)
40 Heuvelmans, B., *Cryptozoology*, Vol. 5, pp. 1-26 (1986)
41 Bate, D.M.A., *PZSL*, pp. 315-23 (1905)
42 Lavauden, L., *Comptes Rendus de l'Academie des Sciences*, Vol. 189, pp. 1,023-4 (2 December 1929)
43 Scharff, R.F., *Proceedings of the Royal Irish Academy B*, Vol. 26, pp. 1-12 (1906)
44 Chalmers, P., *The Field*, Vol. 178, p. 672 (6 December 1941)
45 MacDermott, A., ibid., Vol. 179, p. 16 (3 January 1942)
46 Andrews, W., *Proceedings of the Dublin Natural History Society*, Vol. 1 (1890s)
47 Wood, J.G., *Illustrated Natural History: Mammalia* (Routledge, Warne & Routledge, 1859-63)
48 Hamilton, E., *PZSL*, pp. 211-14 (3 March 1885)
49 Lloyd, A.T., *Carnivore Genetics Newsletter*, Vol. 3, pp. 373-7 (1979)
50 Tegetmeier, W.B., *PZSL*, p. 3 (1885)
51 Scharff, R.F., *Irish Naturalist*, Vol. 14, p. 79 (April 1905)
52 Welch, R., ibid., Vol. 14 (May 1905); Kane, W.F. de V., ibid., Vol. 14, pp.

165-6 (July 1905)
53 Warren, R., ibid, Vol. 14, pp. 135-6 (June 1905) & Vol. 14, pp. 183-4 (August 1905)
54 Scharff, R.F., ibid., Vol. 14, p. 184 (August 1905)
55 Barrett-Hamilton, G.E.H., ibid., Vol. 20, p. 55 (March 1911); Moffat, C.B., *Proceedings of the Royal Irish Academy B*, Vol. 44, pp. 61-128 (1937-8)
56 Stelfox, A.W., *Irish Naturalists' Journal*, vol. 15, pp. 57-60 (July 1965)
57 Holiday, F.W., *The Goblin Universe* (Llewellyn Publishers, Minnesota, 1986)
58 Sutcliffe, A.J., *On the Track of Ice Age Mammals* (Brit. Mus. Nat. Hist., 1985)
59 Ferrant, V., and Friant, M., *Bulletin. Musée National d'Histoire Naturelle (Paris)*, Series 2, Vol. 11, pp. 508-12 (1939)
60 Fisher, J., Simon, N., and Vincent, J., *The Red Book* (Collins, 1969); Jaekel, O., *Zoologischer Anzeiger*, Vol. 70, pp. 225-36 (1927)
61 Mazak, V., *Zeitschrift für Säugetierkunde*, Vol. 35, pp. 359-62 (1970)
62 Kurten, B., *Pleistocene Mammals of Europe* (Weidenfeld & Nicolson, 1968)
63 Rousseau, M., *Archéologia*, No. 40, pp. 81-2 (May-June 1971)
64 Rousseau, M., *Mammalia*, Vol. 35, pp. 648-57 (December 1971)
65 Berlitz, C., *Atlantis* (Macmillan 1984)
66 Begouen, H., *Bulletin de la Societé d'Histoire Naturelle (Toulouse)*, Vol. 56, pp. 469-71 (1927); Astre, G., ibid., Vol. 56, pp. 471-4 (1927)
67 *Doubt*, No. 17, p. 260, and No. 18, p. 269 (1947); Chartrain, D., *Amazone*, No. 1, p. 17 (October 1982)
68 Magin, U. *Pursuit*, Vol. 17, pp. 114-15 (autumn 1984)
69 *Matin* (Nice), 16 and 18 February 1983; *Fortean Times*, No. 43, p. 47 (spring 1985)
70 *Fortean Times*, No. 42, pp. 41-2 (autumn 1984)
71 Brodu, J-P, and Meurger, M., *Les Félins-Mystère* (Pogonip, Paris, 1984)
72 Lüps, P., *Mitteilungen der Naturforschenden Gessellschaft in Bern* Vol. 28, pp. 71-3 (1971); Lüps, P. *Jahrbuch des Naturhistorischen Museums Bern*, Vol. 7, pp. 195-9 (1981); Lüps, P., Unpublished report (1983)
73 Ragni, B., *Natura Montagna* Vol. 30, pp. 41-3 (1983)
74 *The Field*, Vol. 82, p. 263 (12 August 1893)
75 Ibid., Vol. 82, p. 302 (19 August 1893)
76 Burton, R.G., ibid., Vol. 82, p. 882 (9 December 1893)
77 Pietila, A., *Sun* (Baltimore, Maryland) 15 February 1987
78 Keswal., *The Field*, Vol. 83, p. 127 (27 January 1894)

3 Multicoloured Tigers and Mint-Leaf Leopards

Asia

Through the Jungle very softly flits a shadow and a sigh –
He is Fear, O Little Hunter, he is Fear!
Rudyard Kipling, *The Song of the Little Hunter*

In terms of felid diversity, the continent of Asia is unrivalled, laying claim to a total of fourteen species of Small Cat, the systematically singular clouded leopard and no fewer than four species of Big Cat (tiger, leopard, lion and snow leopard).[1] In addition, a tiny number of Asian cheetahs exist in the Middle East[1] (most recently, reports have emerged concerning a small population rediscovered in Iran's Yeylaq mountain region, bordering Iraq[2]).

Many of these felids are striking, handsomely marked creatures, but none more so than the tiger *Panthera tigris*, surely the living embodiment of Asia itself – exotic, elusive, majestic, mysterious. Eight modern subspecies are recognized, ranging in shade and size from the pale Amur (Siberian) tiger *P. t. altaica*, of average total length 11 ft/330 cm, to the dark orange Bali tiger *P. t. balica*, not generally exceeding 7 ft/210 cm. In addition, there is much evidence to suggest that the 'burning bright' black-and-orange pelage which illuminated the imagination of William Blake is far from being the only colour-combination which can be exhibited by the tiger.

White and Red Tigers

The most familiar of all aberrant tigers are the famous white tigers of the old Indian state of Rewa (now part of Madhya Pradesh), well known from various priceless specimens displayed at several of the world's major zoos.[3] These tigers are partial albinos – specifically, they are homozygous for the full colour gene's recessive chinchilla mutant allele. In such tigers, their coat's background colour is creamy white and overlaid by ash-grey stripes; in addition, their eyes are blue.[4] White tigers of this type, though most widely known from Rewa, have been documented from various other Indian states too, and even beyond India[5] (e.g. China, Korea[6]), though sadly they now appear to be extinct in the wild state.

Having been well documented and well studied, these chinchilla white tigers are no longer anomalous. Conversely, the possible existence of pure white tigers is a subject still shrouded in mystery and controversy. In his definitive work *Le Règne Animal*, the eminent eighteenth-century French naturalist Baron Georges Cuvier described a white tigress whose stripes were visible only when viewed from certain angles,[7] implying that this was a true albino individual (i.e. homozygous for the full colour gene's recessive complete albino mutant allele).[8] A comparable specimen was on display in London during the 1820s and was described in the Reverend J.G. Wood's *Illustrated Natural History* as follows: 'The color of this animal was a creamy white, with the ordinary tigerine stripes so faintly marked that they were only visible in certain lights.'[9] Clearly another complete albino. Yet, surprisingly, some years later the famous British zoologist Richard Lydekker still doubted whether such tigers really existed,[10] a doubt which persisted in the minds of some other authorities too – until 1922. During that year, two pure-white sub-adult tigers were shot in the former north-east Indian state of Cooch Behar. And, as confirmation of their genetic status, they possessed the characteristic trademark of all complete albinos – pink eyes,[11] for in such mutants (irrespective of species) even the pigment of the eye's iris is absent.

In addition to the chinchilla and the complete albino forms described above, somewhat darker versions of white tiger also exist, in which the coat's background colour is a very pale counterpart of that of normal tigers, while the stripes are dark brown rather than black. These very unusual, pallid tigers are referred to loosely as 'red tigers'[5] (produced by chinchilla-related alleles?[8]). And according to Roy Robinson, the colouration of a brown tiger with stripes only a little darker than its coat's background shading (recorded by Reginald Pocock[12]) may be due to expression of the extension of black gene's non-extension mutant allele.[8]

In a letter published in *The Times* during 1936, W.H. Carter commented that, in one of the official gazetteers of Bengal, a local tiger form was mentioned which does not possess stripes at all but is instead uniformly brown. Carter suggested that this would serve as camouflage in the open sandy tracts of Sunderbans which it inhabits.[13] Further data on tigers with reduced striping has been documented by Willy Schroeter.[14]

Blue Tigers

Even more exotic and ethereal than red or white tigers is the concept of a blue tiger, yet it would seem that such a felid form exists not only in reverie but also in reality, at least as far as Harry R. Caldwell was concerned – for he almost shot one! Moreover, as both a Methodist missionary and a very experienced big-game hunter who bagged dozens of tigers during his stay in China, Caldwell was nothing if not a reliable eyewitness.

In September 1910, while in the Futsing region of Fujian (formerly Fukien) Province in south-eastern China, he was watching a goat when an attendant directed his attention to something else: 'I glanced at the object, which appeared to be a man dressed in the conventional light-blue garment and crouching.... I simply whispered to the cook, "Man," and again turned my attention to watching the goat. Again the cook tugged at my elbow, saying, "Tiger, surely a tiger," and I once more looked.... Now focusing upon what I had altogether overlooked in my previous hurried glances, I saw the huge head of the tiger above the blue which had appeared to me to be the clothes of a man. What I had been looking at was the chest and belly of the beast.'[15]

Caldwell described this uncanny tiger as follows: 'The markings of the animal were marvellously beautiful. The ground colour seemed to be a deep shade of maltese, changing into almost deep blue on the under parts. The stripes were well defined, and so far as I was able to make out similar to those of a tiger of the regular type.'[15]

Just as Caldwell was about to pull the trigger on this near-fairytale felid (which he had aptly nicknamed 'Bluebeard'), he perceived that it was clearly very interested in something in the ravine beneath the spot where it was sitting. Caldwell was unable to spy the subject of the tiger's attention, so he leaned forward to obtain a better view and spotted two boys gathering bundles of vegetation. Caldwell realized that, if he shot the tiger from his present location, he might endanger the children, so he decided to move to a different one to alter the direction of his shot. This he did, but upon arrival there he discovered to his horror that the tiger had silently departed, leaving Caldwell with only a memory of his encounter with what must surely be the most marvellous of all mystery cats.[15]

In his book *Blue Tiger* (published in 1925), Caldwell noted that other sightings of such creatures had been reported in this region of China[15] – reiterated more recently by Dr Heuvelmans.[16]

Science has yet to examine one of Fujian's blue tigers but, judging from Caldwell's precise description, I feel that it is likely that this form is homozygous for both the recessive non-agouti mutant allele of the agouti gene and the recessive dilute mutant allele of the dense pigmentation gene. This combination yields a notably blue-hued pelage generally termed 'blue dilution'.

Black Tigers

Melanism in felids is most frequently exhibited by tropical species, as exemplified by the leopard and jaguar. Consequently, one would expect the tiger to exhibit an all-black morph too. Yet, very surprisingly, not a single specimen of a melanistic tiger has ever been submitted for official scientific examination. Indeed, in recent books dealing with felids, mention of black tigers is either omitted or limited to a couple of lines in which alleged sightings of such cats are generally discounted as panther misidentifications. Supported as it is, however, by a very extensive history of observations and reports, the subject of black tigers is one which should not be dismissed so lightly.

Probably the most significant black tiger record was provided by the noted eighteenth-century artist James Forbes. In a *Country Life* article,[17] Charles Stonor noted that, among the many watercolours by Forbes then housed within the museum of the seminary at Oscott College near Walsall, one, dating back to 1772, depicted in very great detail a black tiger and was painted in south-west India during the period when Forbes was in the service of John Company in India. A description of this felid featured in his painting also exists, contained in one of Forbes' own handwritten letters from that same period. He wrote:

> I have also the opportunity of adding the portrait of an extraordinary Tyger, shot a few months ago by the Nairs in this neighbourhood, and presented to the Chief as a great curiosity. It was entirely black yet striped in the manner of the Royal-Tyger, with shades of a still darker hue, like the richest black, glossed with purple. My pencil is very deficient in displaying these mingled tints; nor do I know how to describe them better than by the difference you would observe in a black cloth variegated with shades of a rich velvet.[17]

The current whereabouts of this painting is unknown; in October 1987 I learnt from Oscott College's rector, the Rt. Rev. Mgr. Michael J. Kirkham, that in 1965 the entire Forbes collection was sold at Sotheby's, and no record appears to have been kept of the black tiger painting's new owner.

A follow-up letter concerning black tigers, written by Lieutenant-Colonel N.M. Hughes-Hallett,[18] appeared in *Country Life* three weeks after Stonor's article and referred to a book entitled *Sophie in London, 1786*, published in 1933. In this, the lady in question recorded her impressions of a trip to the Tower of London's menagerie, mentioning lions, leopards, tigers and wolves, and also noting: 'The all-black Tiger, which Mr Hastings brought with him from the East Indies is most handsome, but his tigery glance is horrible.' Another eighteenth-century black tiger?

The next report which I have is a short item from *The Observer* for 27 January 1844, which records that a black tiger (originally intended as a present from the King of Java to Napoleon) was currently on display at Kendrick's collection of exotic animals opposite St James's Church, Piccadilly.[19]

Two years later came an account from the noted naturalist C.T. Buckland. Early in 1846, a black tiger was reported from the Chittagong hills, in what is now Bangladesh, which was not only raiding cattle but had also killed a local villager. In March Buckland recorded in his diary that news had reached him of its dead body's having been discovered, lying near the edge of a road; it had been killed by a poisoned arrow. In the company of a number of other interested persons, Buckland set out to view it. Upon arrival, they inspected the carcase closely, and Buckland described it as follows:

> It was a full-sized tiger, and the skin was black, or very dark-brown, so that the stripes showed rather a darker black in the sunlight, just as the spots are visible on the skin of a black leopard ... by the time that we arrived the carcase was swollen, the flies were buzzing about it, and decomposition had set in so that those of our party who knew best, decided that the skin could not be saved.... Captain Swatman, who was in charge of the Government elephant kheddas, and Captain Hore (afterwards Lord Ruthven), of the 25th N.I., were well-known sportsmen, and had each of them killed many tigers. No doubt was expressed about the animal being a black tiger.[20]

Moving into the twentieth century, T.A. Hauxwell (then the Conservator of Forests at Maymyo, Burma) recorded in 1914 the wounding of a supposed black tiger at a range of 15 yards/13.5 m by his son, in the Bhamo district. At first his son took the all-black creature to be a pig, while his shikari insisted that it was a bear. Upon approaching very cautiously the area in which the growling wounded beast was moving, however, they observed enormous round pug-marks, measuring 20 in/50 cm in circumference, which in their judgement seemed closely similar to those of a tiger. Sadly, the body of this mysterious animal was never recovered.[21]

In 1928 the editors of *The Field* noted that a dead black tiger had been reported in the Lushai Hills, south of Assam; frustratingly, this specimen's skin was too decomposed to be saved.[22]

During the early 1930s, a reward was offered for the destruction of a savage creature inhabiting India's Imphal Manipur state. When eventually dispatched, the latter proved to be an adult black bear – but the Mikirs insisted that it was a black tiger. In the opinion of J.C. Higgins, however, this peculiar classification was largely influenced by the fact that the reward to be gained if the creature proved to be a tiger was more than twice that on offer for a bear.[23]

Also during the 1930s, a series of letters concerning black tigers appeared in *The Times*. The earlier items dealt with cases noted above, but the later letters provided several additional examples. Captain Guy Dollman of the British Museum (Natural History) reported that a young black tiger had been shot in the Central Provinces some years earlier and had possessed a dark brown background coat colour, overlaid by black stripes. He also commented that a magnificent black tiger had been shot in 1915 by some natives in Assam, east of Dibrugarh – of especial interest was the fact that this specimen was completely black, no vestige of striping being visible even in sunlight.[24,25]

Colonel S. Capper placed on record a very clear sighting of a black tiger made through a deer-stalker's telescope by himself and his hunting companion C.J. Maltby on 11 September 1895, on the Cardoman Hills of southern India. The tiger was initially lying on a rock at the jungle's edge, but eventually it rose and disappeared from sight into the latter. Upon arrival at this spot, Capper and Maltby discovered the clear pug-marks of a tiger – both men were well acquainted with tiger and leopard spoor.[26]

The first few lines of a letter to *The Times* in January 1937 by R.G. Griffiths contained the news which science had been awaiting so long – a black tiger had been captured alive! A colossal creature, 12 ft/360 cm long, it had been caught on 4 September 1936 in the vicinity of Dibrugarh. So far so good. As one might have expected of a mystery felid, however, the truth – as Griffiths revealed in the lines that followed – was rather different.[27] Further enquiries (made by Dr Baini Prashad, director of the Zoological Survey of India at Calcutta's Indian Museum[28]) not only revealed that it was a lot shorter than claimed but also discovered that it was not a tiger at all. Instead, it was nothing more than an 8 ft/240 cm-long black panther.[27] This muddled melanistic mammal was later sold and transferred to Calcutta, where

Griffiths had recently seen it; further details were given by Captain Dollman.[25]

Regrettably, it seems as if the misidentified panther of Dibrugarh sounded the death-knell for the bona fide black tigers; until then, the existence of such cats had never been seriously doubted, but following this sorry episode the black tiger appeared to fall out of fashion.

In a letter published by *The Field* on 9 January 1937, Dunbar Brander recorded that a couple of years earlier the sportsman and Calcutta barrister J.A. Clough had seen, in the deputy commisioner's bungalow at Betul, Central Provinces, a tiger skin whose background colour was chocolate brown. When questioned concerning this, the deputy commissioner mentioned that a second tiger of this type had been sighted in the area where his own specimen had been killed.[29]

By and large, however, reports dried up, and the black tiger became yet another felid of fiction and fable rather than fact.

To complete this account, I will come full circle, back to the 1964 *Country Life* article by Charles Stonor. In this, Stonor also included a personally collected report of particular interest. He recalled that, whilst in the Mishmi Hills, at the foot of the Assam Himalayas, he had learnt from a local headman that the Mishmi tribespeople knew of an occasionally seen creature referred to as the 'bear tiger', which resembles a normal tiger in all respects but one – it is completely black. At Stonor's suggestion that it could simply be a panther, the headman reasserted vehemently that it was a black tiger – stating that not only was it of full tiger stature but also, when observed in sunlight, one could discern the familiar tiger pattern of stripes upon its otherwise inky coat.[17]

Very recently, I was informed by Phil Bennett that in India, during 1952, the people of one village complained that an exceedingly large black tiger was killing their cattle. According to these villagers, the cat in question was between 20-24 ft/600-720 cm in length! Although the authorities searched for this extraordinary beast in vain, some unusually large pug-marks were found, which could not be explained. Further reports of this animal continued to emerge until 1967 (Bennett, pers. comm.).

With the exception of this latter colossus (whose length is clearly an immense exaggeration on the part of the locals, its size presumably increasing in direct proportion to their fear of it), the alleged black tigers which figure in the above collection of reports conform to a standard appearance. The only degree of variation on record concerns the pelage's background colour – dark brown in some individuals, totally black in others – but such variation is commonly seen amongst melanistic individuals of other species too, including the leopard.

Is it possible, therefore, that genuine melanistic tigers do occur? Let us first consider some other phenomena which could explain alleged black tiger sightings.

For example, could they be, as with the captured Dibrugarh specimen from 1936, nothing more than misidentified panthers? This could certainly be the case with sightings involving only the briefest of observations, or made in conditions of poor lighting or deceptive shade, or made by observers with little or no experience of tigers. Conversely, most of the reports mentioned in this section have taken place in good light, with ample observation time (in some cases the specimen was dead, and hence unlikely to run away!), and sometimes involving eyewitnesses with superb credentials. These latter include: experienced tiger-hunters Captain Swatman and Lord Ruthven, naturalist and Fellow of the Zoological Society of London C.T. Buckland, and painter and Fellow of the Royal Society James Forbes. The two reports incorporating these eyewitnesses' accounts are in themselves enough to verify that black tigers as well as black leopards exist. The experience of various eyewitnesses in distinguishing readily between tiger and leopard spoor also supports the validity of tiger identifications in relation to certain other black tiger reports.

In addition, the description of black tigers contained in the reports given here – a tiger-sized black (occasionally dark brown) cat whose stripes can be discerned in sunlight – is exactly that which we would expect for a true melanistic (non-agouti) tiger.

Certainly it is inconceivable that anyone could fail to distinguish (at least on a dead specimen) between the cryptic spots of a panther and the long, continuous shadowy stripes of a melanistic tiger. This being the case, how did the infamous Dibrugarh 'black tiger' fiasco come about? Most probably not through any morphological muddle or misconception but through an error of etymology, for, as E.P. Gee points out, *bagh* – the word for 'tiger' in various parts of India – is, in fact, commonly used for almost any cat species. In short, the locals will refer in their language to a 'striped tiger' (the true tiger), a 'spotted tiger' (leopard) and so on, right down to the smaller cat species.[30] Consequently, when the Dibrugarh 'tiger' was captured, it would simply have been referred to locally as a 'black tiger', even though it was a black leopard, and even though the locals *knew* it to be a black leopard. The error came from the loose translation of *bagh* not being familiar to non-locals, who naturally took 'black tiger' to mean just that.

It is also worth noting that in the early nineteenth century British people referred to both tiger and panther as 'tiger', with the epithet 'royal' being added when speaking of the genuine striped tiger. Thus the Piccadilly 'black tiger' was probably a black panther – this may also have been the identity of the specimen noted in *Sophie in London, 1786*.

Excluding etymological ambiguities, however, it is evident that few of the black tiger reports documented here could have been based upon panther sightings.

Another explanation sometimes put forward to deny the existence of genuine black tigers is that sightings of such were really of normal tigers whose coats had become darkened in various ways by external factors. One such manner involves deceptive shadows cast upon terrestrial beasts in dense jungles during early morning and evening.[31] However, such shadows cannot account for the skins of dead black tigers reported here, which were examined carefully by competent observers. A suggestion by Dunbar Brander is that black tigers are actually normal tigers that have rolled in the charcoal and ashes of forest fires.[32] If this were true, the cryptic stripes so characteristic of the black tigers reported would have been totally hidden by the charcoal. Moreover, observers of the dead specimens would surely have noted the presence of charcoal on such skins – no mention of its presence, however, has ever been made.

Dunbar Brander once watched a large tiger devouring a kill and, in so doing, becoming covered with its victim's blood, which rapidly turned from red to black. He commented that, had he not seen this transformation taking place before his very eyes, he would have been firmly convinced that he had stumbled upon a genuine black tiger.[30,33] Once again, however, such an occurrence would hide the cryptic stripes clearly observed by many black tiger eyewitnesses. This is equally true relative to yet another of Brander's suggestions.[29] In various jungle pools used by tigers for bathing and by tanners for skin-preservation, certain tree barks are introduced to poison fish that become marooned there when the pools shrink during hot weather; these barks also stain fur a deep brown shade and could be responsible, according to Brander, for reports of brown tigers, dead or alive. Elegant, but unsatisfactory.

Only one plausible possibility is left – that sightings of alleged black tigers have really involved melanistic tigers after all, and why not? As vouched for by felid geneticist Roy Robinson, the descriptions of cryptic stripes provide the most telling piece of eyewitness evidence in favour of such creatures' existence.[8]

What remains to be explained is why they should be so rare, in contrast to the relative abundance of the melanistic morph in leopards and other tropical felids. The answer is probably connected to the fact that, whilst such species have normally originated in the tropics, the tiger evolved in a much colder climate, invading Asia's tropical zones only in relatively recent times (geologically speaking). Black is the most efficient heat radiator, hence black coat colouration is advantageous to a felid inhabiting a tropical locality, for it would assist it effectively to release heat from its body, especially in shade, where dark colours operate most efficiently. Consequently, melanistic coat colouration would be selected as a result of this inherent survival advantage, and thus the frequency of the non-agouti mutant allele would increase within populations of leopards etc. Once the tiger also entered such locations, this same allele would then begin to increase through selection in tiger populations. Yet because this allele would have been exposed to positive selection for far less time than in populations of leopard etc (due to the tiger's much more recent settlement in the tropics), its frequency (and hence its expression in the form of black tigers) would not be as great as in longstanding tropical felids – and therefore far fewer black tigers would be born.

Moreover, due to the extremely severe depletion of the normal tiger in recent times (a proportion of which must be heterozygous for the mutant non-agouti allele to explain the origin of black tigers in the first place), the numbers of black tigers being born would again be reduced.

Finally, it is worth noting that most black tiger reports derive from localities in fairly close proximity to one another and to the north-east of the Bay of Bengal – such restricted distribution (unusual for a simple mutant) presumably marks its origin (cf. the king cheetah, white lion, blue tiger).

In short, everything points to reports of black tigers being based upon melanistic specimens. Ironically, the black tiger nowadays could in fact be a felid of fable after all, for this fascinating mutant form may have slipped quietly and tragically into extinction while science has been casually contemplating whether or not it ever existed in the first place.

The Harimau Jalor

Natives of the Malaysian state of Trengganu have repeatedly informed Lieutenant-Colonel A. Locke of the *harimau jalor*, a larger-than-normal form of tiger immediately distinguished from all others by the fact that its stripes do not run downwards (from back to underparts) but instead stretch longitudinally (from head to tail). No one has apparently seen a dead *harimau jalor* but, as it is so frequently mentioned by the natives, Locke feels reluctant to dismiss its existence totally. Nonetheless, he considers that an optical illusion may be responsible, involving normal tigers viewed head-on (thereby concealing their stripes) and overlain by longitudinal shadows from branches overhead.[34]

Island Tigers

Three of the tiger's eight modern subspecies are confined to islands. Two of these – the Sumatran tiger *P. t. sumatrae* and the Javan tiger *P. t. sondaica* – are exceedingly rare. Neither, however, is more so than the third, the Bali tiger *P. t. balica*, For many authorities believe that this is now extinct.

The Bali Tiger

The Bali tiger is (or was) indigenous to Bali, and during the early part of the twentieth century it was believed to be relatively abundant, but it was decimated by the spates of uncontrolled killing by locals and Dutch colonials alike which occurred throughout the island during the years between the two World Wars. Indeed, by the middle of the 1930s hardly any tigers were left in West Bali, though others allegedly survived in its north-western and south-west regions. At the close of the decade, however, the Bali tiger seemed to have become extinct throughout the island; the last known specimen, an adult tigress, had been shot at Sumbar Kima in West Bali on 27 September 1937.[35]

Nevertheless, unsubstantiated rumours continued to circulate for many years that a few specimens still survived in a West Bali reserve, thereby suspending this subspecies in an uncertain limbo between existence and extinction for over thirty years.[36]

Then in 1972 two visitors to Indonesia reported that during conversations with Balinese Forestry Department officials they had learnt that at least one tiger had been seen very recently.[37] Nevertheless, by 1975 zoological explorations of central and western Bali, instigated in search of this individual and any others that might also exist, were forced to concede defeat. Similarly, although animals apparently killed by flesh-eating creatures were discovered in north-western Bali, there was no positive indication that tigers were responsible.[38] Another dead end. But in 1980 more encouraging news emerged. The World Wide Fund For Nature (WWF, at that time known as the World Wildlife Fund) announced that clawmarks had been observed on trees in Bali at a height which made them compatible with those of a tiger; they had been made between six and eighteen months earlier.[39]

Worth noting, incidentally, is that its continuing existence is not the only mystery surrounding the Bali tiger. Some authorities have declared that the tiger is not native to Bali in the first place but has been introduced here from some other Asian locality. Arguing against this, however, is the longstanding familiarity of the tiger to the Balinese people, plus the singular appearance of Bali tiger skins and skulls, which can be readily differentiated from those of other subspecies.[40]

Iriomote Felids

South-east of Japan lie the Ryukyu Islands, a long chain whose principal member is Okinawa and whose southernmost member is a dot called Iriomote. Belying its apparent insignificance, however, this tiny isle could be home to a completely unknown form of tiger. Indeed, the name Iriomote is already more than familiar to all felid researchers due to a very dramatic discovery made there in the 1960s.

During the winter of 1965, Japanese naturalist Yukio Tagawa visited Iriomote to carry out some work. Whilst doing so, he also followed up stories which he had heard concerning a strange cat form which existed there, known locally as *pingimaya*. His efforts were, however, somewhat hampered by the regrettable tendency of the natives to eat any specimen of this mystery felid which they happened to trap. Nevertheless, his perseverance paid off, and eventually, with the help of Okinawan zoologist Dr Tetsuo Takara (Professor of Ryukyu University), a skull and two skins were at last obtained and sent to Japanese zoologist Dr Yoshinori Imaizumi of Tokyo's National Science Museum.[41,42] Following his detailed studies of these preserved specimens, together with further collected material and at least one living cat, in 1967 Imaizumi published a formal scientific description of the Iriomote cat, revealing that it was indeed a new species – which he named *Mayailurus iriometensis*[42] (more recently, *Mayailurus* has been demoted from genus to sub-genus, so that this species is now called *Felis iriomotensis*). Significantly, the Iriomote cat appears to be the most primitive of all living cat species, most closely related to the leopard cat *F. bengalensis*[43] but curiously sharing similarities with some of the smaller South American felids too.[42]

As can be imagined, the scientific world was quite astonished to learn that a totally new cat species had been discovered so recently, but even more startling news was to follow, for, according to the Iriomote inhabitants, the *pingimaya* is not the only felid form known to them on this island. Apparently a very much more sizeable cat also exists there, which they refer to as *yamamaya*. From their descriptions, this still-unknown felid is as large as a sheepdog and looks like a tiger![41] In view of the Iriomote cat's own recent discovery, plus the fact that Iriomote is virtually unexplored and almost completely covered in dense, mountainous rainforest whose fauna has received hardly any scientific attention, the existence there of an unrecorded tiger form would certainly not be impossible. Further proof of this is the equally surprising discovery on that island during the early 1970s of a hitherto unknown type of dwarf wild pig.[44] Clearly the superficially insignificant little island of Iriomote may hold further highly significant surprises in store for zoology.

Clouded Leopard Controversies

Known scientifically as *Neofelis nebulosa*, in English as the clouded leopard and in Chinese as the mint-leaf leopard (all three names are derived from the shape of the ornate blotches decorating its very handsome coat), this specialized species occupies an entire genus to itself, on account of its perplexing combination of Big Cat and Small Cat characteristics.[45] It has a wide distribution across South-East Asia and is split into two modern subspecies.[33] Judging from various reports, however, it may exist even further afield, and in some forms currently unknown to science.

For example, as an alternative to the possibility mentioned earlier that the mysterious *yamamaya* of Iriomote is an unclassified subspecies of tiger, Dr C.A.W. Guggisberg has suggested that it may in fact be a form of clouded leopard.[33] Though the latter is certainly comparable in size with that reported for the *yamamaya*, it is difficult to conceive how the blotches of the clouded leopard could be interpreted as tiger-like markings – unless a race has evolved on Iriomote in which the blotches have become more elongate in shape.

It is not generally supposed that the clouded leopard exhibits a melanistic morph. Yet around April 1946, the skin and lower jaw of a pure-black Bornean specimen were obtained and placed on record three years later.[46] Another black specimen was supposed to have existed at one time on Mount Matang.[46] Moreover, six reports of large black cats were recorded during a WWF faunal survey of Sabah in 1982, while in 1986 three such cats were sighted in Sarawak and a further account recorded from Sabah.[47]

Anomalous and Unexpected Leopards

Today, science recognizes just one species of true leopard – *Panthera pardus*. Yet until the 1920s, only those individuals with relatively short tails were actually classed as such; any which had tails equalling or exceeding their head-and-body lengths were classified as a separate species – the panther. One authority went even further, splitting off those individuals of very small total length to yield a third leopard species – the pantherette. It is now recognized that leopards come in all shapes and sizes, and the term 'panther' is generally restricted in present-day usage to melanistic individuals.[33]

Doglas

Taking into account the controversial pygmy leopard *P. p. nanopardus* from the Somali Republic, East Africa, the leopard normally ranges from 3-5 ft/90-105 cm in head-and-body length, with a further 2-3 ft/60-90 cm of tail. Nonetheless, much larger specimens have also been recorded occasionally, including one tiger-sized individual from India that measured a mighty 9 ft 4 in/280 cm in total length.[32,33]

As noted by F.C. Hicks in 1910, it is popularly believed by natives throughout India that the largest male leopards often mate with tigresses, to yield mysterious hybrids known as '*doglas*'. Moreover, some sizeable leopards have been recorded which bear very prominent stripes on their underparts, which the natives allude to as support for this belief. Nonetheless, Hicks doubted very much whether individuals such as these were truly of interspecific origin. This opinion was based on personal experience, for he once shot a felid that was quite evidently a bona fide leopard × tiger hybrid, and this was very different morphologically from those leopards identified as *doglas* by the natives. Hicks described his specimen (later lost or stolen) as follows:

> ... the spotted head of a panther [old usage of term] of extraordinary size pushed its way through the grass, followed by the unmistakable striped shoulders and body of a tiger, though looking a bit dirty as if it had been rolling in ashes. I succeeded in dropping this extraordinary creature dead with a shot in the neck, and, on examining it, I found it to be a very old male hybrid, with both its teeth and claws much worn and broken; its head and tail were purely that of a panther, but with a body, shoulders and neck-ruff unmistakably that of a tiger, the black stripes being broad and long though somewhat blurred and breaking off here and there into a few blurred rosettes, the stripes of the tiger being the most predominant on the body. One of the peculiarities of this creature which I particularly noticed was that, though it was male, it had the feet of a female and measured a little over 8 feet in length [240 cm].[48]

Could it have been not only a hybrid but also a hermaphrodite? Intersexual tigers[36,49] and leopards[32] have been recorded. Notwithstanding, it possessed an undeniable combination of tiger and leopard characteristics. Hicks admitted that, if such hybrids were fertile themselves and capable of breeding in turn with leopards, this could then explain the *doglas* of the Indian natives. However, most of the Big Cat hybrids on record have been found to be sterile,[50] hence this prospect is very unlikely.

A Melange of Morphs, and a Mystery from Malabar

In any event, when dealing with the leopard, the fact that some individuals have striped underparts should come as no surprise; for not only does this species vary in colour from subspecies to subspecies (one of the palest of these, the Sinai leopard *P. p. jarvisi* was rediscovered in 1974 after having been written off as extinct for many years[51]), it also exhibits an unparalleled variety of morphs and freakishly marked types over its equally wide distribution range. In Asia alone the leopard extends from Asia Minor to China and Korea (but not Japan – *P. p. japonica*, the so-called Japanese leopard, was described from a single skin that was almost certainly derived not from Japan but from either China or Korea[33]), and as far south as India, Sri Lanka, Malaysia and Indonesia.[33] Its most familiar morph is its melanistic (non-agouti) morph[52] – the black panther. This is very abundant in Asia but most frequently found in humid, densely forested areas.[33]

Cream-coloured leopards with pale markings and blue eyes (chinchilla mutants) have been documented from the Indian states of Dumraon and Hazaribagh and from southern China.[53] In addition, an orange-coloured (erythristic) specimen, in which the spots were virtually assimilated into the pelage's background colour, was reported by Pocock from India[54] (probably a non-extension of black mutant). Even jaguar-like leopards have been recorded, whose rosettes each contain one or more central spots.[54,55]

Few of these variants, however, can compare with the magnificent and mysterious skin purchased in December 1912 by Holdridge Ozro Collins from G.A. Chambers of Madras. Its predominant colour was an elegant glossy black and was described in 1915 by Collins: 'The wide black portion, which glistens like the sheen of silk velvet, extends from the top of the head to the extremity of the tail *entirely* free from any white or tawny hairs....'[56] He goes on to say: 'In the tiger, the stripes are black, of an uniform character, upon a tawny background, and they run in parallel lines from the center of the back to the belly. In this skin, the stripes are almost golden yellow, without the uniformity and parallelism of the tiger characteristics, and they extend along the sides in labyrinthine graceful curls and circles, several inches below the wide shimmering black continuous course of the back. The extreme edges around the legs and belly are white and spotted like the skin of a leopard.... The skin is larger than that of a

Leopard but smaller than that of a full grown Tiger.'[56]

The cat had been killed in Malabar, south-western India, earlier in 1912, and so unusual was its exceedingly handsome skin that Chambers had been totally unable to classify it, so that he wondered whether it could actually represent some hitherto unknown form of felid. To obtain an answer, Chambers had sent it to Madras's Government Museum for official identification. He subsequently received a letter from J.R. Henderson of the museum, who stated that, although the species was certainly leopard, it constituted a variety which he had never before seen. Collins also sought scientific advice concerning its status, and learnt from Dr Gerrit S. Miller Jnr, curator of the Smithsonian Institute's Division of Mammals, that it was indeed a black leopard, but not of the normal melanistic type.[56]

In fact, this remarkable skin was that of a pseudo-melanistic leopard, a rare mutant known only from a handful of specimens. In a normal melanistic leopard (i.e. black panther), its coat's background colour is abnormally dark, but its coat's rosettes are unchanged (so that they can often still be spied in shadow-like form against its dark pelage). Conversely, in a pseudo-melanistic leopard, its coat's background colour is normal (orange-yellow) but is largely obliterated by abnormal fusion (nigrism) and multiplication (abundism) of the rosettes. In extreme cases of pseudo-melanism, as demonstrated by Collins's specimen, this fusion and multiplication of the rosettes can be so extensive that virtually the entire upper body is covered in a mass of black colour, with only occasional gaps through which the normal background colour is visible (appearing as orange streaks or spots). Faced with such a bizarre skin, it is little wonder that its owners had wondered whether it constituted a major zoological discovery.

Nelliampatti and Bali Leopards

Nevertheless, Asia may indeed still harbour undescribed leopard types. For example, as noted by S.H. Prater, it is possible that a small, dark race of leopard from Cochin's Nelliampatti Hills awaits formal scientific recognition. Attention to this form was first directed by R.C. Morris, but it has yet to be described.[57]

When the WWF announced that evidence for the Bali tiger's survival had been obtained in the late 1970s, this was not the only surprise that it unveiled concerning felids, for news also emerged that in 1979 a leopard had been heard calling at night in northern Bali and that a leopard's fresh pug-mark had been discovered in a dried-up river bed by zoologists working within the area in question.[36,39] This created great zoological excitement, because science had not previously been aware that the leopard actually existed on Bali. Moreover, it later transpired that a full four years earlier, on Bali, in the Prapat Agung area, two officers of the Indonesian Nature Protection and Wildlife Conservation Service had reported seeing a cat that seemed to be a black panther.[36] Suddenly, instead of being devoid of Big Cats, Bali now appeared to have two different species – a tiger subspecies resurrected from extinction, and a race of leopard raised from obscurity.

All of which serves well in demonstrating once again just how very elusive felids can be – even large ones on a relatively small island like Bali.

Hong Kong Mystery Cats

During the last two weeks of October 1976, more than twenty dogs (some sizeable) were bitten to death in Pik Uk and Junk Bay, in the Hang Hau area of Sai Kung (within Hong Kong's New Territories). A police search was instigated but drew a blank. And a gleaming-eyed, long-tailed beast sighted by villagers in this same vicinity on 30 October was thought by them to be a large leopard, not a dog. Yet its fur was described as blackish-grey in colour (not even a black panther's fur matches this). During late November/ early December, a villager alleged that within the past ten days he had twice seen a creature referred to by him as a tiger, 'about 3 ft [90 cm] high, 4 ft [120 cm] long, and of a dark colour' (surely too small and the wrong colour – especially for a species which does not officially exist in Hong Kong anyway). Once again a police search was made, and this time some pug-marks were discovered, after which the subject was referred to the Agriculture and Fish Department and was not heard of again.[58]

Even if the above two incidents did involve the same animal (which is far from certain), it was surely neither tiger nor panther – but until (if ever) further information becomes available, little more can be said.

A second, equally odd offering from the Orient serves to conclude this chapter – the strange tale of a tiger which barked! Set once again in Hong Kong's New Territories, as described in an article published by the magazine *Animals*,[59] it all began in July 1965 when a senior pupil of the Diocesan Girls' School, on a picnic with schoolfriends upon the slopes of the mountain Taimoshan, saw a tiger stalking through the undergrowth nearby. She was quite naturally alarmed but also very surprised (as tigers are not supposed to exist here). A search-party was organized at once but succeeded only in spotting some flattened grass where the creature may have rested. Inevitably, further sightings were soon reported, and so for the next three months hunting-parties trekked far and wide on the track of this evanescent animal – by now referred to as the Shing Mun tiger after the valley it was allegedly raiding – but always in vain.[59]

During the last week of October it was sighted at the village of Shatin, near the Chinese border (and the site of a fully authenticated tiger account fifty years earlier), but the eyewitness in question, local builder Chan Pui, caused confusion and consternation by stating flatly that the animal was not a tiger at all – it was a wolf. This identification found little favour, especially with the original schoolgirl eyewitness, who was adamant that she had seen a tiger, while a naturalist announced that wolves did not exist in that region. In reply, Chan Pui retorted that he would vindicate his statement by capturing the creature – and to everyone's surprise, he proclaimed on 1 November that he had done just that. Moreover, he described the fabled Shing Mun tiger as being a fierce wolf with eyes that 'burn like lamps', and allowed interested (albeit apprehensive) newspaper reporters to photograph the savage creature.[59]

Yet the final metamorphosis in this tale of tiger-into-wolf was still to come, for, upon his inspection of the ambiguous animal, zoologist Dr I.W.B. Thornton announced that it was nothing more fabulous or fearsome than an alsatian-chow crossbreed! And far from being a rapacious predator, it was only too happy to lick the hand of another of its visitors, a representative of Hong Kong's Society for the Prevention of Cruelty to Animals.[59]

Clearly it is most unlikely that this docile dog was really the same animal as the creature responsible for the schoolgirl's sighting and the Shing Mun raids. Almost certainly the genuine culprit, tiger or whatever, had simply moved on, with the capture of the dog being nothing more than coincidence. Also, as seen in various earlier cases documented here, once a mystery beast has been sighted several times there is a marked tendency for the episode to be brought to an 'official' end by the capture or shooting of *something* – regardless of whether it actually bears any resemblance to the original creature reported. Such 'substitutions' (whether accidental or deliberate) are very frequent components of a cryptozoological case and can cause a great many problems for the investigator attempting to distinguish the relevant from the inconsequential.

When Oscar Wilde wrote 'The truth is rarely pure and never simple', I doubt very much that he was contemplating any cryptozoological conundrum. Yet even if he had been doing so, he could hardly have encapsulated its vital essence within a more accurate and appropriate epigram.

Abbreviations: JBNHS = *Journal of the Bombay Natural History Society*
PZSL = *Proceedings of the Zoological Society of London*

1 Corbet, G.B., and Hill, J.E., *A World List of Mammalian Species*, (second edition) (Brit. Mus. Nat. Hist., 1986)
2 *The Independent* (London), 10 June 1988; *Express and Star* (Wolverhampton), 10 June 1988
3 Reed, T.H., *National Geographic*, Vol. 119, pp. 628-41 (1961); Gee, E.P., *Animals*, Vol. 3, pp. 282-6 (1964); Cherfas, J., *Zoo 2000* (BBC, 1984)
4 Thornton, I.W.B., Yeung, K.K., and Sankhala, K.S., *Journal of Zoology*, Vol. 152, pp. 127-35 (1967); Robinson, R., *Genetica*, Vol. 40, pp. 198-200 (1969); Thornton, I.W.B., *Journal of Zoology*, Vol. 185, pp. 389-94 (1978)
5 Gee, E.P., *JBNHS*, Vol. 56, pp. 581-7 (1959)
6 Weigel, I., in Grzimek, B., (ed.), *Grzimek's Animal Life Encyclopedia*, Vol. 12 (Van Nostrand Reinhold, 1975), p. 348.
7 Cuvier, G., *Le Règne Animal* ..., 16 Volumes. (Roulin & Valenciennes, 1836-49)
8 Robinson, R., *Genetica*, Vol. 46, pp. 1-31 (1976)
9 Wood, J.G., *The Illustrated Natural History: Mammalia* (Routledge, Warne, & Routledge, 1859-63)
10 Lydekker, R., *The Game Animals of India, Burma and Tibet* (Rowland Ward, 1907)
11 Narayan, V.N., *JBNHS*, Vol. 28, p. 1124 (1922)
12 Pocock, R.I., ibid., Vol. 33, pp. 505-41 (1929)
13 Carter, W.H., *The Times*, 16 October 1936
14 Schroeter, W.K.H., *Sitzungsberichte Ges. Naturf. Freunde Berlin*, Vol. 12, pp. 154-8 (1973)
15 Caldwell, H.R., *Blue Tiger* (Duckworth, 1925)
16 Heuvelmans, B., *Cryptozoology*, Vol. 5, pp. 1-26 (1986)
17 Stonor, C., *Country Life*, Vol. 136, p. 691 (17 September 1964)
18 Hughes-Hallett, N.M., ibid., Vol. 136, p. 926 (8 October 1964)
19 *The Observer*, 27 January 1844
20 Buckland, C.T., *The Field*, Vol. 73, p. 422 (23 March 1889)
21 Hauxwell, T.A., *JBNHS*, Vol. 22, pp. 788-9 (1914)
22 Editors, *The Field*, Vol. 152, p. 657 (25 October 1928)
23 Higgins, J.C., *JBNHS*, Vol. 35, pp. 673-4 (1932)
24 Dollman, G., *The Times*, 19 October 1936
25 Dollman, G., ibid., 4 February 1937.
26 Capper, S., ibid., 20 October 1936
27 Griffiths, R.G., ibid, 19 January 1937
28 Prater, S.H., *JBNHS*, Vol. 39, pp. 381-2 (1937)
29 Brander, A.A.D., *The Field*, Vol. 169, p. 80 (9 January 1937)
30 Gee, E.P., *The Wild Life of India* (Collins, 1964)
31 Burton, R.G., *The Field*, Vol. 152, pp. 656-7 (25 October 1928)
32 Turnbull-Kemp, P., *The Leopard* (Bailey Bros & Swinfen, 1967)
33 Guggisberg, C.A.W., *Wild Cats of the World* (David & Charles, 1975)
34 Locke, A., *The Tigers of Trengganu* (Museum Press, 1954)
35 Day, D., *The Doomsday Book of Animals* (Ebury Press, 1981)
36 Wood, G.L., *The Guinness Book of Animal Facts and Feats*, third edition (Guinness Superlatives Ltd, 1982)
37 Sitwell, N., *Animals*, Vol. 14, p. 389 (September 1972)
38 *Wildlife*, Vol. 17, p. 187 (April 1975)
39 Ibid., Vol. 22, p. 17 (February 1980)
40 Sody, H.J.V., *JBNHS* Vol. 36, pp. 233-5 (1932)
41 *Animals*, Vol. 10, pp. 501-3 (March 1968)
42 Imaizumi, Y., *Journal of the Mammalogical Society of Japan*, Vol. 3, pp. 75-106 (1967)

43 Wurster-Hill, D.H., Dol, T., Izawa, M., and Oni, Y., *Journal of Heredity*, Vol. 78, pp. 105-7 (1987)
44 *Wildlife*, Vol. 17, pp. 87-8 (February 1975)
45 Pocock, R.I., *Catalogue of the Genus Felis* (Brit. Mus. Nat. Hist., 1951)
46 Harrisson, T., *Malayan Nature Journal*, Vol. 4, pp. 70-6 (1949)
47 Davies, A.G., and Payne, J.B., *A Faunal Survey of Sabah* (WWF Malaysia, Kuala Lumpur, 1982); Rabinowitz, A., Andau, P., and Chai, P.P.K., *Oryx*, Vol. 21, pp. 107-11 (April 1987)
48 Hicks, F.C., *Forty Years Among the Wild Animals of India* (Pioneer, Allahabad, 1910)
49 Fraser, C., *JBNHS*, Vol. 43, p. 99 (1942)
50 Gray, A.P., *Mammalian Hybrids* second edition, (Commonwealth Agricultural Bureaux, 1972)
51 *Wildlife*, Vol. 17, p. 232 (May 1975)
52 Robinson, R., *JBNHS*, Vol. 66, pp. 423-9 (1970); O'Grady, R.J.P., *Proceedings of the 4th Symposium of the Association of British Wild Animal Keepers*, Vol. 4, pp. 32-41 (1979)
53 Fooks, H.A., *JBNHS*, Vol. 42, pp. 435-6 (1941)
54 Pocock, R.I., ibid., Vol. 34, pp. 64-82, 307-36 (1930)
55 Lydekker, R., *PZSL*, pp. 1-3 (14 January 1908)
56 Collins, H.O., *Bulletin of the South Californian Academy of Science*, Vol. 14, pp. 49-51 (1915)
57 Prater, S.H., *The Book of Indian Animals*, third edition (Bombay Natural History Society, Bombay, 1971)
58 *Fortean Times*, No. 25, p. 35 (spring, 1978)
59 *Animals*, Vol. 9, pp. 16-17 (May 1966)

4 Cheetahs With Stripes and Lions With Spots

Africa

Ex Africa semper aliquod novi – There is always something new out of Africa.

Pliny the Elder, *Natural History*, VIII (altered)

As far as cryptozoological cats are concerned, the above quotation is singularly apt; for, in addition to possessing seven species of Small Cat and two species of Big Cat (lion and leopard), plus the taxonomically aloof cheetah,[1] there is substantial evidence to suggest that the Dark Continent is also sheltering a number of other types of felid – felids which still await formal scientific recognition. Yet there should be no reason for considering such a possibility unlikely. Almost all the last hundred years-worth of major zoological discoveries from Africa – e.g. pygmy hippo, okapi, mountain gorilla and giant forest hog – have occurred as a result of explorers' following up native reports of creatures not resembling any species known to science at that time. Yet, bewilderingly, by continuing today to dismiss as superstition and folklore this primary source of information concerning the possible existence of undiscovered African animals, science clearly demonstrates that it has still not learnt its lesson.

The King Cheetah

Consequently, reports of a strange and exceedingly shy forest creature, described by the native Zimbabwean people as being half-leopard and half-hyaena and termed by them *nsui-fisi* (leopard-hyaena), were simply rejected by scientists as fantasy during the early part of the twentieth century.[2] Such notions would, however, soon be revised, for in 1926 *The Field* published a short letter and accompanying photograph sent by Major A.C. Cooper of Salisbury (now Harare) which concerned a most unusual skin,[3] obtained from a peculiar felid trapped near Salisbury and presented to its Queen Victoria Memorial Library and Museum by a Mr Donald Frazer.[4] It should be noted here that, despite Major Cooper's original statement that this cat had been trapped in the Umvukwes Range, the museum's records reveal that it had actually originated from Macheke, about 62 miles/100 km south-east of Salisbury;[4] apparently it was one of several specimens of this cat form sighted there.[3] Cooper suggested that it was a hybrid of leopard and cheetah, and described it as follows: '... a very stockily built leopard, with powerful limbs and a comparatively short thick tail. As against this there are the non-retractile claws of the cheetah, also the ruff round the neck, which is totally absent in the leopard. The background of the skin is the full yellow of the leopard, not the sandy yellow of the cheetah. The markings are like nothing on earth (note the longitudinal stripes down the back and shoulders).'[3] Its markings were indeed exceptional. A series of longitudinal black stripes extended from its neck along the entire length of its back to the upper part of its tail, while its flanks and upper limbs were ornately decorated with thick black blotches and curved stripes of irregular shape and size, plus notable rings around much of its tail's length. Cooper wondered if any similar skins had been recorded.

His letter came to the attention of felid expert Reginald Pocock, who judged from the photograph (which did not reveal the ruff and non-retractile claws) that the cat was most probably an aberrant leopard.[5] When the skin was subsequently lent to the British Museum (Natural History) for his direct examination, however, Pocock realized immediately that it was not a leopard at all but a most remarkably patterned cheetah with unusually long, silky fur and a prominent mane. In view of the latter feature and its regal appearance as a whole, Pocock formally named it *Acinonyx rex* – the king cheetah, classifying this striped form as a distinct species in its own right, totally separate from the normal spotted cheetah.[6]

As a result of Major Cooper's zealous researches, further king cheetah skins were discovered and publicized, and one was bought for £150 by Lord Rothschild. This later skin was particularly interesting in that its markings were less ornate than those of other king cheetahs, so that it bore more of a resemblance to the typical spotted form than did any of the earlier 'kings', as noted by Pocock in 1928.[7] Indeed, this somewhat intermediate specimen inspired Abel Chapman to voice the opinion that the king and spotted cheetahs belonged to the same species after all.[8]

Over the next few years, an increasing number of zoologists

subscribed to this view, until in 1939 Pocock himself finally conceded that the king cheetah was indeed most likely a freak variety of the normal cheetah.[9] In just over a decade the king had been crowned and dethroned. It was now referred to simply as *Acinonyx jubatus* var. *rex*, and scientific interest waned.

Nonetheless, skins and sightings of king cheetahs continued to emerge, and almost invariably from Zimbabwe. In 1962 Sir Archibald James listed eight skins (of which three had been lost or destroyed),[10] and by 1980 the total had risen to thirteen.[4] By 1987 thirty-eight specimens were known, recorded south of the Zambezi in a triangular portion of Africa enclosing eastern and southern Zimbabwe, northern South Africa and eastern Botswana, with the habitat housing the kings consisting of thorn forest and woodland, usually of high elevation – very different from the typical savannah habitat of normal cheetahs.[11,12]

This latter feature was not lost upon the researchers responsible for the recent upsurge of scientific interest in the king cheetah – biologist Lena Bottriell and her husband Paul. Until the late 1970s, the only known photograph of a living king cheetah was one that had been taken in the Kruger National Park in 1974.[13] In 1979, however, with the aid of a hot-air balloon the Bottriells conducted an intensive aerial investigation of king cheetah country in its triangle of distribution. Moreover, they succeeded in tracking down and photographing a number of skins as well as filming live specimens, and also discovered a most surprising fact concerning this cheetah form.[11,14,15] Hair samples which they had submitted to the Institute of Medical Research in Johannesburg revealed that the cuticular scale pattern of king cheetah guard hair compared much more closely with that of leopards than with that of spotted cheetahs.[11] If the king cheetah were nothing more than a freak colour morph of the normal cheetah, one would have expected its hair structure to correspond (or at least to be most similar) to that of the latter felid. The striped cheetah mystery deepened.

It was no longer simply an abnormally marked mutant: it also differed from the spotted form in the structure and texture of its fur; it inhabited forests rather than savannahs; and, as the Bottriells also discovered, it tended to be more active during the night than did the typically diurnal spotted cheetah.[11,12]

Worth noting here is that, according to East African legend, leopards and cheetahs will sometimes mate.[16] Arguing against a hybrid identity for the king cheetah, however, the Bottriells have remarked that leopards actively attack cheetahs,[11] and even if they did mate, the two species are so different genetically that the production of offspring would be quite impossible.

In May 1981 a litter of cubs was born to normal cheetah parents at the de Wildt Cheetah Breeding and Research Centre of Pretoria's National Zoological Gardens. One of these cubs proved to be a king cheetah, thereby proving categorically that this form was neither hybrid nor separate species. A few days later, a king cheetah was also born in a litter produced by the sister of the first litter's mother.[14] Now, by carrying out monitored breeding studies, the genetics of king cheetah production could be studied.

By 1984 a recessive mutant allele was suspected to be responsible,[17] and in 1986 a formal scientific paper on the subject appeared, containing the findings of king cheetah researchers Dr R.J. van Aarde and Ann van Dyck.[18] They proposed that this felid's remarkable coat pattern was indeed due to a recessive mutant allele, one quite probably homologous (equivalent) to that responsible for the blotched tabby pattern in the domestic cat.[18] In short, the entire king pattern was due to a single genetic difference.

Lena and Paul Bottriell, however, were not satisfied with this as a complete explanation; for, as they point out, the morphological change from spotted to king in the cheetah involves several markedly different components (body stripes, body blotches, more pronounced mane, distinctive hair, striped upper tail, and rings round the remainder of the tail), hardly compatible with either a single colour change (as in albinos or melanistic individuals) or the single markings change (as from stripes to blotches in domestic tabby cats) which normally results from a single allele change.[11,12] Moreover, whereas blotched tabbies are born everywhere, king cheetahs have a very precise and limited distribution within the total range known for the cheetah as a whole.[11,12]

In combination with the king cheetah's environmental and behavioural idiosyncracies already noted, all these anomalies led the Bottriells towards a single and inevitable, albeit startling, conclusion: namely, that the king cheetah is demonstrating evolution before our very eyes – the development within a specific region of a completely new race of cheetah, adapted not for daytime sprinting across open grasslands as its hunting mode but for nocturnal stalking through dense forests, where its more heavily patterned coat would provide it with excellent camouflage.[11] In short, natural selection has acted upon the original 'freak' king individuals to bring about a habitat extension for the cheetah, which (given sufficient time and continuous isolation between spotted and king individuals) will result in so great a genetic and morphological divergence between the two forms that they will ultimately cease to belong to the same species.[11]

Thus the king cheetah would seem to be more than a mere freak – as labelled in the title of the Bottriells' presentation at the 1987 ISC Annual Members Meeting, it may well be a new race in the making.[19] The Bottriells' hypothesis, presented fully in Lena Bottriell's stimulating book *King Cheetah*,[11] is eminently plausible and fits the facts very succinctly. The *nsui-fisi* has been vindicated after all!

The Woolly Cheetah

While the king cheetah is enjoying a well-earned scientific renaissance, a second, equally perplexing cheetah form seems to have vanished without trace into the mists of scientific obscurity.

In 1877 Philip Sclater, secretary of the Zoological Society of London, recorded in its *Proceedings* the acquisition by London Zoo of a most unusual cat – male and apparently not fully grown – which he described as follows:

> It presents generally the appearance of a cheetah (Felis jubatus) [its old scientific name], but is thicker in the body, and has shorter and stouter limbs, and a much thicker tail. When adult it will probably be considerably larger than the Cheetah, and is larger even now than our three specimens of that animal. The fur is much more woolly and dense than in the Cheetah, as is particularly noticeable on the ears, mane and tail. The whole of the body is of a pale isabelline colour, rather paler on the belly and lower parts, but covered all over, including the belly, with roundish dark fulvous blotches. There are no traces of the black spots which are so conspicuous in all of the varieties of the Cheetah which I have seen, nor of the characteristic black line between the mouth and eye.[20]

Evidently this brown-blotched felid appeared very different from the usual form – to the extent that Sclater stated that it was impossible to associate it with this. Instead, he proposed for it the temporary name of *Felis lanea*, the woolly cheetah. It had been obtained from Beaufort West, South Africa, and, as Sclater himself remarked: 'It is difficult to understand how such a distinct animal can have so long escaped the observations of naturalists.'[20]

One other matter is also difficult to understand, and remains a source of confusion concerning this mystery cat. Sclater referred to its markings as 'blotches', but in the painting which accompanied this report the creature was depicted with numerous tiny spots!

A year later, Sclater noted in the Society's *Proceedings* that he had received a letter from a Mr E.L. Layard, informing him that a second woolly cheetah was currently preserved in the South African Museum. Like the first, it had been procured from Beaufort West. It had been killed by Arthur V. Jackson who, like

Layard himself, assumed that it was an erythristic (abnormally red) variant of the normal cheetah. At the end of this item, in answer to an enquiry by Layard, Sclater recorded that the claws of the London Zoo specimen were non-retractile.[21]

Sharing Sclater's own bewilderment as to how so large and unusual an animal could have evaded scientific detection until then, many zoologists had grave reservations concerning his optimism that the woolly cheetah constituted a totally separate species. In 1881 St George Mivart commented that the noted zoologist Elliot regarded this felid simply as a variety of the known cheetah species[22] (curiously, Mivart added a stripe to one side of the woolly cheetah's muzzle in his book *The Cat*, not mentioned by Sclater and in any event highly abnormal, thereby confusing the issue even further). By then, London Zoo's specimen had died, and Elliot's opinion received support from the discovery by Oldfield Thomas of the British Museum (Natural History) that this cat's skull did not differ from that of any other cheetah.[23]

In 1884 Sclater recorded a woolly cheetah skin sent to him by the Reverend G. Fisk, again obtained from Beaufort West. In comparison with the zoo specimen, this example was more distinctly spotted, less densely furred and rather smaller in size. Reverend Fisk believed that these differences were due to the specimen being a female, an explanation accepted by Sclater, who felt that this new skin consolidated his opinion concerning the woolly cheetah's separate status.[23] The rest of the scientific world, conversely, remained unconvinced, so that since then it has been regarded as nothing more than an unusual variant of the typical cheetah species.

According to mammalogists Daphne Hills and Dr Reay Smithers, this odd form no longer occurs in Beaufort West.[4] Presumably, therefore, it is extinct, and the chance to investigate further its precise taxonomic status similarly lost. Or is it? The British Museum owns the skin of the zoo specimen – perhaps it may be possible to carry out genetic tests upon small samples of this.

The woolly cheetah may indeed be nothing more surprising than an atypical colour morph – perhaps, as suggested by Lena Bottriell and others, a partial albino.[11] At the same time, Sclater's more radical views can also be appreciated, for this cat form differs from the typical cheetah not only in colour and markings but also in fur density and even in relative limb length. Simple colour variants do not generally exhibit such pronounced differences as these from normal individuals of the same species. Its shorter limbs suggest a non-cursorial life – could it possibly have been a forest form? It is worth noting that a 'lion-like forest cheetah' known as the *kitanga* was described in this century's early years to Major G. St J. Orde-Brown by the Embu natives of south-eastern Kenya[24,25] and that a comparable felid has occasionally been reported from the little-explored forests of Senegal, West Africa, where the typical cheetah *A. j. hecki* is extremely rare (Owen Burnham, pers. comm.).

As already discussed with the king cheetah, the possibility of a cheetah form becoming modified for life in this type of habitat is by no means implausible. On the contrary, even the normal spotted form is not an exclusive denizen of the savannahs.[26] This was well demonstrated in March 1983, when Lise Campbell spied a single cheetah at a height of 2½ miles/4 km in the vicinity of the Sirimon Track in the moorland zone of Mount Kenya; she had a second sighting later that day of what may have been the same animal, even higher, amidst the tufted high-altitude grass.[27]

In 1921 Pocock brought to public attention the skin of an extremely unusual cheetah. Its mane was very sparse, and it possessed very few spots over its shoulders and neck, whilst those on its body were remarkably small.[28] Even more striking must have been the blue-spotted specimen brought to the Mogul naturalist Jahangír at Agra, probably a partial albino.[26] In 1925 a black cheetah was observed by H.F. Stoneham in Kenya's Trans-Nzoia District, and a second such cat was sighted in the company of a normal cheetah by Vesey-Fitzgerald in Zambia.[26] Thus the king and woolly cheetahs are by no means the only unexpected cheetah forms on record.

In view of the wide range of colours and markings exhibited by certain other felids, notably the leopard, one could be forgiven for seeing little reason to be surprised at a similar trend in the cheetah. However, as discovered by Dr Stephen O'Brien and co-workers via certain protein examinations (isoenzyme analyses), African cheetahs display a conspicuously low degree of genetic variation (lower than that for lions, tigers and leopards), i.e. the cheetah populations are very inbred – especially those from South Africa.[29]

Consequently, one would hardly expect the appearance of genetic variants as markedly different from the normal type as are the king and woolly cheetahs (both inhabiting South Africa too), which makes the reconciliation of these as mere freaks all the more difficult to accept. Even though we know that the king cheetah is not a separate species, the fact that this form and the woolly cheetah actually derive from South Africa suggests very strongly that they must be very much more delineated genetically from the normal cheetah than most taxonomists currently believe. Certainly, in view of the latter's depauperate genetic variation, it is very difficult to explain away these forms as simple mutants.

Evidently, cheetah genetics hold quite a few more surprises in store for science.

Spotted Lions

As with the woolly cheetah, at least one form of spotted lion is known to science via preserved skins; hence its actual existence is not in doubt. What *is* in question is its precise identity.

Reports of such creatures had filtered into Europe from East Africa as long ago as 1903, via Colonel Meinertzhagen, soon to be immortalized in zoological circles as the discoverer of the Congo's giant forest hog.[24] Moreover, according to an Irish adventurer called C.J. McGuinness, in his book *Nomad*, one of the hunters employed by the famous animal-collector Carl Hagenbeck had himself sighted a spotted lion.[30] Nonetheless, the scientific world took little notice of these. When, in 1931, Kenyan game warden Captain R.E. Dent observed four lions crossing a track ahead of him at a height of just under 11,000 ft/3,300 m near the headwaters of Mount Kenya's Garcita River, he noticed that they seemed to be darker and smaller than normal lions, but simply assumed that this impression was due to a trick of the light. Yet some months later his native attendants informed him that they had trapped a strange cat on the Aberdare Mountains which seemed intermediate in appearance between lion and leopard – unfortunately they had not preserved its skin.[31,32]

This situation was remedied a little later by Michael Trent, when he shot two lions which had raided his Aberdares farm, above Tomson's Falls. He was very surprised, upon examination of the bodies, to discover that, although they were both adults (one male, one female), each possessed a very heavily spotted coat. Normal lions display varying degrees of spotting when cubs, but this is generally lost by adulthood and in any event never approaches the intensity and extent of spotting possessed by these two, covering neck, back, flanks and legs. Equally perplexing was the presence in the male of only the sparsest of manes.[31,32]

Very fortunately, Michael Trent preserved these remarkable skins, which in themselves demonstrated unequivocally that adult lions with conspicuous spotting did indeed exist. At the same time, however, as he did not retain their skulls or skeletons, their precise taxonomic identity could not be conclusively established.[32]

Nevertheless, the spotted lion saga was steadily gaining momentum, for Trent's pair of pelts attracted the interest of wealthy young adventurer Kenneth Gandar Dower, who brought this felid to popular attention in the West by preparing an illustrated article, published by *The Field* in 1935.[31]

In addition, he was so attracted to the possibility of a new species of lion awaiting formal scientific discovery that he organized an expedition to the Aberdares in search of this mottled mystery cat – which, it transpired, was well known to the region's natives, who referred to it as the *marozi*. He was accompanied by renowned hunter Raymond Hook, but despite their perseverance the quest did not succeed in its ultimate objective of obtaining a specimen. Nonetheless, some unusual tracks *were* sighted, which seemed too small in size for a lion's and too large for a leopard's, whilst appearing to be thinner in shape than those of a young lion. Undaunted, Dower made further recourses to the Aberdares, and on one occasion, due to a misunderstanding, he missed the opportunity of observing some spotted lions by a mere twenty-four hours.[33,34]

Despite his very understandable frustration and disappointment at such events, in 1937 he published a very interesting and well-written book called *The Spotted Lion*,[24] in which he described his search and included an appendix written by Reginald Pocock concerning Trent's male specimen. Pocock had examined this personally and, like other observers, had been struck by its exceptional degree of spotting, which he went so far as to describe as being 'jaguarine' in quality. Furthermore, he confessed that not even the British Museum (Natural History) had anything to compare with this felid. Even so, he preferred to reserve final judgement concerning its taxonomic status until he could examine skeletal material from such lions. A skull had been passed to him which was supposedly from one of Trent's specimens, but this has never been officially confirmed. It seemed to be that of a young lioness, though Pocock did not totally rule out the likelihood that it had come from a form of diminutive lion.[35] Quite plainly, the scientific world was somewhat bemused by these paradoxical pelts.

The interest which Dower's exploits and explorations had stirred amongst the hunting and wildlife fraternities, as well as amongst Kenyan inhabitants, resulted in a welter of new information and accounts of such animals coming to light. Dower himself, for example, was informed that in the Virunga Mountains a man had encountered a lion which had resembled a jaguar (as in Pocock's use of the word 'jaguarine' in relation to Trent's skins?); he also received word from a lady curious to know why he was so excited about 'the ordinary common or garden Spotted Lion of the Aberdares which everybody had known about for years'![24]

The Field published much correspondence on this subject during the 1930s and 1940s. On 1 June 1935 it reproduced a photo and accompanying letter by Andrew Fowle, regarding a normal-sized lion aged two years but still possessing distinct spotting.[36] Nevertheless, it did not compare with that exhibited by Trent's cats. Towards the end of 1937 a letter appeared by B.V. Richardson, who did not share Dower's optimism that Trent's specimens represented something more than a freak form of normal lion; for, although his own safaris to the Aberdares did not traverse higher than the mountains' foothills and plateau, he had made contact with most settlers and a fair proportion of the natives who had at some time travelled through areas covered by Dower's searches; yet he had never heard any of these people speak of spotted lions. He also remarked that the natives were liable to exaggerate in an attempt to please their masters, fostering their hopes of locating something that might well not even exist.[37] Could this be the origin of the *marozi*?

Apparently not. In 1948 G. Hamilton-Snowball informed *The Field* that, many years before Dower, he too had learnt of the *marozi* – from Kikuyu attendants in the Aberdares, who considered it to be a creature very different from the typical lion, being smaller, spotted, hunting in pairs and living only at very high altitudes.[38] In addition, during the spring of 1923, whilst crossing the Aberdares on foot across the Kinangop plateau from Liakipia to N'jabini, at a height of 11,500 ft/3,450 m, at about 4 p.m., he observed a pair of strange cats approximately 200 yards/180 m away. The light was poor, and he thought at first that they were 'two very tawny and washed out looking leopards',[38] but when he turned to his bearer for his rifle, he overheard an excited murmuring from his native attendants and the repetition of an unfamiliar word – '*marozi*'. Before he could bag either of these curious cats, they had turned away, bounding to safety within the nearby forest belt. Upon questioning, his attendants firmly denied that lions ascend to such mountainous heights but affirmed that, '*Marozis* live here.'[38]

A further spotted lion letter appeared in *The Field* later in 1948, written by J.R.T. Pollard, an acquaintance of Raymond Hook. Pollard recalled that Hook believed the spotted lion as such to be largely mythical, though he did suggest that the existence of a small race of lions, possibly descended from the plains form and driven by European settlements to take refuge in the mountainous forests of Kenya, would not be impossible. As far as a fully fledged spotted race was concerned, however, Hook felt that at present there was insufficient evidence to support this.[39]

In contrast, Pollard himself was sympathetic to the mooted existence of an unknown felid in Mount Kenya's upland rain-forests.[39] He recollected that Powys Cobb of Elementeita (who possessed a wide knowledge of Africa's larger carnivorous mammals) had given chase to an unusual cat trespassing on his farm, near the Mau Forest's edge. Cobb observed that the felid was intermediate in size between a lion and leopard and left behind spoor resembling a small lion's; thereafter he remained convinced that an unknown cat did indeed survive in that little-explored region.[39]

Conversely, G. Flett suggested that Cobb had been deceived by shadow effects into believing that he had seen a spotted felid. Flett based his opinion upon personal experience, for on two separate occasions in Kenya this particular optical illusion had temporarily persuaded him that the lions which he had been watching at close range were genuinely spotted.[40]

During 1950, *The Field* published a full-page review of the spotted lion saga, written by Major W. Robert Foran.[41] Whilst greatly enjoying Dower's book, Foran remained highly sceptical of its subject's existence as a full-blown spotted race or subspecies of lion. Instead he favoured the idea that some individuals of the modestly sized Somali lion *Panthera leo somalica* (which has little in the way of a mane) had somehow wandered into Kenya and up into the Aberdares and included amongst themselves some freak members with intense spotting.[41] He concluded his review by stating that he would await further developments in the attempt to solve this riddle conclusively, but sadly no such development has occurred.

Reports of *marozis* were recounted by various persons in the Aberdares during the Emergency (Aberdares invasion by Mau-Mau) in 1952,[42] but since then popular interest in the spotted lion has faded; it is nowadays remembered chiefly as a whimsical wildlife novelty of the World War II period. Yet is this really all that it was? The product of romantic dreams of adventure on the part of Dower,[25] triggered by a pair of freak skins, perpetuated by optical trickery? All of these may well be involved, but the simple facts of this cryptozoological case, coupled with relevant information drawn from parallel zoological situations, suggest that something much more substantial was also present. Consider the following possibilities.

1) Trick of the Light?

Though optical illusions may certainly be responsible for some spotted lion reports, the skins of Trent demonstrate unequivocally that they clearly cannot be offered as an explanation for all of these.

2) Native Invention?

The suggestion that natives say anything to please their masters may be true on occasion, but it must be remembered that, when Hamilton-Snowball sighted those two strange cats in the 1920s, his

Woolly cheetah exhibited at London Zoo during the 1870s

Pseudo-melanistic leopard – this illustration is based upon skin described by Dr Günther in 1885

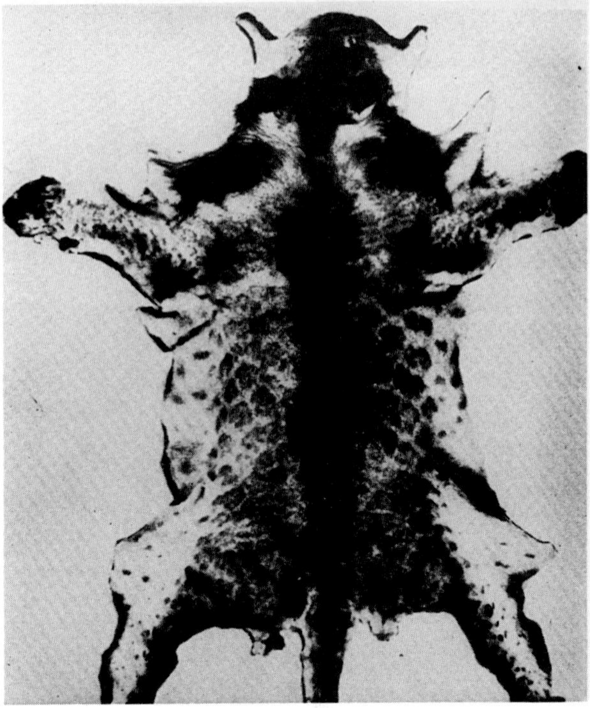

Skin of one of the two spotted lions shot by Michael Trent in the Aberdares

Leopon (lion × leopard hybrid) exhibited at Koshien Zoo, Japan; perhaps the true identity of Africa's spotted lions?

White (*chinchilla* mutant) lion cub Bella and normal brother Danie, born at Johannesburg Zoo on 12 February 1982

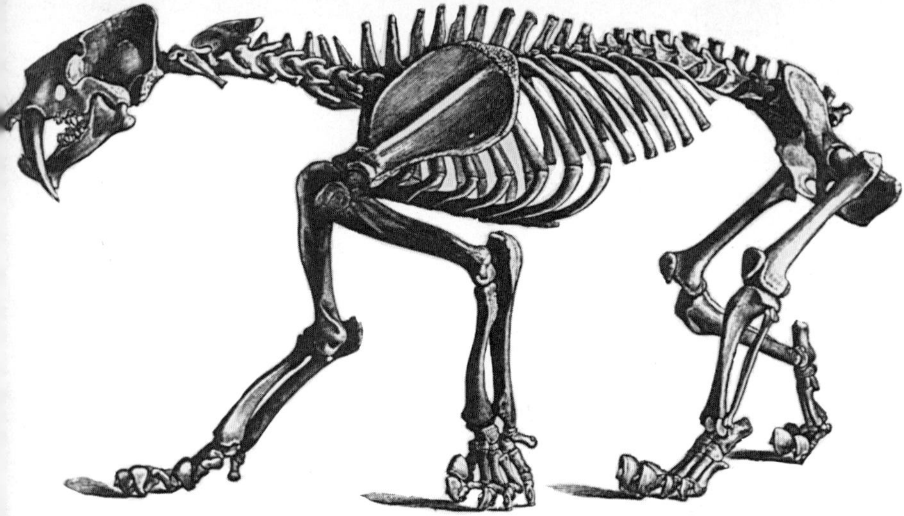

Skeleton of *Smilodon fatalis*, the great sabre-tooth of North America's Pleistocene – are smaller relatives still alive in tropical Africa and South America?

Left: Van Etten swamp monster, based upon eyewitness description. *Right:* The bush-dog – perhaps this is the true identity of the Guyanan *warracaba* tiger

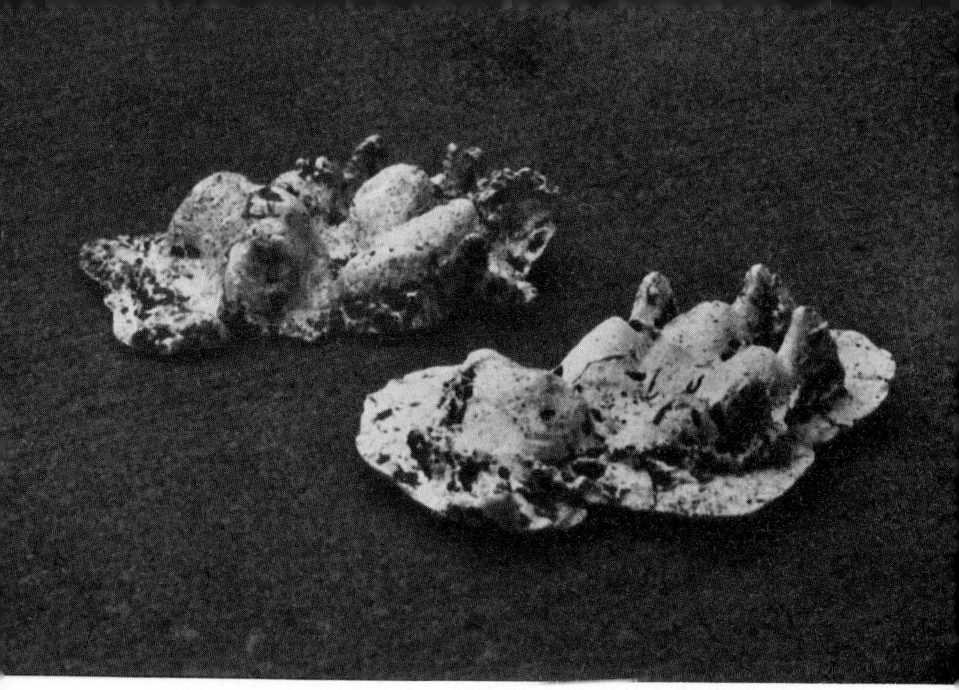

Casts of spoor discovered by Charles and Helen Marks near their trailer court in Westerville, Michigan, on 10 June 1979

The *jaguarete* – an inaccurately drawn black jaguar or an unknown cat form?

Joseph Shirk's *onza*, photographed alongside Dale and Clell Lee in 1938

Normal and black (melanistic) jaguars – the latter may be responsible for reported sightings of black panthers in North America

Queensland tiger, based upon eyewitness descriptions

Skull of Pleistocene marsupial lion, *Thylacoleo carnifex*. The Queensland tiger may be a modern thylacoleonid

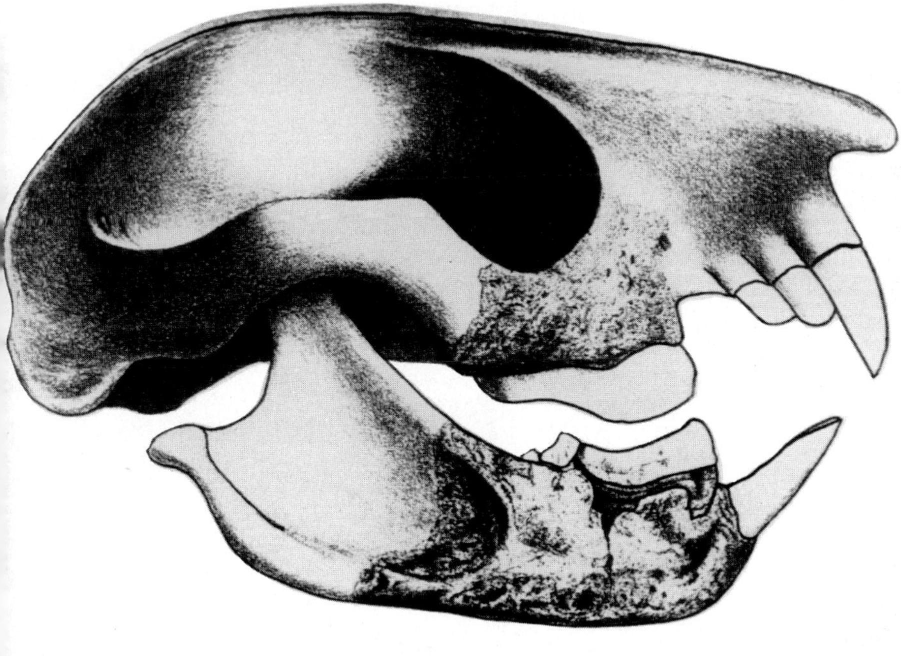

Thylacine (Tasmanian wolf). The Queensland tiger may be a short-faced mainland thylacine

Ozenkadnook tiger – thylacoleonid, thylacine, canid or something quite different from any of these?

native attendants murmured '*marozi*' amongst themselves, not directly to him. Their reaction appeared to have been spontaneous, triggered by their surprise at seeing the cats, rather than as a means of pleasing Hamilton-Snowball. The vast number of native reports which have led to major new animal species being discovered should also be borne in mind here.

3) Freak Individuals?

Fowle's photo demonstrated that spotting can be retained well into adulthood by normal lions, but the extent of spotting displayed by this specimen was much less than that of Trent's cats. Furthermore, its normal body size conflicts with their stunted appearance, and the meagre mane of the male member of Trent's pair has also to be explained. An ordinary lion cub may sometimes retain its juvenile pelage into maturity, but when it also retains its juvenile size and fails to develop one of its species' most characteristic sexual features, it is time to look for a better explanation.

4) Leopons?

A possible solution which on first sight possesses rather more potential than the above set is that that the spotted lion may represent a natural hybrid of lion and leopard. Such hybrids, known popularly as leopons, have been bred on several occasions in zoos, especially in Japan's Hanshin Park Zoo[16] and Koshien Zoo,[43] as well as in Italy more recently.[44] These very striking animals bear more than a passing resemblance to the descriptions of *marozis* – possessing heavily spotted bodies and poorly developed manes and attaining an overall size intermediate between leopard and lion.

According to North African legend, lion × leopard interbreeding does occur in the wild. However, their offspring, though exhibiting a leopard-like pelage, are supposed to be fully maned and as powerful as the lion[45] – a far cry from the *marozi*. In any event, naturalist Henry Scherren pointed out that wild-born leopons would probably not be produced, as an encounter between a wild lion and leopard would most likely result in the leopard's death.[46] This is very feasible, for numerous reports exist of interspecific felid aggression. But the biggest obstacle of all to be surmounted when attempting to reconcile spotted lions with leopons is the fact that such hybrids are almost certainly sterile – very few Big Cat hybrids have ever been obtained that have themselves succeeded in producing viable offspring.

A notable exception is the mystery felid supposedly from the Congo and of a hitherto unknown species which was offered for sale to London Zoo in 1908. Subsequent investigations revealed that it had been bred in America and was actually a complex crossbreed, the offspring of a lion and a jaguar-leopard hybrid.[47]

Nevertheless, it is virtually impossible that an entire population of leopons could develop and be maintained in the wild state.

5) Separate Taxonomic Form?

Could the spotted lion really be a distinct race, subspecies or even full species of lion? The plain fact, though generally 'overlooked' by *marozi* sceptics, is that its appearance as described by many observers with no knowledge of zoology or ecological principles is exactly that which a zoologist or ecologist would predict for a leonine type adapted for inhabiting dense forests – namely, a smaller, less stocky form with dappled pelage, a more primitive hunting-technique and, even in the male, little or no mane.

A bulky felid would not move so effectively through thick forests and would not be effectively hidden from its intended prey with an unpatterned pelage. The vast open spaces of the African savannahs have facilitated the evolution in the normal lion of social hunting[48] – not carried out by any other felid, for such activity would be far less effective in densely wooded areas. Similarly, as it would obviously be very difficult for the sexes of the lion to identify one another across huge expanses of grassland via the normal subtle signals and colour differences exhibited by other felids, the development of highly visible and distinctive morphological features are required – hence the male lion's unique mane.[48] With a lion inhabiting deep forests, conversely, this feature would be superfluous (in fact, the mane may even be deleterious, attracting the attention of would-be prey).

From this it can be seen that the *marozi* fits the bill very well as a forest lion, morphologically and behaviourally. Moreover, there is nothing unusual in the concept of a given mammalian species existing in different forms according to habitat. The African elephant exists in two recognized subspecies – one large and inhabiting plains and bush, the other smaller and inhabiting rainforests. In the Cape buffalo, its savannah subspecies is huge, black and aggressive; its forest form is small, reddish and reclusive. Similarly, the bushpig's forest subspecies is light red, whilst its bush equivalent is very much darker.[49] Compared with these, a somewhat small and spotted forest lion is nothing extraordinary at all.

Finally, if the spotted lion truly comprises a separate race, rather than a few freak individuals, we might expect it to occur in parallel with the plains lion across Africa, at least in relatively undisturbed forests. And sure enough, felids closely resembling the Kenyan *marozi* have indeed been reported from various mountainous forests distributed widely across Africa.[50]

Ikimizis and Wonder-Leopards

For example, in the Mufumbiro Volcanoes region of Rwanda we have the *ikimizi*, a mystery cat which in 1921 attracted the attention of Prince William of Sweden, who later included the following description of it (based upon native reports) in his book *Among Pygmies and Gorillas*: 'The ikimizi is said to be a cross between a lion and a leopard. No white man has ever seen it, and only a few black ones. It is said to be grey in colour, with darker spots and a beard under its chin.'[51]

Despite the Prince exploring the area where one such animal had been seen some time previously, and putting out bait in the hope of luring a specimen, the *ikimizi* did not reveal itself, which dissuaded him from believing in its existence. Nonetheless, he did note that this felid even had its own native name, in spite of the fact that the natives' language had a very restricted vocabulary. This in itself implies that the *ikimizi* is indeed very different in appearance from other cats known to them (lion, leopard, serval etc).

A similar animal, referred to as the *bung bung*, has been reported from the Cameroons;[50] a comparable creature was described by East Africa's Akamba tribe to the Swedish ethnographer Gerhard Lindblom;[52] and an Ethiopian equivalent is known as the *abasambo*.[50] Even the Embu natives' alleged forest cheetah (*kitanga*) may be a spotted lion.

In the Central African Republic's Ubangi region, Dr E. Gromier heard tales of a strange and extremely fierce cat form called the *bakanga*, said to be intermediate between a lion and leopard. Though in overall appearance it was comparable with a maneless lion, its reddish-brown pelage was supposedly dappled like a leopard's. Its most curious feature, however, was that it did not roar but barked rather like a dog. Though promised skins of the *bakanga* by white hunters, Gromier never received any, and his subsequent researches failed to uncover anything further regarding this very peculiar beast.[53]

In Uganda, the spotted lion is represented by the *ntarargo*. In fact, the term *ntarargo* (sometimes spelt *ntarago* or *enturargo*) is a plural noun, of which *ruturargo* is the singular – at least, according to Captain Charles Pitman (game warden and African wildlife authority). Nonetheless, so many reports use *ntarargo* as a singular noun that it will be used in this sense here too for the sake of conformity. Also worth noting is that another version of this name exists – *kitalargo*, which Captain Phillips concluded was a contraction of *kitalo-engo*, wonder-leopard.[54] Regardless of its name, however, its appearance follows the same familiar pattern: 'This creature is said to be a cross between a lion and a leopard [with] a long tail, a slightly spotted skin, and retractile claws.' This is the description given by the Kichwamba natives to E.A. Temple-Perkins.[55] Moreover, he once heard a most peculiar animal voice in this region which was harsh and guttural, most closely resembling the cough of a leopard but with an additional gurgling quality. Four different natives, questioned independently of one another by Temple-Perkins, stated without hesitation that the creature he had heard was the *ntarargo*.[55]

There seems little doubt that Africa possesses a distinct race of diminutive spotted lion, whose preferred habitat – remote mountain forests – is surely a major reason for its continued neglect by science; certainly its addition to the catalogue of creatures formally recognized and classified by science is long overdue. Indeed, in an attempt to rectify this, Dr Heuvelmans has actually proposed an official scientific name for it, *Panthera leo maculatus*,[56] thereby considering it to be of subspecific status. All that is now required is a complete specimen to determine definitely whether this felid is truly more than a freak and a fable. Perhaps someone with the exuberance and diligence of the late Kenneth Gandar Dower will one day complete his quest and bring back to the West a living spotted lion.

White, Black, Striped – and Green? – Lions

The spotted lion is certainly not the only unexpected variation upon the basic leonine theme to attract widespread attention. This was strikingly demonstrated in 1977, when zoologist Chris McBride revealed to stunned pressmen across the world that for the past two years, on a private South African game reserve called Timbavati, he had been studying and protecting three blue-eyed, snowy white lions.[57] In fact, sightings of white lions in the Kruger National Park and from the neighbouring Transvaal had been reported for many years prior to this,[11,58] but the Timbavati trio were the first to receive extensive media publicity and official recognition; several more have been formally documented since.[58] And by breeding normal-coloured animals with two of the Timbavati specimens (now in captivity themselves after the third was killed by a poacher in the wild[58]), white lions have since been born in zoos too. [58-59] These lions are chinchilla mutants, leonine equivalents of Rewa's famous white tigers.[60]

A light-grey cub, also labelled (tentatively) as a chinchilla mutant, had been born at Alabama's Birmingham Zoo in 1974, but this specimen was darker than those from Timbavati.[61]

Paralleling the situation with tigers, whilst white lions are now known and studied, the likelihood of black lions existing is still undetermined. According to W.L. Speight, in 1940, an experienced game warden once stated that he had spied a whole pride of pitch-black lions in the Kruger National Park.[62] Half a century earlier, a very dark brown specimen had been killed by soldiers of the Luristan Regiment and was seen by archaeologist Sir Henry Layard at Ispahan in what is now Iran.[63] And an account of a black lioness observed at very close quarters was included in *Okavango*, by June Kay.[64]

During 1975, at Glasgow (formerly Calder Park) Zoo in Scotland, a lion cub named Ranger was born which had a black chest and one black leg. According to media news of the time,[65] the zoo's director, Richard O'Grady, planned to mate him when old enough with his mother, Kara, in the hope of producing an all-black specimen. I have since learnt from Mr O'Grady that such matings occurred on several occasions, but despite both lions being in excellent health, Kara never conceived and has now died. Ranger has also been mated with another lioness, but again without success, suggesting that he could be sterile. Nonetheless, the fact that Ranger possesses these sizeable areas of black pigment (probably an example of mozaicism) implies that it is not beyond the realms of possibility that one day a totally black lion may be born.

In addition to white and black lions, reddish-brown individuals have also been reported[50] but what of the *green* lion supposedly seen by a prospector in the forests of western Uganda?[53]

Guggisberg notes[26,53] that some lion cubs' spots are arranged in distinct vertical lines, and occasional examples have been recorded in which these spots have merged to yield definite stripes. Exceptionally, these are retained into adulthood – a good photograph of one such felid is included in Ivan Heran's *Animal Coloration*.[66] Otherwise, however, the nearest animals to striped lions known from actual specimens are various zoo examples of lion × tiger hybrids – known as ligers (if sired by a lion) or tigons (if sired by a tiger).

A Bewilderment of Black Leopards

In spite of the expansive array of colours and patterns exhibited by the leopard in Asia, its African equivalents are even more dramatically diverse. On a morphic (as opposed to a subspecific) level, these range from red leopards,[45] cream leopards[67,68] and striped leopards[69] to jaguar-rosetted leopards,[67] buff leopards with orange rosettes[68] and even leopards without any distinct rosettes,[68] to mention but a few.

Surprisingly, however, and in stark contrast to the extremely abundant black panther of Asia, very few records exist of African melanistic leopards. Considering that this continent has numerous localities whose habitats and climate correspond closely with those in Asia that support panthers, the reason for this anomaly is quite obscure. In fact, the only areas from which true (non-agouti) black leopards have been recorded with certainty are Ethiopia[70] and the Cameroons, plus the forests of Mount Kenya and the Aberdares[26] (clearly the places to be when seeking unexpected African felids).

Yet, if we also take heed of the many unconfirmed reports of predominantly black, leopard-like cats from several other African regions, it would seem that African panthers are more widespread – and varied – than science supposes.

The Grahamstown Mystery Cat

A mysterious felid of quite remarkable appearance was killed during the 1880s at Grahamstown, South Africa, and its skin was sent to Dr A. Günther. Its coat's background colour was tawny, brightening to a rich orange gloss on the shoulders. Rosettes were virtually absent, being replaced mostly by numerous small separate spots, but these had coalesced dorsally to yield an unbroken expanse of black, stretching from its head right along to its tail base. In contrast to this specimen's richly hued upperparts, however, its underparts were principally white with large black spots, as in typical leopards, and it also bore the facial markings characteristic of this species. Its total length was 6 ft 7 in/197.5 cm (including a 2½ ft/75 cm tail).[71]

Günther had initially entertained the possibility that this singular cat was some bizarre hybrid. However, his detailed examination of its skin ultimately revealed certain very specific but taxonomically significant features which, in combination with its already-noted leopard features, persuaded him that, despite its exotic colour scheme, its owner had indeed been nothing more than a leopard after all[71] – albeit of a very spectacular pseudo-melanistic variety (comparable with the Malabar specimen noted in Chapter 3). A year later, Günther received a second, even darker specimen of this form (sometimes referred to as *Panthera pardus* var. *melanotica*), again from Grahamstown.[72] Other, less striking pseudo-melanistic examples have been recorded elsewhere in Africa.[26]

Damasia – Dark Leopard or New Species?

Well worth considering is whether a comparable variety could be the explanation of a still-unidentified African felid known as the *damasia*, which dwells – not surprisingly? – in the Aberdares. The *damasia* was referred to in the previously mentioned letter to *The Field* by G. Hamilton-Snowball concerning his sighting of spotted lions on these mountains.[38] In this, he also recalled that during the 1920s he had shot a creature which he had taken to be a leopard, albeit a very large, dark specimen. Yet when his Kikuyu attendants saw it, they announced that it was not a *chui* (leopard) but a *damasia*, and that a *damasia* was as different from a leopard as a *simba* (lion) was from a *marozi*. Apparently the *damasia* is well known to the Aberdares natives but is always mistaken by non-locals for a leopard.[38]

Tropical Africa's native tribes frequently classify animals by way of criteria very different from those used by scientists. Often an individual animal which is of a colour or size different from that of normal specimens of the same species, or an individual which is notably more aggressive than others of its own species, is given an entirely separate name by the natives and thought of as being of a form totally different from the more typical members of its species. Therefore it is certainly possible that, despite the Kikuyus' firm denial, the *damasia* really is just a dark-coloured (pseudo-melanistic?) leopard. Since genuine black leopards are on record from the Aberdares, it would be interesting to learn whether the natives class them as leopard or *damasia*. Alternatively, considering that the Aberdares' primeval forests already house one mystery cat, in the form of the *marozi*, it is conceivable that they are hiding further zoological surprises too.

Kibambangwe and Uruturangwe – Cats or Composites?

The same may be true of Bufumbira County, mountain home of a quite ferocious beast which supposedly hunts by day and by night and which is known as the *kibambangwe*. Its name translates as 'snatcher', a term assigned to hyaenas in other parts of Africa where Bantu is spoken, but is this the true identity of the *kibambangwe*? As recorded by Captain Pitman in his book *A Game Warden Among His Charges*,[54] during the 1920s one of these animals created terrible havoc in this region but was never captured. Suggested identities ranged from a notably dark-coloured giant hyaena (in itself very deserving of cryptozoological attention, surely), to a melanistic leopard. Unfortunately, hardly any morphological details concerning the *kibambangwe* have been recorded, other than its possession of blackish markings and short ears – not much on which to base a zoological identification. Pitman also recalled a story regarding a pair of these creatures which once existed in lava caves sited loftily on the mountains and which every so often descended to the plains to ravage the local inhabitants' livestock. Eventually, in desperation, the locals banded together and upon their next encounter with the *kibambangwes* entered into a fierce battle with them, as a result of which both animals were finally destroyed.[54]

Then there is the bloodthirsty *uruturangwe*, allegedly inhabiting the forests around Mount Muhavura and Mount Sabinio in Rwanda. It apparently resembles the leopard in size but possesses a hyaena-like pelage. According to the natives, it can enter a hut by a very tiny hole (just like the leopard) and kills its human victim by suffocation – lying on him and taking his entire face and throat within its jaws. Pitman noted that this behaviour again compares well with the leopard's mode of killing. Moreover, the *uruturangwe* is supposed to have a long tail and retractile claws – neither of these is a typical hyaena characteristic.[54] Yet, paradoxically, when a skull said to be from an *uruturangwe* was brought forward for scientific examination, it was found to be that of a spotted hyaena, albeit an exceedingly large one.[54]

The most plausible explanation for this inconsistency of identity is one which has already been aired in relation to the so-called British Big Cat and exemplified by reference to the mystifying Nandi bear of Africa – namely that the *uruturangwe* is probably a non-existent composite creature rather than a real entity. Certainly, as if it were not complex enough already, the Nandi bear melange has even encroached upon various mystery cat reports on occasion, e.g. the skin of a supposed *ntarargo* was identified by Pocock as that of a young spotted hyaena.[73] Comparably, it is only too simple to visualize sightings of abnormally large hyaenas and killings made by savage leopard specimens in the same area being attributed by the latter's alarmed native population to a huge and ferocious mystery beast, requiring the creation of a new name. The same applies to the equally vaguely defined *kibambangwe*.

Ndalawo – Black and Grey Mystery Cat of Uganda

This Ugandan mystery carnivore was described by Captain William Hichens as follows: '... a fierce man-killing carnivore, the size and shape of a leopard, but with a black-furred back shading to grey below'.[2] An *ndalawo* skin was actually procured but was sent out of the country before it could receive formal scientific attention. Consequently, its identity was never ascertained, and its whereabouts are now unknown. Pitman recorded that it seemed to be a 'partly melanistic leopard' (note the word 'partly', indicating that it was not a normal black panther), practically devoid of spots but displaying a few typical leopard markings on the extremities and round the lower jaw.[54] This more detailed description is reminiscent of that cited by Günther for *P. pardus Var. melanotica*;

certainly, pseudo-melanistic leopards have paler underparts, unlike the uniformly dark black panthers. Based upon pelage cc isiderations alone, it is not implausible that the *ndalawo* may indeed prove to be a pseudo-melanistic leopard (albeit a less showy version than those from South Africa). However, there is more than just its pelage to consider: the *ndalawo* exhibits some rather unexpected traits for a mere leopard. For example, it allegedly hunts in threes or fours and whilst hunting gives voice to a most peculiar laugh.[54] These are indicative of a hyaena. Yet, as Hichens pointed out, the *ndalawo* is very greatly feared as an exceedingly ferocious beast, while even the oldest woman in a native kraal is more than prepared to shoo away a hyaena that comes too close.[2] If the *ndalawo* is a form of leopard, it is a very unusual one; in fact, out of all the black mystery cats of Africa discussed here, the *ndalawo* is surely the one most likely to represent a hitherto unknown felid species.

Mngwa – Tanzania's 'Strange One'

An even stranger felid – even its name, *mngwa*, comes from the Kiswahili for 'strange one'[32] – may still survive within the temperate coastal forests of Tanzania (formerly Tanganyika). Also known as the *nunda*, this is a quite monstrous beast by all accounts, described by natives as being as big as a donkey and striped with grey like a domestic tabby cat.[2]

The history of the *mngwa* extends far back into Swahili legend, appearing in many of its sayings and songs (including a very early warrior's song, dating back to *c.* AD 1150 and attributed to the Swahili hero Liongo Fumo wa Ba-Uriy[74]), and features prominently in the legend of the Sultan Majnun documented in *Swahili Tales*[75] by Edward Steere in the nineteenth century. As a result of its frequent occurrence in folktale and myth, the *mngwa* was dismissed out of hand as purely imaginary by British inhabitants of Tanzania – until the raw reality of a horrific episode in the 1920s demanded a very different view to be taken.

In 1922 Captain Hichens was Native Magistrate at a small Tanzanian coastal village called Lindi, the site of the following gruesome occurrence:

> It was the custom for native traders to leave their belongings in the village market every night, ready for the morning's trade; and to prevent theft and also to stop stray natives sleeping in the market-place, an askari or native constable took it in turns with two others to guard the market on a four-hour watch. Going to relieve the midnight watch, an oncoming native constable one night found his comrade missing. After a search he discovered him, terribly mutilated, underneath a stall. The man ran to his European officer,

> who went with me at once to the market. We found it obvious that the askari had been attacked and killed by some animal – a lion, it seemed. In the victim's hand was clenched a matted mass of greyish hair, such as would come out of a lion's mane were it grasped and torn in a violent fight. But in many years no lion had been known to come into the town.[76]

Hichens was still perplexed the next morning, when he was visited by an old native governor of the district and two men brought with him. This latter pair seemed very frightened – and for good reason, as Hichens soon discovered, for he learnt that on the night of the askari's death these two men '... had slunk by the market-place lest the askari should see them and think them evil-doers; and as they crept by they were horrified to see a gigantic brindled cat, the great mysterious nunda which is feared in every village on the coast, leap from the shadows of the market and bear the policeman to the ground'.[76] The native governor added that this creature had visited the village on several previous occasions and was neither lion nor leopard, being bigger than both.[76]

Until then, Hichens had disbelieved such accounts – the previous evening's events, however, were only too real. And so, to be absolutely safe, he kept watch himself on the market the following evening, accompanied by two armed askaris – but nothing happened. Consequently the next morning he delivered a severe lecture to the askaris on the foolishness of superstition – little knowing just how soon he would be regretting his impatience. That same evening saw the slaughter of another askari, and when his hideously mangled body was examined, more of the same grey matted fur was discovered. For the next month, similar killings were reported up and down the coast at a number of small villages, and despite the authorities' sending-out search-parties, setting down traps and laying out poison, the ferocious felid responsible was never obtained. Instead, it simply failed to appear one night and did not return again – and the killings stopped. Fur samples sent for analysis were identified very non-specifically – as cat.[76] Had the hair-analysts taken the trouble to record how comparable the fur seemed in relation to that of lion and of leopard, this would have been far more useful.

In the 1930s a further outbreak of nefarious killings began; needless to say, this time Hichens was far less sceptical – especially when a horribly mauled man was carried on a stretcher to him at Mchinga, another small coastal village in Tanzania, and informed him that his attacker had been a *mngwa*. The man was a renowned hunter who had frequently tracked and killed lions and leopards;

hence it was most unlikely that he would mistake either of these familiar felids for anything else or invent some far-fetched tale.

In any event, to testify even further how distinct a creature the *mngwa* is from lion and leopard in the eyes of the coastal Tanzanian people, there is a famous native hunting-song in which all three of these large-sized cats are mentioned within a single verse, clearly demonstrating that there is no confusion between these felids.[2]

Hichens was not the only Westerner with experience of *mngwa* activity. Patrick Bowen actually saw the spoor of one such cat which had carried off a small child from another coastal village. He tracked the creature without success but did find some brindled hair on the stakes through which it had forced its way into the kraal to reach the child. The hair appeared to be quite unlike that of either lion or leopard. And the spoor? Bowen stated that it compared with that of a leopard as large as the largest lion.[74] Any leopard of leonine proportions would truly be a creature to fear!

So is this the identity of the *mngwa* – an abnormally large leopard? Its coat morphology argues against this theory, for, diverse though the leopard's pelage can be, it is still very difficult to conceive how it could mutate into the brindled appearance described for the *mngwa*, as commented by Dr Heuvelmans in his own consideration of this mystery cat.[32]

During the Pleistocene epoch, Africa housed a number of notably large felids now extinct. These included the formidable *Panthera crassidens* and a lion-sized felid with a tiger-like lower jaw.[48] If either of these has persisted into the present day in Tanzania's little-penetrated coastal forests, it may well make the mystery of the *mngwa* somewhat less incongruous.

Another identity on offer is one proposed by Dr Heuvelmans in his cryptozoological checklist[50] – namely, that the *mngwa* could constitute a hitherto undescribed giant form of the African golden cat. He gave no reasons for his opinion, but from a zoological standpoint it is not difficult to comprehend why he favours this identity.

Known scientifically as *Felis* (sometimes *Profelis*) *auratus* and measuring 3½-4½ ft/105-135 cm in total length (i.e. twice the size of a large domestic cat), with markedly long limbs and tail, the African golden cat is one of the most beautiful, yet least-known of all felids. Its most notable feature is its pelage, which exhibits a quite outstanding range of variation – from the rich golden hue which has earned it its English and scientific names to all manner of reds, browns, greys (even an occasional melanistic example), and sometimes adorned with varying degrees of dark spotting too.[26]

The golden cat's lifestyle and distribution remain a notable mystery. For example, traditionally thought of as a predominantly West African felid, it gave science quite a jolt when Raymond Hook's investigations revealed that it also inhabited Kenya's Mau Forest;[34] more recently, in 1979, an Aberdares record was documented.[77] Worth considering is whether brief sightings of speckled individuals of this elusive species may even be responsible for some *marozi* reports.

Although it approaches neither lion nor leopard in body size, the golden cat inspires extraordinary fear and tribal superstition amongst the natives throughout its range[78] – as observed, for example, by Gerald Durrell when collecting animals in the Cameroons.[79] Similarly, okapi-discoverer Sir Harry Johnston was informed by Liberians that the golden cat was very bloodthirsty – they even referred to it as 'the leopard's brother'.[80]

How much greater then would be the terror of natives if faced with a golden cat which *was* comparable in size with a lion or leopard? Equal, perhaps, to the fear roused by the *mngwa*? Additionally, of all African felid species, the bewilderingly variable pelage of the golden cat affords the greatest chance of giving rise to a colour variant possessing the unusual brindled appearance described for the *mngwa*. Also, though not officially chronicled from Tanzania so far, its relatively recent discovery in Kenya and its known occurrence in neighbouring Uganda suggest that it is not in any way improbable that this evanescent species may also exist in Tanzania.

There is one further *mngwa* feature which, though seemingly insignificant in itself, gives the golden cat identity very great impetus in combination with all the other correspondences mentioned here. In a *Wide World* article, Captain Hichens mentioned in passing that, when making its exit with its mutilated victim, on several occasions the *mngwa* has been heard purring![81] Although the Big Cats can purr between breaths, the cats with the correct throat structure and capability for normal continuous and loud purring are the Small Cats. The golden cat is a Small Cat and is perfectly capable of purring loudly and continuously, and young specimens in particular purr profusely when contented. Consequently, the purring prowess of the *mngwa* provides important evidence in favour of a Small Cat identity.

Like the *mngwa*, the golden cat is believed to be primarily nocturnal and hunts crepuscularly (at dawn and dusk), with arboreal tendencies and the capacity to kill animals as large as medium-sized antelopes.[26] Yet until more specific details regarding its lifestyle can be ascertained, it is both difficult and unwise to speculate too closely upon whether circumstances could exist whereby a giant-sized form would or could evolve. At present, the most which can be stated with safety is that such a felid would certainly comprise a persuasive *mngwa* identity. In any event, only an actual *mngwa* specimen can verify (or disprove) this theory, but if the latter mystery cat *is* found to be a giant golden cat, the fact that the world's largest felid form (which is what the *mngwa* may well be) is a Small Cat rather than a Big Cat will undoubtedly represent one of the most startling zoological revelations for a very long time.

Wobo and Abu Sotan – Tigers in Africa?

Although Asia possesses a small number of lions, it is surely too audacious to suggest that Africa houses an entourage of tigers –?

Theodor von Heuglin and other nineteenth-century explorers of Ethiopia (formerly Abyssinia) learnt of an extremely dangerous wild beast which was called *wobo* by the Amhara and *mendelit* by the Tigre inhabitants. It was described as being larger than a lion, yellowish-brown or grey-brown in colour and decorated with black stripes. King Theodoros informed von Heuglin that for some considerable time a *wobo* skin had adorned the principal cathedral of Eifag, and many people claimed to have seen it.[82,83] What could the *wobo* skin be from? In *Simba*, C.A.W. Guggisberg speculated that it might have been a tiger pelt from Asia that for some unknown reason had made its way ultimately to Ethiopia.[53] This is possible, but it does not explain the widespread native knowledge of such a creature, unless we assume that all of this evolved from knowledge of the skin at Eifag.

There is a fundamental problem with this idea, in that the *wobo* is not an isolated case, for von Heuglin also noted that a similar carnivore appeared to occur in neighbouring Sudan, where it was referred to as the *abu sotan*. Inhabiting rocky mountains near the River Rahad, it was described as being marked with great black blotches or stripes.[83] Perhaps, as von Heuglin suggested, the *wobo* and *abu sotan* belong to a currently unknown species.[83] Certainly it is very difficult to suggest a known African species which possesses stripes – ironically, of all African cats, it is the equally mysterious *mngwa* which in terms of both brindled pelage and huge size comes closest to these! Curiouser and curiouser, as Alice would have said!

And what are we to make of a lion-clawed, tiger-headed, leopard-rosetted felid on the rampage in the Mayanja district of Kenya during early 1974, and likened in some reports to a giant cheetah? This anomalous amalgam allegedly devoured many domestic animals during its reign of terror, while eluding with ease the many hunting-parties that went in search of it. Its identity was made particularly mystifying by the fact that leopards are very rare in this region, whilst the last reported lion here was killed more than twenty years earlier.[84] Nor was it ever killed – unless it happened to be one and the same individual as 'the beast of Bungoma', an equally ferocious felid which hit the headlines a little later, when it was held responsible for the deaths of hundreds of farm animals in Kenya's Bungoma district. A very large and savage leopard was ultimately trapped by forestry rangers, but whether this was really the Beast is unknown.[85]

Mountain Tigers

One of the greatest losses for the modern mammalogist must surely be the huge-fanged sabre-toothed cats. The African Pleistocene epoch possessed a number of sabre-tooth genera, including *Megantereon, Machairodus, Therailurus* and *Afrosmilus*;[48] in life they undoubtedly constituted a sight more awe-inspiring than even the most magnificent of today's lions, tigers, jaguars and other large cats.

As it happens, there are many Africans alive today who may actually have first-hand knowledge of such experiences, for it could be that a few sabre-tooths still exist. Take, for example, the unidentified mountain tiger of Chad – concerning which I am exceedingly grateful to Michel Raynal for supplying me with much information from his files.[86] The Zagaoua people of Ennedi, northern Chad, tell of a cat form (known to this region's French-speaking people as '*tigre de montagne*') that is definitely not known, at least in the living state, to modern science. For they describe it as being larger than a lion but lacking a tail, possessing red fur banded with white stripes, plus long hairs on its feet, and – most interesting of all – teeth that protrude from its mouth. It inhabits the Ennedi mountains and caves and is so strong that it can bear away sizeable antelopes.[86]

Whilst in the company of an old game-tracker in the Ouanda-Djailé area during the 1960s, a French hunting guide heard a terrible roar near a large cavern, a roar which was totally unlike anything known to him, despite his very considerable experience with animal calls. His companion *had* heard it before and identified it as that of the *tigre de montagne*; his subsequent description of this beast suggested a sabre-toothed cat. And sure enough, when the hunting guide returned to that area a year later, armed with drawings of modern and fossil animal forms, his game-tracker acquaintance positively identified the picture of the extinct African sabre-tooth *Machairodus* as the mountain tiger.[86]

This is not the only information on record concerning such cats, either. A similar beast, the *hadjel*, is known to the Hadjeray of

Chad's south-west Ouadai district[50] and also to the Central African Republic's Youlou tribe, who call it *coq-ninji* or *coq-djingé* (while this region's French speakers again use the term *tigre de montagne*).[50] And in other, unidentified languages of this latter country, the same creature is apparently referred to as the *gassingram* or *vassoko*.[50] In 1937 Lucien Blancou, formerly Chief Game Inspector in French Equatorial Africa, was informed by the village chief of Ouanda-Djailé that the *gassingram* was reddish-brown in colour, larger than a lion and with equally over-sized footprints. Primarily nocturnal, with eyes that shone like lamps in the darkness, it bore its prey to mountainous caves.[32] In view of its close correspondence with the *tigre de montagne* of Ennedi, the *gassingram* is surely one and the same species.

Amphibious Sabre-Tooths?

Certain other reports from the Central African Republic, but this time derived from localities to the north of its capital, Bangui, describe creatures which, although comparable in some ways with those mountain-dwelling forms discussed above, are nonetheless most probably of a quite separate species, for they display a most unexpected and singular behavioural attribute – they are predominantly aquatic!

The marked predominance of this feature is acknowledged in the various native names given to these animals by different Central African Republic tribes. Thus the Banda speak of the *mourou n'gou* or *muru-ngu* (meaning water leopard), the Baya speak of the *dilali* (water lion), the Sangho of the *ze-ti-ngu* or *nze ti gou* (water panther) and the Zandé of the *mamaimé* (water lion) or *ngoroli* (water elephant).[50,86] Judging from all but the last-mentioned term, these creatures are quite clearly feline, an assumption supported by the various descriptions of these on record.

According to an old Banda tribesman called Moussa, interviewed by Lucien Blancou in 1934, the *mourou n'gou* was somewhat larger than a lion (Moussa estimating its length at about 12 ft/360 cm), with an overall body shape and pelage background colour reminiscent of a leopard's but additionally adorned with stripes. Curiously, its paw-print was described as 'containing a circle in the middle'.[32] Apparently, Moussa at some stage had observed one of these emerging from the Koukourou river in close proximity to a soldier in a canoe. The *mouro n'gou* seized the hapless man and dragged him down into the water. As a result of this incident, the detachment to which the beast's victim had belonged decided not to cross the river at this point thereafter but at a new location some considerable distance to the east.[32]

In 1945 a native gunbearer called Mitikata drew a sketch of the *mourou n'gou*, which showed a small-headed, large-fanged creature about 8 ft/240 cm long, with a plump, uniformly brown-coloured body and a panther-like tail.[32]

Blancou also learnt a little concerning the *dilali*, which, according to an interpreter at Bozoum in eastern Ubangi-Shari, possessed the body of a horse and the claws of a lion, as well as large, walrus-like tusks (this last-noted feature was mentioned to Blancou by a Zandé native guard).[32]

Then there is the *nze ti gou*, a nocturnal beast of leopard stature, having red fur marked with pale stripes or spots, living within hollows in large rivers and emitting a thunderous noise.[86] Such creatures are not limited to the Central African Republic either.

The Mbunda tribe of eastern Angola speak of the *coje ya menia* (water lion), which attracted the interest of Ilse von Nolde during her sojourn there in the early 1930s. Like the *nze ti gou*, this beast is well known to the natives for its loud, rumbling vocals and, though principally aquatic, sometimes ventures forth onto dry land. Like the other beasts mentioned here, it is armed with large canine teeth or tusks and supposedly kills hippos with them, despite its own smaller body size. The observations and dealings of von Nolde with this region's natives convinced her that the *coje ya menia* was not based upon misidentified sightings of crocodiles or hippos, or of these species' spoor; on the contrary, the natives were very adept at identification and interpretation of spoor.[32,87] She was equally convinced of the sincerity of a Portuguese lorry-driver who told her that, in the company of some natives, he had actually tracked a *coje ya menia* which had chased after and killed a hippopotamus. Sure enough, the tracks of the two beasts had led to the mutilated carcase of a hippo – yet no part of it had been eaten. The tracks of the *coje ya menia* were smaller than those of the hippo and, while in shape somewhat reminiscent of an elephant's, they additionally contained the impression of toes.[87] Worth noting here is that as far back as the 1940s the renowned cryptozoologist Dr Ingo Krumbiegel had suggested a surviving sabre-tooth as a possible identity for this *Löwe des Wassers*.[88]

Moving to southern Zaire, we meet reports of yet another similar animal, known variously as *simba ya mai, ntambue ya mai* and *ntambo wa luy*, all of which translate once again as 'water lion'. Further mystery beasts apparently belonging to this same type include the Kenyan *ol-maima* and the Sudanese *nyo-kodoing*.[50]

Even though from description and native nomenclature a feline identity seems probable, and from their formidable upper canines a sabre-tooth is clearly intimated, the existence of an aquatic version remains a very bizarre concept. Certainly there is no evidence from fossil sabre-tooth finds to suggest that any extinct form ever became adapted for this kind of lifestyle. So is it really possible that such a creature is the explanation for the various mystery beasts described here?

In *Les Derniers Dragons d'Afrique*,[89] Dr Heuvelmans asserted that it was not only possible but was, to his mind, more than likely. The principal arguments he put forward in support of this can be summarized as follows:

1) Despite popular belief, many cat species are not afraid of water.[89]

2) The very effective utilization by walruses of their own huge upper canines for anchorage, dragging themselves onto land or ice floes and ploughing up the sea-bed sediment in search of modest-sized prey demonstrates that the sabre-tooth's enlarged canines would be of great benefit for an aquatic existence.[89,90]

3) Conversely, on land such teeth would surely have been a great handicap to the sabre-tooth when attempting to tear off and devour pieces of meat from its prey.[89]

4) Due to this, sabre-tooths would have faired badly in competition with true felids of comparable size, e.g. lions and leopards, and ultimately would have been forced to move into ecological niches unoccupied by such cats – namely, remote mountains and aquatic realms[89] (the very environments from which reports of alleged modern sabre-tooths are emerging).

Consequently, Heuvelmans believes that sabre-tooths could exist very readily in an aquatic environment simply by paralleling the walrus's lifestyle. Moreover, if challenged by potential rivals, such as elephants or hippos, the sabre-tooth would be more than equipped to dispose of them and could even the drink the blood spurting from any vanquished opponent's neck (some authorities believe that the fossil terrestrial sabre tooths were themselves sanguivorous). Its carcase could serve as a food source too, for, if dragged under water by the sabre-tooth and allowed to decompose, the carcase's meat would eventually soften, enabling it to be torn off in pieces and devoured more readily by the sabre-tooth, thereby cancelling out the problems which the felid could otherwise experience due to its cumbersome canines.[89]

Once again, this suggestion is supported by walrus activity: some walruses have been reported killing seals and small whales, and lumps of blubber and seal remains (soft and/or from decomposing beached carcases – hence easy to tear) have been found in the stomach of some walruses.[89,90]

Nor have we come to the end of walrus parallels. Any sabre-tooth modified via evolution for an aquatic existence that compared closely with that of a walrus behaviourally would very likely follow a similar course morphologically too (convergent evolution).

Other than eyewitness reports of the various mystery beasts mentioned here, is there any evidence for a walrus-like creature in tropical Africa? The answer is both affirmative and rather stunning, for a cave painting discovered at Brackfontein Ridge, Orange Free State, depicts an animal which bears a startling resemblance to a walrus, from its rounded head displaying two very large downward-curving tusks to its elongated, tapering body and paddle-like limbs. It differs primarily from the walrus in possessing a long tail.[89,91] Over its 23-million-year evolution from originally terrestrial ancestors, the walrus has lost its tail; conversely, as the known fossil sabre-tooths of Africa's Pleistocene epoch (2 million years ago) displayed terrestrial-related morphology, any amphibious development must have occurred since then. It is rather unlikely that as drastic a change as the complete loss of a tail via evolution would have occurred in so short (geologically speaking) a space of time. And so the painting is precisely what we would expect a recently evolved amphibious sabre-tooth to look like – a more streamlined version of its terrestrial counterpart with limbs modified for an aquatic life but with the tail not yet lost. Also worth noting is that such a sabre-tooth may be expected to be larger than land-living species, as the accompanying weight increase would be buoyed by its surrounding liquid environment; this would explain the notable size of some of the mystery beasts reported in this section.

Many years ago, an Ituri Forest pygmy identified a picture of a walrus shown to him by John A. Hunter as a savage, nocturnal beast which lived in the deepest parts of the forest. Not surprisingly, Hunter dismissed this as nothing more than the pygmy's desire to please him.[92] Nonetheless, in view of the Brackfontein painting and this section's unidentified animals, it may be prudent not to discount it totally. Also worth keeping in mind is a certain Ngona Horn folktale of the Wahungwe, Zimbabwe, documented in *African Genesis*[93] by Professor Leo Frobenius and Douglas Fox, for it refers to some very odd felids – 'lions under the water' – and is itself entitled *The Water Lions*. Comparable with nearby Angola's *coje ya menia*?

Clearly the concept of aquatic felids is not at all alien to native Africans. And the close correspondence in such creatures' descriptions over so far-reaching an expanse of Africa – cutting across many different tribal cultures and histories – is indicative that there is something more substantial and fundamental to their accounts than folktale and superstition.

The mysterious Kenyan *dingonek* – an aquatic beast of generally feline appearance, familiar to the Wa-Ndorobo tribe and allegedly shot at by adventurer John Alfred Jordan – is another possible member of the aquatic sabre-tooth association. It possesses one feature which initially seems to exclude it from such an identity – namely, a body covered in scales.[94] Heuvelmans, however, considers it more likely that these are optical illusions produced by light shining on a particularly reflective pelage, and one which also bears tufts of hair that have adhered together as a result of the animal's having been submerged in water, thereby creating the effect of scales.[89] Another aquatic mystery beast, the *chipekwe* of Zambia's Lake Bangweulu,[95] has also been put forward as a possible water-dwelling sabre-tooth;[89] unlike the *dingonek*, however, most reports of the *chipekwe* imply a reptilian (possibly dinosaurian) identity rather than anything mammalian.

Madagascan Mystery Cats

South-east of the African mainland lies the island of Madagascar, a zoological time-capsule, for it is the home of a vast variety of creatures extinct elsewhere or totally unique, a wonderland of lemurs and tenrecs, falanoucs and vanga-shrikes. It has no native canids or felids; instead, the viverrids reign supreme here, of which the largest species – and the creature which assumes on Madagascar the ecological roles occupied elsewhere by sizeable felid species – is the peculiar fossa *Cryptoprocta ferox* (not to be confused with the Madagascan civet, whose scientific name is *Fossa fossa*). Despite its viverrid relationship, the puma-sized fossa is strikingly cat-like in appearance, comparable with the South American jaguarundi.

In addition, Madagascar may possess an unknown species of true felid. In a report published by *Le Chasseur Français* in October 1939, Paul Cazard recalled that whilst in Madagascar he had been informed by civil engineer Mr Bélime that native tales originating from areas of the island still unexplored by white men told of giant lions which lived in caves and which ravaged the island's other fauna as well as the inhabitants of these regions' native villages.[96] Cazard wondered whether these lions of the rocks could possibly be living sabre-tooths and if it would be feasible for an expedition to be mounted to seek out these mighty beasts. Feasible or not, no such expedition has set out on their trail to date, so that their identity remains unknown. Needless to say, zoogeographically speaking it would be a great jolt to scientific conceptions if a true cat form were to be discovered there – but it would certainly not be without precedent, as the discovery of so many hitherto unknown and highly unexpected animals already within the twentieth century can verify.

I began this chapter with a quotation from Pliny the Elder. I end it now with a riddle from another philosopher (one whose words seem to have lived on long after the memory of his name ceased to exist):

> What is the world's most cunning animal?
> That which no man has ever seen.

I have a strong feeling that Africa still houses many comparably cunning animals.

Abbreviation: *PZSL* = *Proceedings of the Zoological Society of London*

1 Corbet, G.B., and Hill, J.E., *A World List of Mammalian Species*, second edition (Brit. Mus. Nat. Hist., 1986)
2 Hichens, W., *Discovery*, Vol. 18, pp. 369-71 (December 1937)
3 Cooper, A.L., *The Field*, Vol. 148, p. 690 (14 October 1926)
4 Hills, D., and Smithers, R.H.N., *Arnoldia Zimbabwe*, Vol. 9, pp. 1-23 (1980)
5 Pocock, R.I., *The Field*, Vol. 148, p. 707 (21 October 1926)
6 Pocock, R.I., *PZSL*, pp. 245-52 (1927)
7 Pocock, R.I., *The Field*, Vol. 151, p. 593 (15 April 1928)
8 Chapman, A., ibid, Vol. 151, p. 654 (19 April 1928)
9 Pocock, R.I., *The Fauna of British East India Including Ceylon and Burma. Mammalia Vol 1. Primates & Carnivora*, second edition (Taylor & Francis, 1939)
10 James, A., *The Field*, Vol. 219, pp. 1018-19 (24 May 1962)
11 Bottriell, L.G., *King Cheetah. The Story of the Quest* (E.J. Brill, Leiden, 1987)
12 Bottriell, L.G., *Excellence*, Vol. 3, pp. 52-6 (April 1987); *GEO*, No. 3, pp. 179-82 (March 1987)
13 de Graaf, G., *Custos*, Vol. 3, p. 2 (1974)
14 *Wildlife*, Vol. 24, p. 73 (February 1982)
15 Oakes, P., *The Mail on Sunday – YOU Magazine*, pp. 36-7, 10 May 1987
16 Hallet, J-P., and Pelle, A., *Animal Kitabu* (Elek Books, 1967)
17 Sayre, R., *Audubon*, Vol. 86, pp. 26-7 (1984)
18 van Aarde, R.J., and van Dyck, A., *Journal of Zoology A*, Vol. 209, pp. 573-8 (1986)
19 Bottriell, L.G., and Bottriell, P., Paper presented at the ISC Annual Members Meeting, Royal Museum of Scotland, 26 July 1987
20 Holdsworth, E.W., *PZSL*, pp. 532-4 (19 June 1877)
21 Sclater, P.L., ibid., pp. 655-6 (18 June 1878)
22 Mivart, St G., *The Cat* (John Murray, 1881)
23 Sclater, P.L. *PZSL*, p. 476 (4 November 1884)
24 Dower, K.C.G., *The Spotted Lion* (William Heinemann, 1937)
25 Goss, M., *Fate*, Vol. 39, pp. 78-91 (June 1986)
26 Guggisberg, C.A.W., *Wild Cats of the World* (David & Charles, 1975)
27 Campbell, L., *East African Natural History Society Bulletin*, pp. 34-5 (May-June 1983)
28 Pocock, R.I., *The Field*, Vol. 137, p. 352 (19 March 1921)

29 O'Brien, S.J., et al., *Science*, Vol. 221, pp. 459-62 (29 July 1983); *New Scientist*, Vol. 114, p. 27 (9 April 1987)
30 McGuinness, C.J., *Nomad* (Methuen, 1934)
31 Dower, K.C.G., *The Field*, Vol. 165, p. 388 (23 February 1935)
32 Heuvelmans, B., *On the Track of Unknown Animals* (Rupert Hart-Davis, 1958)
33 Dower, K.C.G., *The Field*, Vol. 166, p. 21 (6 July 1935)
34 Pollard, J.R.T., *African Zoo Man* (Robert Hale, 1963)
35 Pocock, R.I., in Dower, K.C.G., *The Spotted Lion*, op. cit., pp. 317-21
36 Fowle, A., *The Field*, Vol. 165, p. 1361 (1 June 1935)
37 Richardson, B.V., ibid, Vol. 170, p. 1515 (11 December 1937)
38 Hamilton-Snowball, G., ibid., Vol. 192, p. 412 (9 October 1948)
39 Pollard, J.R.T., ibid., Vol. 192, p. 553 (13 November 1948)
40 Flett, G., ibid., Vol. 193, p. 76 (15 January 1949)
41 Foran, W.R., ibid., Vol. 196, p. 535 (30 September 1950)
42 Simon, N., *Between the Sunlight and the Thunder* (Collins, 1962)
43 *Daily Mirror*, 28 January 1970
44 Florio, P.L., *International Zoo News*, Vol. 30, pp. 4-6 (1983)
45 Turnbull-Kemp, P., *The Leopard* (Bailey Bros & Swinfen, 1967)
46 Scherren, H., *The Field*, Vol. 111, p. 711 (25 April 1908)
47 Ibid., Vol. 111, p. 711 (25 April 1908); Pocock, R.I., ibid., Vol. 159, p. 149 (30 January 1932)
48 Kingdon, J., *East African Mammals. An Atlas of Evolution in Africa*, Vol. IIIA (Academic Press, New York, 1977)
49 Haltenorth, T., and Diller, H., *A Field Guide to the Mammals of Africa Including Madagascar* (Collins, 1980)
50 Heuvelmans, B., *Cryptozoology*, Vol. 5, pp. 1-26 (1986)
51 Prince William of Sweden, *Among Pygmies and Gorillas* (Gyldendal, 1923)
52 Lindblom, G., *The Akamba in British East Africa*, second edition (Appelbergs Botryckeri Aktiebolag, Uppsala, 1920)
53 Guggisberg, C.A.W., *Simba. The Life of the Lion* (Bailey Bros & Swinfen, 1962)
54 Pitman, C.R.S., *A Game Warden Among His Charges* (Nisbet, 1931)
55 Temple-Perkins, E.A., *Kingdom of the Elephant* (Andrew Melrose, 1955)
56 Heuvelmans, B., *Sur la Piste des Bêtes Ignorées*, Vol. 2 (Plon, Paris, 1955)
57 McBride, C., *The White Lions of Timbavati* (Paddington Press, 1977); McBrie, C., *Operation White Lion* (Collins & Harvill Press, 1981)
58 Smuts, G.L., *Lion* (Macmillan, 1982); Smuts, G.L., *Custos*, Vol. 8, pp. 6-7 (March 1979); Stevenson-Hamilton, J., *The Field*, Vol. 197, p. 358 (1951)
59 *Daily Mail*, 31 March 1982; Myer, L., *Zoon*, No. 16, pp. 4-5 (1983)
60 Robinson, R., and de Vos, V., *Genetica*, Vol. 60, pp. 61-3 (1982)
61 Robinson, R., *Carnivore Genetics Newsletter*, Vol. 2, p. 236 (1974)
62 Speight, W.L., *Empire Review*, Vol. 71, pp. 223-8 (1940)
63 Layard, H., *Early Adventures in Persia, Susiana and Babylon* (John Murray, 1887)
64 Kay, J., *Okavango* (Hutchinson, 1962)
65 *The Sun*, 3 November 1975
66 Heran, I., *Animal Coloration: The Nature and Purpose of Colours in Vertebrates* (Hamlyn, 1976)
67 Pocock, R.I., *PZSL*, pp. 543-91 (1932)
68 Robinson, R., *Genetica*, Vol. 46, pp. 1-31 (1976)
69 *Illustrated London News*, Vol. 188, p. 1,012 (6 June 1936); Ansell, W.F.H., *Arnoldia Rhodesia*, Vol. 3, pp. 1-6 (1967)
70 Burton, W., *PZSL*, p. 346 (28 April 1908); M.A.B., *Journal of the East African Natural History Society*, Vol. 16, pp. 223-4 (1942)
71 Günther, A., *PZSL*, pp. 243-5 (3 March 1885)

72 Günther, A., ibid., pp. 203-5 (6 April 1886)
73 Pocock, R.I., *Natural History*, Vol. 2, pp. 162-9 (1930)
74 Lane, F.W., *Nature Parade*, fourth edition (Jarrolds, 1955)
75 Steere, E., *Swahili Tales. As Told by Natives of Zanzibar* (1870; reprinted by Kraus-Thomson Organization Ltd, Nendeln/Liechtenstein, 1970)
76 'Fulahn' (Hichens, W.), *Chambers's Journal*, Ser. 7, Vol. 17, pp. 692-5 (1927)
77 Hardy, I.W., *East African Natural History Society Bulletin*, pp. 111-12 (September-October 1979)
78 Pitman, C.R.S., *Annual Report of the Game Department for the Year Ended 31st Dec, 1950* (Entebbe, 1951)
79 Durrell, G., *The Bafut Beagles* (Rupert Hart-Davis, 1954)
80 Johnston, H., *Liberia* (Hutchinson, 1906)
81 Hichens, W., *Wide World*, Vol. 62, pp. 171-6 (December 1928)
82 von Heuglin, T., *Reise noch Abessinien, den Gala-Ländern, Ost-Sudan, und Chartum in den Jahren 1861 u. 1862* (H. Costenoble, Jena, 1868)
83 von Heuglin, T., *Reise in Nordostafrika*, Vol. 2 (G. Westermann, Braunschweig, 1877)
84 Ryan, J., *San Francisco Examiner & Chronicle*, 17 February 1974
85 *Daily Mirror*, 24 April 1974
86 Raynal, M., Personal communications (1987)
87 von Nolde, I., *Deutsche Kolonialzeitung*, Vol. 51, pp. 123-4 (1939)
88 Krumbiegel, I., *Kosmos*, Vols. 42 and 43, pp. 143-6 (1947)
89 Heuvelmans, B., *Les Derniers Dragons d'Afrique* (Plon, Paris, 1978)
90 Whitfield, P., *The Hunters* (Hamlyn, 1978)
91 Stow, G.W., and Bleek, D., *Rock Paintings in South Africa* (Methuen, 1930)
92 Hunter, J.A., *Hunter* (Hamish Hamilton, 1952)
93 Frobenius, L., and Fox, D.C., *African Genesis* (Turtle Island Foundation, Berkeley, 1983)
94 Bronson, E.B., *In Closed Territory* (A.C. McClurg, Chicago, 1910); Jordan, J.A., *The Elephant Stone* (Nicholas Kaye, 1959)
95 Hagenbeck, C., *Beasts and Men* (Longmans, Green & Co, 1909); Hughes, J.E., *Eighteen Years on Lake Bangweulu* (*The Field*, 1933)
96 Cazard, P., *Le Chasseur Français*, p. 664 (October 1939)

5 Panthers Aplenty and Bobcats of Blue

North America

Velveteen silhouette, silent and sinister;
Satin-furred midnight on ebony paws.
Eyes hewn from emeralds, seeking a sacrifice;
Death to deliver with ivory claws.

Patrick Krushenk, *The Panther*

Although North America also houses the Canadian lynx, the bobcat and a few rarer and more exotic species too,[1] the feline personification of this continent must surely be the puma *Felis concolor*. Not only is it undoubtedly the most familiar of America's cat species, demonstrated by its long list of common names (including cougar, mountain lion, catamount, painter and panther) but it is also its most widely distributed. Until the twentieth century, the puma's range extended from British Columbia to Patagonia – over 8,700 miles/14,000 km. Nowadays, however, it has been exterminated from much of South America's more densely settled areas as well as from many of its former North American haunts.

The Eastern Cougar

Two US puma subspecies in particular have suffered greatly in modern times. The Florida cougar *F. c. coryi* is now represented by fewer than twenty specimens lingering in the Everglades (the shooting of one of these recently rightly caused great consternation amongst American conservationists[2,3]), but the plight of the Eastern cougar *F. c. couguar* (sometimes called the Eastern panther too) has been even more severe. It once ranged from the eastern US to provincial Canada west to the edge of Alberta and the Plains, but by the early part of this century most zoologists believed that it had been hunted into extinction in the

USA and virtually eliminated in Canada too.[4] Yet sightings and occasional killings of pumas in eastern North America continued to be reported, attracting in particular the attention of Robert Downing[5] and Bruce Wright.[6] Their writings are essential reading on the Eastern cougar and proved invaluable during my preparation of this section.

Comparable reports are still being made, and due to the Eastern cougar's perpetuating suspension between existence and extinction within the USA, it has ultimately gained the status of a cryptozoological cat – hence its inclusion here.

Of the various accounts on record for the first two decades of this century, the following couple are particularly important, as they are supported by preserved specimens. In 1903 a mounted puma from Georgia's Bulloch County was displayed (a photo taken of it is still held at the University of Georgia),[5,7] and two years later a puma was collected near Vidalia, Louisiana, and housed in the US National Museum.[5] Other notable reports of eastern specimens killed during this period (but not preserved afterwards) were documented from Maryland, Maine, Pennsylvania and Wisconsin.[5]

During the 1920s, a puma cub was killed in Maryland's Garrett County, and it is now ensconced at the US National Museum,[5] while in 1927 an adult was dispatched at Shutesbury, Massachusetts.[5] Reputable reports of killed pumas in the east during the 1920s and 1930s also emerged from Georgia, Louisiana, North Carolina, Tennessee and Maine.[5]

The last official killing of a puma in Missouri took place during 1927, but in January 1938 a puma scare occurred near Lamar, when strange sounds believed to be those of a 'painter' (to use the Ozark vernacular) were reported by several local farmers. Nevertheless, despite many searches and forays, the creature responsible remained aloof and unidentified. A few coyotes were flushed from cover, but no sign of a puma (or even of a bobcat) was discovered.[8]

Moving momentarily to Canada, in 1931 a puma was shot at Mundleville in New Brunswick – the last specimen shot in this area and actually preserved dated back to 1881.[9] Later in the 1930s New Brunswick was involved in another Eastern cougar incident, though on this occasion the site of procurement was in the USA. In January 1938 (perhaps a couple of years earlier, according to one opinion[9]), a puma was trapped east of Little St John Lake, Maine, by Rosarie Morin. Preserved as a mounted exhibit, it was ultimately sold in 1960 to New Brunswick's Northeastern Wildlife Station, whose director was Bruce Wright.[6,9]

One of the most compelling of eastern US accounts from the

1940s is the report by Fred Barkalow that a 109 lb/49.5 kg specimen was killed in northern Alabama's TVA lakes region in 1942, and that during this same year several other pumas were flushed from cover while the lake bed was being cleared for the construction of Fontana Dam.[5,10] Also worthy of note is an account documented by Herbert Sass of a puma hit and killed by a truck driven by Alan Broun Jnr in South Carolina's Georgetown County sometime during 1942-3.[11]

As far as pumas in Arkansas were concerned during this period, the official Arkansas Guide Book published in 1941 stated that, 'Only a few remain, and these in the most remote sections',[8] but Ronald Nowak notes the killing of one specimen near Mena, Poke County, in 1948.[12]

On 29 March 1947, in the company of two colleagues and travelling on skis and snowshoes on the border between Albert and St John counties in New Brunswick, Bruce Wright discovered a set of unmistakable puma tracks, clearly belonging to a large male. Investigating these, Wright observed that they were joined just 200 yards/182 m further along by two more sets of tracks – belonging to a female with a one-third-grown cub. In short, the spoor of an entire puma family! Wright took several photos of these tracks. On 29 July Dr Paul F. Elson discovered large cat tracks in this same area. On this occasion, casts as well as photographs were taken, and all were sent by Wright to the US National Museum, where they were confirmed to be puma. Wright was most excited by these finds – and with every reason, for they comprised the first puma tracks unequivocally recorded in eastern Canada for more than a century.[13]

Back in the USA, in 1949, just over a decade after the trapping of the Little St John Lake individual, Maine produced a further specimen in the shape of a skull submitted to Safari Club International.[5]

The 1940s also saw the publication of Young and Goldman's definitive book *The Puma: Mysterious American Cat*.[14] Judging from its hide-and-seek tactics in the eastern US, their book had been very adroitly titled.

By the 1950s, scores of alleged puma sightings were emerging each year from many of these states. Indeed, in Vermont an entire association was founded by people willing to testify that they had observed pumas there, whilst puma pandemonium in Minnesota (where officially the puma has been extinct since 1875) reached such proportions in one county that a sheriff's posse and a National Guard Unit were called out to investigate reports.[11]

Several killings of pumas were also reported during this decade, including at least three in North Carolina (1950, 1952 and 1959),[5] a roadside victim at Charleston, South Carolina, in 1952,[11] and a specimen from Alabama's Tuscaloosa in 1953.[5]

Moving into the 1960s, at least four specimens in the eastern US (in Louisiana, Arkansas, Oklahoma and Pennsylvania) were killed and preserved.[5,15] However, Robert Downing notes that one of these – now housed at the Carnegie Museum – possessed deformities suggestive of a former existence in captivity,[5] and it was allegedly traced back to an Ohio zoo.[16]

1971 saw the publication of Bruce Wright's major work *The Eastern Panther*.[6] Also in that year, whilst deer-hunting north of Crossville, eastern Tennessee, a Mr Buckner shot a puma and arranged for its body (including the skull) to be preserved as a permanent exhibit.[17] It was partly as a result of this latest specimen to be obtained that in 1973 the US Department of the Interior changed its official classification of the Eastern cougar from 'extinct' to 'endangered'.[17]

In April 1974 a puma was photographed in the Adirondacks by New York teacher Alex McKay,[18] and a year later the Arkansas Game and Fish Commission offices gained a mounted puma – a 118 lb/53.5 kg male that had been killed in Logan County during 1975.[5] Additionally, reports of killings unsubstantiated by physical evidence emanated from several other states.[5]

In Canada, a puma sighting on the Bruce Peninsula in Ontario was recorded by Provincial Police Constable Art King in 1978, followed a month later by a similar sighting made by writer John Kerr on the banks of the Saugeen River – casts taken of spoor left behind were confirmed to be those of a puma by Ontario's Ministry of Natural Resources.[19,20]

On 10 June 1979 Charles and Helen Marks, co-managers of the Lake Estates trailer court in Michigan's Westerville, paid close attention to more than 200 large pawprints which had been discovered in a grassy muddy field and alongside a small lake nearby. Some of the prints showed claws, others did not. The Marks took casts of the most dramatic ones – those with claws – and showed them to the police. They were identified as dog spoor, but the Marks were sure that they were puma prints. And within hours, three boys who knew nothing about these spoor reported seeing a very large tan-coloured felid in a tree behind the trailer court. It jumped down from the tree and fled but was later seen again by the boys on a roadway close by. Only after this second appearance of the mystery cat did the boys learn of the prints.[21]

The early 1980s were memorable on the Massachusetts mystery carnivore front for 'the beast of Truro', believed by many locals to have been either a wild or escaped pet puma. In September 1981 several mutilated domestic cat carcases were found in the vicinity of Truro, a town amid scrub pine forests and sand dunes, ensconced within the National Seashore Park at the tip of Cape Cod. During the next few months, further livestock killings were reported, and two hogs belonging to police officer David Costa were severely clawed. At first these attacks were attributed to feral dogs, but this theory was abandoned when piercing screams began to ring out at night, and sightings of puma-like beasts were reported. Also worth noting is that Costa's hogs had been clawed horizontally, implying that their attacker had jumped onto their backs.[22,23] Moreover, whilst walking along a path near the parking-lot in the Cape Cod National Seashore Park one day in late September/early October 1981, William and Marsha Medeiros were convinced that they saw a puma about 50 ft/15 m further along the path. It weighed 60-80 lb/27-36 kg and had short ears and a long, slender tail held low but curling upwards at its tip (a puma characteristic). Surprisingly, when the animal saw its human observers, it showed no alarm, simply sauntering unconcerned into the nearby woods, within which it soon disappeared from view. Similarly, on 7 February 1982, Truro police officer Rodney Allen claimed that a cougar crossed in front of his cruiser.[22,23]

Certainly there is more than enough undeveloped woodland around Truro to conceal such a cat, while a pet puma identity could explain the unfrightened attitude of the animal sighted by William and Marsha Medeiros (wild pumas are notoriously shy of humans). However, extensive searches of the entire area by Park Rangers failed to uncover any positive signs to verify the presence there of a large felid. No more reports emerged from Truro either. Another mystery animal had made its escape.[22,23]

The Pennsylvania Association for the Study of the Unexplained (PASU) has been investigating suspected puma sightings in this state for a number of years, and in February 1987 a selection of some of the more recent of these were published by *PA Woods & Waters* in the form of a report written by PASU director Stan Gordon.[24] Of particular interest was the discovery made by a PASU team on 25 July 1984 of a short trail of pawprints near South Buffalo township in Armstrong County. A cast was made of the best spoor, which bore three lobes on the plantar pad's posterior edge (a felid characteristic). No dimension for the spoor was given, but according to Gordon, several wildlife experts (unnamed) have identified it as a puma print.[24]

More recently, the dog of John Galinat, from Chaplin, Connecticut, treed a small-headed, large-bodied felid roughly 40 lb/18 kg in weight with spots on its body and a lengthy ringed tail. As luck would have it, Galinat had a film-loaded camera with him and took some photos of this unexpected cat, which depict an animal resembling a young puma (immature pumas do have spotted pelages and rings round their tails).[25]

By autumn 1987, John Lutz's Eastern Puma Research Network based in Maryland had recorded seventy puma sightings so far that year, plus ninety-seven in 1986,[26] with West Virginia supplying the largest number, together with further reports stretching into 1988.[26,27] And at the 1988 ISC Annual Members Meeting, held at Maryland University, Robert Downing presented an Eastern cougar update.[28]

From the accounts recorded above, there can be no doubt that pumas do still occur not just in eastern Canada but also in several regions of the eastern USA. Less evident, however, is whether these constitute remnant breeding populations of the genuine Eastern cougar or whether they are isolated stragglers, perhaps even wanderers from more westerly locations or escapees from captivity. In addition to the Carnegie Museum specimen already noted, other escapee examples may include an individual apparently killed and photographed near Kentucky's Central City in 1960 and rumoured to have escaped from a roadside zoo,[5] and the killing of one puma and capture of another in West Virginia during 1976 – Robert Downing notes that these were shown to possess behaviour and parasite loads indicative of recent captivity.[5]

Misidentification of other species is another important consideration. Downing, for example, records that certain 'puma' carcases and skeletons have proved to be those of dogs or bobcats.[5] And there is always the possibility of deliberate hoax being responsible for some reports – as exemplified by three episodes from the 1950s in West Virginia which proved to be hoaxes perpetrated with Western and Mexican pumas, plus a newspaper April's Fool hoax in Tennessee.[5]

Nonetheless, it still seems very unlikely that *all* Eastern cougar reports are due to Western invaders, escapees, misidentifications and hoaxes. When dealing with a species as elusive as the puma, one should never be too hasty in declaring it extinct.

American Mystery Panthers

Creatures closely resembling black panthers but appearing in totally unexpected locations are not restricted to Britain and mainland Europe. A vast dossier could be compiled from all the reports of such creatures which have been filed in North America too. Moreover, regardless of the States in which they have been recorded, the eyewitness descriptions of these felids' morphology is always the same – namely, a powerful jet-black creature of pantheresque outline and build, with a head and body of

4-5 ft/120-150 cm and height of 2-3 ft/60-90 cm. The head is relatively small, with short, pricked ears and bright greenish-yellow or orange (occasionally even red) eyes; the limbs are fairly (though not markedly) long, and the tail is lengthy and slender. Spoor left behind is generally cat-like in outline, but sometimes claw impressions are present. Many eyewitnesses have stated categorically that the beast which they have seen was not a dog but a large, unmistakably feline animal. As a result of such marked morphological uniformity, in the following necessarily brief selection of reports (an entire book could be devoted to reports of American black panthers and still not do the subject justice) to avoid tedious repetition it should be understood that, unless stated otherwise, the creatures seen fitted the above description. Also, as it has not been demonstrated conclusively so far that these mystery cats are bona fide black panthers (i.e. melanistic leopards), inverted commas around the term 'black panther' should be understood throughout the following reports.

The leading investigator of these unidentified American felids is research consultant Loren Coleman, whose writings (especially *Mysterious America*[29]) comprise the most detailed documents available on this subject and contain full coverage of certain accounts mentioned here.

Local inhabitants in several US regions claim to have seen black panthers in their vicinity for decades, but it was not until the end of World War II that these animals gained widespread attention from the general public and the media – thereby making this period a convenient point at which to begin our coverage.

On 4 September 1946 Harry McClain of Lebanon, Indiana, claimed that a black panther which had been terrorizing the area for some time had been shot by his assistant, Roy Graham, but that its body had fallen into a creek and could not be recovered. Just a fortnight later, two black panthers made an appearance near Oquawka, Illinois, but a 150-man search three days later (assisted by an aerial reconnaissance of the region via three aeroplanes) found nothing.[30]

As reported by Coleman in a *Fate* article published during 1971, the state of Illinois is a rich source of black panther incidents, of which one in particular could have provided an answer to the panther phenomenon. On 25 October 1955 a black panther was unexpectedly encountered near Decatur by game warden Paul G. Myers, who promptly shot it – but not fatally, for the panther escaped; its body was never found.[31] A large cat, described as very dark brown, possibly black, was the subject of many reports from at least three different localities in Illinois's Champaign County during 1963, and eluded even a 300-man search posse. Its tracks, however, *were* discovered and were described as being between a dog's and a puma's in size.[29,31] In 1965 panther accounts re-emerged from Decatur's environs.[29]

Two adult panthers were observed in 1964 near Ventura, in California's Conejo Valley,[32] while on 12 December 1967 a specimen was sighted there by Henry Madrid and three companions – but due to the investigating sheriff deputies' car becoming bogged down in a marshy field, the panther was readily able to avoid further enquiries.[32]

1970 saw further panther sightings near Decatur,[29] including a bizarre incident that occurred on the evening of 10 April. Whilst investigating the reason for his car's sudden engine trouble a mile south of Olive Branch, Alexander County, Mike Busby was attacked by a macabre beast resembling a black panther but walking *on its hind legs!* It was frightened off by an approaching truck, and Busby later received medical attention for his wounds.[29,31] This is not the only record of a bipedal panther-like beast: a comparable individual was recorded from South Carolina's White Oak Swamp in autumn 1948,[33] and another from Queens County in Canada's New Brunswick on 22 November 1951.[34]

Also noteworthy: in December 1970 a large black panther and cub were sighted twice in a field near Decatur by Clarence Runyon and family.[29]

Three years on and over 1,850 miles/2,900 km further west, a large cat described as a 5 ft/150 cm-long black panther or very dark puma was the quarry of a posse of police and County Animal Control officers in the eastern foothills of California's San Jose Hills, south of San Francisco. Local ranchers believed that it had been roaming the area for two or three months and allegedly had even been treed on one occasion by a collie belonging to Navy Lieutenant Commander Thomas Mantei.[35]

On to the spring of 1977 and to Ohio's Allen County, the scene of many panther sightings and ferocious sheep-killings. Spoor discovered in the vicinity of these latter were found to be cat-like in general shape but possessing the clear impression of claws.[36]

Summer 1977 saw the début of New York State's Van Etten swamp monster, apparently inhabiting the 2 mile/3.2 km-long swamp lying between Van Etten and Spencer, and held responsible for the death of several domestic animals. During July and August, many sightings of a black panther in the area were reported by local inhabitants, and State Conservation Officer Charles Winant recalled rumours that such an animal had been there since 1971.[37] On 25 July news emerged of the discovery of strange, claw-lacking spoor by Van Etten gardener John Palomaki, and Cornell

University mammalogist Professor Milo Richmond commented that the absence of claw marks was indicative of a felid identity, though further evidence would be needed for confirmation of this.[37] In the next weeks, however, various scientists questioned the prints' authenticity, arguing that they did not match those of any North American mammal but could have been made by a human.[37] Yet the argument proved ultimately to be academic, for, excluding a brief reappearance in October and December 1977,[38] the Van Etten swamp monster was seen no more.[39]

The 1980s have seen mystery panthers come and go too. Summer 1984, for example, marked the descent of panther pandemonium upon several lower Michigan localities, beginning in the village of Manchester with a good black panther sighting by patrolman Kevin Deacons,[40] though by the end of the year attention had moved on to Cincinnati in Ohio.[41] The usual pattern was prevalent – many sightings, many searches, nothing caught. The closest came during the Michigan outbreak, when paw prints discovered were examined by Dr Stephen P. Schiffer of Michigan University, who confirmed the presence of a black leopard;[40] others went even further by speculating that more than one cat could be involved.[41]

In May 1987 a mysterious cat described as a 'black cougar' and displaying a predilection for posing on peoples' porches in Nauvoo hit the headlines briefly before departing for pastures new[42] and was rapidly replaced by the equally elusive black panther of New Jersey's southern regions. For the past few months livestock killings and eerie screams piercing the night had been reported by the inhabitants of Salem County's rurally sited Pittsgrove township and Cumberland County's Vineland. In June a Pittsgrove township resident informed police that he had seen a large, long-tailed cat resembling a black panther, and a few days later a paw print exceeding 4 in/10 cm in length was discovered near a trap set in Vineland woods by officials of the State Division of Fish, Game and Wildlife. An unnamed wildlife authority identified it as that of a bear, but Vineland Police Captain James Forcinito stated that he would not be surprised to find that the animal concerned turned out to be a black cougar, remarking that reports had been received for years by police regarding such animals in the nearby woods. Yet fur samples ultimately obtained were identified by scientists as canine, and by then some authorities were suggesting that many (if not all) of the slaughtered livestock had died from natural causes.[43,44]

So, in best official traditions, a black panther/puma identity was discounted, in favour of a feral domestic cat. Undoubtedly it is true that an element of panther paranoia had entered into the proceedings, with such felids being seen everywhere – one lady reported a panther prowling behind her home, only to discover that it was her own pet cat.[43] Yet what of the 4 in/10 cm spoor? No domestic cat could have made that. Once again, a cryptozoological case has been concluded with a convenient but clearly incorrect solution having been put forward.

Most recently, Gerald Cameron Jnr of Savannah, Georgia, informed biologist and cryptozoologist Victor Albert (see also Chapter 7) that he had seen a black panther on three separate occasions locally (twice in the Dean Forest Road area, and once near Arnesville). He described them as being 4-4½ ft/120-135 cm in head-and-body length (plus a long, smooth tail), 2½-3 ft/75-90 cm in shoulder height, and weighing about 100-140 lb/45.5-63.5 kg, with feline outline and pure black pelage. Apparently they inhabit the wilder, more remote high woodlands, and according to various of his friends they range down from South Carolina's Charleston to Florida's Tampa region, and come to the edges of Okefenokee Swamp to hunt. They are extremely shy of humans, keeping well away from them, but as a result of their noticeable colouration are frequently seen. Indeed, though happy to answer all Victor Albert's questions concerning these animals, Gerald Cameron remained perplexed as to why he should be so interested in such common animals which everyone knew about (Albert, pers. comm.).

Indisputably, creatures closely resembling black panthers *are* being seen in North America, but what can they be?

Too many eyewitnesses have been adamant that the beasts they sighted were cat-like and not dog-like for a canine identity to be generally tenable in any but the most fleeting of sightings or those made in poor viewing-conditions. Also, it must be remembered that clawed spoor cannot be used to distinguish immediately between felids and canids. Thus, with one notable exception, we should look to the cat family for these animals' identity – or identities, for it is conceivable that more than one is involved here.

1) Fisher?

This is the notable above-cited exception to the 'felids only' list of possible panther identities. Inhabiting Canada and the north-eastern USA the fisher *Martes pennanti* is a mustelid, related to weasels and especially the martens. It attains a total length of up to 3½ ft/105 cm, of which 16 in/40 cm comprises its fairly bushy but tapering tail, and it appears even larger because of its dense pelage. Indeed, as will now be seen, the fisher has great potential for being confused with a modest-sized panther-like cat. Its body is long and slim, its head is rather cat-like in shape, and its ears are small and pricked. In colour it varies from black to dark brown.[45,46] Of particular pertinence to the panther question is the fisher's overall mien, for this is strikingly cat-like – apparent in its fluid movements, in its precise manner of stalking its prey and also in its attitude of intense concentration. Indeed, the above correspondences between fisher and felid are so marked that Indian tribes living within its range of distribution refer to it in their native tongues as 'black cat'.[46,48] Similarly, a friend of Professor Charles Thomas obtained a clear sighting of a fisher whilst in Maine during the early 1980s, and noted in particular its 'general cat-like appearance' and 'sinuous' mode of movement.[49]

Consequently it is by no means unlikely that some panther reports may actually be based upon fisher sightings. Indeed, from the description given by K.E. Ives,[50] *Info Journal* editor Paul Kelsey suggested this identity for the black pantheresque beast spied by Ives on the shore of Oneida Lake sometime prior to 1982;[48] the fisher's distribution does extend as far south as that area.

2) Feral Domestic Cat?

This potential identity has already been covered in Chapter 1 relative to British mystery panthers but is equally applicable to the North American situation. Moreover, although it may seem implausible that domestic cats could be mistaken in the field for much larger, panther-like felids, such misidentifications have indeed occurred. For example, during the 1970s a 'black panther' was sighted and shot near Cosby, Tennessee, and a photograph of the dead animal was later published in a Newport newspaper. However, while still fresh, its carcase had been examined by Park Ranger J.R. Buchanan and Michael Pelton, and it was identified as nothing more than a large domestic cat.[5] Similarly, a 'black panther' killed near Central, South Carolina, in 1979, also turned out to be a domestic cat[5] (an identity rumoured in relation to the San Jose panther of 1973 too). Nonetheless, it is clearly ludicrous to suggest that all panther sightings can be explained in this way.

3) Jaguarundi?

The jaguarundi *F. yagouaroundi* is a slender felid slightly larger than a domestic cat, with a small head, short legs and very long tail. Predominantly thought of as an exclusively Central and South American species, during the early part of this century it was still common in southern Texas too,[46] although an individual killed by a car in Cameron County during 1986 was the first confirmed record of the jaguarundi in that state since 1952.[51] It exists in two colour forms – a red morph, referred to as the eyra, and a grey-black morph, which is the jaguarundi proper. Assuming that it still survives there, this species may be responsible for certain briefly spied 'panthers' recorded from Texas, and also from Florida – the jaguarundi was introduced there during the 1940s and is now present in large numbers.[52]

4) Bobcat?
Also worth consideration relative to reports of black panthers in Florida is whether at least some of these could have been melanistic bobcats, for, in stark contrast to the typical reddish-brown, spotted pelage of this species, some near-black individuals have been recorded from Florida.[53,54] Moreover, the tails of various of these have been extremely long in comparison with those of normal specimens, thereby enhancing a pantheresque appearance.

5) Pumas?
The puma is panther-sized and is superficially similar to this felid in general outline too. Also, it exhibits a wide variety of coat colourations. So could North America's black panthers actually be black pumas? In fact, although melanism has been recorded frequently from a number of different cat species,[55] the puma is not one of these; for, although unconfirmed reports of black pumas in Florida have surfaced from time to time,[56] only one officially confirmed case is on record – an individual shot in the Carandahy River section of Brazil during 1843;[14] sadly its skin was not preserved. Melanism in wild felids is usually associated with tropical climate and dense forests (cf black panthers in south-east Asia, black jaguars in Amazonia), where a black pelage serves as effective camouflage and as an efficient radiator of body heat. Hence there would seem little advantage in (and thus one would not expect) the evolution of a black puma morph within most of the puma's North American range.

However, Florida contains sub-tropical forest and is therefore more likely than anywhere else in North America to give rise to black felids – demonstrated by its black bobcats. Although it is extremely unlikely that a melanistic puma morph could arise from a few escapee pumas (as would be needed, for example, to reconcile Britain's pantheresque mystery cats with pumas), it is far less implausible that such a morph could arise in its native land and in an environment such as Florida's sub-tropical zone, which would seem well suited for such felids. So perhaps black pumas may indeed be responsible for panther reports in Florida.

But what of other North American regions? Very dark brown pumas could explain some black panthers reported from those areas, especially any which were associated with eerie screams, for, although leopards and panthers can indeed give voice to screeching caterwaulings,[57] the puma is indisputably the felid *par excellence* for producing blood-curdling screams and shrieks. At one time, scientists considered that its renowned scream might be nothing more than a myth. However, a director of Cincinnati Zoo saw and heard one of the zoo's captive pumas give vent to a fine example of this vocal variation, and Robert Beam of the Chicago Zoological Park announced that the park had never owned a female puma which had *not* screamed.[57] Since then, the puma's scream has been classed as fact rather than fable – in some instances it has even been described as a roar,[58] but in truth the puma's Small Cat throat structure prevents it from producing a true roar.

An intriguing panther theory which involved pumas but not genuinely black pumas was contemplated by Bruce Wright: could normal-coloured pumas appear black when wet? To investigate this, Wright took the fresh hide of a newly killed puma from Vancouver Island, suspended it by its edges, filled it with water and left it overnight. When he examined it the following morning, however, despite viewing and photographing it from every conceivable angle, he was unable to make it appear black in colour.[59] He also considered the possibility that backlighting of normal pumas could create the illusion of black fur, but this, when checked, proved untenable too.[59]

Thus it would seem that, if pumas *are* involved in the American black panther phenomenon, they are bona fide black pumas (or at least very dark brown ones). Such cats can even explain those bizarre bipedal panthers – a little-known facet of puma behaviour is that it occasionally stands erect.[11,14]

6) Melanistic Leopards or Jaguars?

In *Mysterious America* and other writings, Loren Coleman has noted that America's mystery panthers often appear more aggressive than the extremely shy puma. With respect to morphology, there is no doubt that a bona fide black panther (i.e. a melanistic leopard) provides the closest correspondence between America's panthers and a known modern felid species (see p.170 for my reasons for dismissing as a contender any unknown or extinct felid form). And as leopards are indeed more belligerent and less afraid than pumas when confronted by man, this identity is supported on behavioural grounds too. Consequently the exotic escapee theory comes into force once more. This subject has already been discussed in detail relative to black panthers in Chapter 1, and the points raised there are equally valid in an American context.

A second possibility involving a melanistic Big Cat is that America's panthers could, in fact, be black jaguars. From an escapee point of view, this is less likely, if only because there are far fewer black jaguars than black leopards in captivity to begin with. Counterbalancing this, however, is the fact that, at least until fairly recently, the jaguar was actually native to certain regions of the USA, comprising a distinct subspecies known as the Arizona jaguar, *Panthera onca arizonensis*.[60]

In the mid 1800s, this felid was known from southern Texas, most of Arizona, parts of New Mexico and California (where it was known as *Hut'-tē-kul* – 'big spotted lion'[61]) and possibly North Carolina, Florida and Louisiana too.[62,63] It was never a common felid, and excessive hunting resulted in this subspecies' apparent extinction by 1905.[62] Yet many reports of jaguars, sometimes supported by actual specimens, have continued to emerge from certain of its former US haunts since that date.[63,64]

If jaguars do still exist in the USA it is possible that some black specimens could be amongst their number. Of great relevance to this is the fact that melanism in the jaguar is controlled by a dominant mutant allele (rather than the recessive non-agouti mutant allele responsible for melanistic individuals in other felids).[65] In short, one might expect black jaguars to be relatively common.

In Chapter 1 it was noted that some cryptozoologists have little faith in the escapee theory as a solution to any mystery animal reports, in which case the idea of at least some of America's mystery panthers being black panther escapees would find little favour with these. Similarly, on account of the jaguar's extreme rarity in the USA (assuming that it exists there at all nowadays), the possibility that black jaguars are present in numbers sufficiently large to explain panther sightings would seem on the face of things rather remote. In any event, to my knowledge, no panther sighting currently documented contains any mention of the eyewitness's having observed spots or rosettes on the creature itself (melanistic leopards and jaguars possess cryptic markings often visible at close range against their dark pelage). One conceivable reason for this is that observers have chosen not to get near enough to the felids themselves to be able to see such markings! Be that as it may, without such information, the escapee black panther and the escapee/native jaguar identities for America's mystery panthers are somewhat intangible.

The second American mystery panther report very kindly brought to my attention by Victor Albert (pers. comm.) is thus of particular interest and importance; it has not previously been published.

As in the first account, the location is Savannah, Georgia, and one of the principal witnesses was Karen Lingle Purser, one of Victor Albert's cousins, who lives in the area on a 500-acre/200 ha farm consisting of about 200 acres/80 ha of pasture and 300 acres/120 ha of woodlands (some dry, some swampy). During the 1960s she was aware that the woods contained a very large cat, which she often heard at night giving voice to loud, fairly harsh cries. Intriguingly, by imitating these sounds, she was sometimes able to lure it out of the woods and into the pasture close to the farm, from where she could view it (she saw it six or seven times via this method). Apparently it had been killing some of the farm goats, however, so eventually it was decided that it must be disposed of.

Whilst her father and others (including Gerald Cameron's father) hid in the pasture one night in/around 1968, Karen imitated the beast's cries in the hope of enticing it out of the woods. This she did, and when the animal had approached to within 10 ft/3 m or so of her lookout point at a window of the farmhouse, she shone a spotlight directly onto it. She described the animal as being big and black but stated that medium-sized spots could also be seen upon it. She compared its size with that of an alsatian and commented that it looked just like one of the black panthers which she'd seen at the National Zoo in Washington DC. She was adamant that it was a large cat, that it definitely did not resemble a dog. On this particular occasion, the coat appeared bluish-black; on some of the previous sightings it had seemed brownish-black (different animals?). Her father and Cameron Snr shot a raccoon and hung it on a tree in the pasture, and when the pantheresque mystery cat drew near to the bait, it was shot dead. Very regrettably, the current whereabouts of this potentially important cat's remains are not known. The cat may have been taken to a nearby patch of ground where dead livestock were left; alternatively it may have been transported away by some unnamed wildlife investigators who subsequently showed an interest in it.

We must hope that Victor Albert may be able to pursue further this most compelling episode – the identity of this large black cat with spots would be of immense interest.

It is clear from the above assessment that America's panthers may actually comprise several different mammalian forms, but there is little doubt that a hard core of sightings genuinely involves very large felids belonging to one or more of the species covered here, but of melanistic rather than of normal colouration.

One further identity has been suggested – again involving a large felid, but one very different indeed from those discussed above, and one which may also be responsible for sightings of the next type of crypto-felid to be examined here: America's maned mystery cats.

Maned Mystery Cats

Black panthers are not the only out-of-place cats being sighted across North America. According to many documented eyewitness accounts from the eastern USA (plus an occasional report from the western states and from Canada too), a number of fully maned lions, not to mention lionesses and lion cubs, are also on the loose there. As with the panthers, the principal sources of information concerning these felids are the writings and researches of Loren Coleman, who has been instrumental in bringing these intriguing mystery cats to the general attention of cryptozoologists.

Possibly the most famous of the earlier US lion episodes concerns a lioness-like creature nicknamed 'Nellie', making headlines in central Illinois during the early summer of 1917 by attacking a butler picking flowers. Despite huge searches being instigated straight away in the Sangamon River region's woodlands nearby, Nellie was never captured, but an interesting discovery *was* made: she appeared to have a maned mate! For a beast whose description closely matched that of a male African lion was sighted during the hunt and several times afterwards – a 'large yellow, long-haired beast', according to eyewitness James Rutherford, who spotted it near a gravel pit on 31 July 1917. Like Nellie, however, this mystery cat was never caught.[66,67]

A similarly shaggy felid pursued a party of four adults and two children at Indiana's Elkhorn Falls in the early evening of 5 August 1948 – happily they escaped unscathed. The eyewitnesses claimed that it resembled a lion, with a long tail and bushy hair around its neck. Two days later, a comparably leonine beast was spied nearby and at close range by two farm boys – and in the company of a second strange cat which apparently resembled a black panther. One of the boys fired his rifle at them, whereupon they turned away, along a lane. The very next day two creatures identical to these were sighted by some farmers north-east of Abington, and the following morning in Wayne County, after which they were heard of no more.[66] And in November 1950 an unseen creature which supposedly roared like an African lion was blamed for the killing and consumption of forty-two pigs, four calves, four lambs and twelve chickens in Peoria County – in a single night![67]

Ceresco, Nebraska, was the scene of a prolonged but unsuccessful lion-hunt just twelve months later. It had been sparked off by a number of reports of a mysterious maned cat in the area, and over the next few years further sightings were made at various locations close by – including Rising City and Surprise (the latter hosting an alleged sighting featuring a lion *and* lioness).[68]

Lions are not exclusive to the USA either, as demonstrated by the observation of a 5 ft/150 cm-long maned felid standing at least 3 ft/90 cm tall and possessing a long tail that terminated in a tufted tip, reported by Leo Dallaire. He spied it on his farm near Kapuskasing, Ontario, during June 1960.[66]

A beast sighted by an Ohio tourist in Oklahoma's Big Cabin country and described by him as being an unmistakable African lion initiated a major lion hunt in mid-March 1961. During the same period an animal identified as a lion was also spotted by two nurses amidst shrubbery in the grounds of Oklahoma State Hospital. Local inhabitants affirmed that it had been in the area for the past two months, claimed to have heard it roar and accused it of having eaten many of their chickens. Rogers County sheriff Amos Ward and Tulsa Zoo director Hugh Davis both felt the mystery beast did indeed exist, and a rumour (albeit unsubstantiated) of a circus truck's having overturned in that vicinity some time earlier was resurrected as an explanation for its origin. Like its predecessors, however, it was never caught and reports petered out.[69]

During the mid-1960s a young African lion was allegedly killed by two deer-hunters near Georgia's Blue Ridge. Its origin is unknown, but it was rumoured to have been a pet which had become unmanageable; a photo of this cat still exists.[5]

In May 1970 Illinois re-emerged as a centre of lion sightings when yet another large-scale lion-hunt was launched. Its quarry was an 8 ft/240 cm-long beast with a mane and long tail, observed at Parthenon Sod Farm near Roscoe by the farm owner, George Kapotas, together with Tom Terry and five of his fellow workers. The creature was not relocated. Nonetheless, a week later a number of livestock on Lyle Imig's farm close by hurtled through two barbed-wire fences as a result of an encounter with a mystery beast which, though remaining unseen itself, left behind some formidable tracks. These were described as being 5 in/12.5 cm long and 4¾ in/12 cm wide, with an inter-print length of 40 in/100 cm.[66]

On or around 1 March the following year, a most peculiar cat was sighted skulking near the home of Howard Baldrige, near Centralia, Illinois. Baldrige described it as resembling a sort of shrunken lion. About twice the size of a large domestic cat and yellow in colour, it had a long tail, very short legs and a face 'like something on television'![67]

In 1976, and at a distance of 50-100 ft/15-30 m, a much larger mystery cat with a mane around its neck was sighted and shot at unsuccessfully by farmer J.H. Holyoak in his pasture within Georgia's Berrien County.[66] The same year saw yet another police lion-hunt too, its quarry having a 'shaggy black mane, light brown body and a black tuft at the end of a long tail', reported by several people in Tacoma, Washington. The best which could be found, however, was a collie-alsatian mongrel called Jake at the city dump.[66]

In the late autumn of 1977, a two-month-old lion cub was discovered by Police Lieutenant Ronald King in Muscatine, Iowa, but despite his putting out a teletype report enquiring whether anyone had lost a lion, the cub's origin remained obscure.[70]

On 23 January 1978 a lady in Loxahatchee, Florida, was taken aback to see a lion just outside her window. Following the by-now-familiar pattern, a police search was duly instigated and returned home empty-handed. Moreover, the nearby Lion County Safari Park and two residents known to keep lions as pets all affirmed that none of theirs was missing.[71]

In August 1979 a lion cub appeared outside a back door in Ohio's West Chester. Though happy to be fed on catfood by the family's children, the unexpected visitor was eventually traced back to an amusement company from which it had escaped.[72]

On 10 November 1979 a growling 300-400 lb/136-182 kg lion prowling through Fremont, California, was sighted by several people and was encountered at close range in the Alameda County Flood Channel by Police Officer William Fontes, but succeeded in eluding the large-scale search-party attempting to track it down.[66]

The late 1970s also saw a 'puma' allegedly killed in the North Carolina mountains turn out to be an African lioness whose body had been rescued from a dumpster.[5] And in 1982 a skeleton found in a ditch, again in North Carolina, proved to be that of a young African lion.[5]

Maned lions are still being reported. One sighting of such a felid was made during July 1984 in a suburb of Cleveland, Ohio. Another was recorded near Texas's Fort Worth Zoo during late February 1985. Needless to say, the zoo itself was checked, but no lions were missing, and although it was later seen by two police patrolmen who identified it unhesitatingly as a lion, it eluded all attempts at capture and was not sighted again.[73]

There would appear to be three identities on offer for America's maned mystery cats.

1) Large Dog?

As we have seen many times already, this is a very popular 'official' explanation for reports of mystery cats. Yet, although it is true that various dog breeds can appear surprisingly panther-like or puma-like under certain viewing-conditions, very few dogs (regardless of viewing-conditions) can be mistaken for a full-sized, fully maned lion.

Probably the closest approximation to a leonine dog is the Chinese chow – and by chance there is at least one episode on record involving a maned mystery cat in which a specific chow *was* put forward as the felid in question. This was during the case of the Fremont lion of November 1979. After Fontes had made his sighting of the mystery beast in the flood channel, a local inhabitant came forward to claim that his own 40 lb/18 kg chow puppy was the animal responsible – to which Fontes soon retorted: 'The puppy in no way resembled the 300 to 400 pound [136-182 kg] animal observed in the flood control channel.'[66] Considering that not even the very largest of adult chows can attain such dimensions, it is hardly surprising that Fontes should so readily dismiss a chow puppy from contention.

Even more remote is the possibility that anyone could confuse a lion with a Brittany spaniel, yet this was a highly regarded 'official' solution to the lion spied near Fort Worth Zoo in 1985.[73] Its police eyewitnesses, however, begged to differ. And who can blame them? Anything less like a lion than a white-and-orange/chestnut/black dog of maximum height 20 in/50 cm and bearing a pair of fluffy pendulous ears would be hard to imagine. Except, perhaps, for mongrel Jake! In any case, though many maned mystery cats have been reported roaring, I have yet to read of a case in which one of these animals barked.

2) African Lion Escapees?

Despite being anathema to some mystery animal afficionados, the exotic escapee theory is a far more reasonable solution to America's maned mysteries. Lions are indisputably very popular animals – not only in public zoos and circuses but also in private animal collections and even as household pets. That escape (or release) of lions from captivity in America does indeed occur has already been demonstrated by the discovery of the various dead specimens recorded above, and it seems highly unlikely that a lion or lioness would have much trouble in surviving in much of North America's countryside. And we have already learnt that cubs are not averse to escaping.

Of great pertinence is the recent horrific revelation that persons in Texas are buying African lions from zoos, circuses and pet owners for the express purpose of inviting would-be big-game hunters to come and shoot them, usually (though apparently not always) within fenced enclosures.[74] Clearly the possibility of escapees must be a very real one. In April 1988, news emerged that two African lion carcases had been discovered on a reservoir site set aside at Texas's Wallisville by the US Army Corps of Engineers and that lion hunts had indeed been occurring there. Yet as lion hunting is technically not illegal here, US Federal officials fear that they can do little to prevent it.[74] If such activity is not limited to Texas, we surely need not look much further for explanations of American maned lions.

Nonetheless, a third explanation *is* on offer – one involving lions that in America are not out-of-*place* but out-of-*time*.

3) Surviving American Lions?

During the upper Pleistocene epoch, the lion *Panthera leo* not only existed throughout much of the Old World but, as a result of the former presence of a Bering Sea landbridge connecting northern Asia with Alaska, it had also penetrated the New World, thriving in North America and Central America and as far south as north-western South America.[75]

The American lion constituted a subspecies separate from its Old World counterparts, and has been named *P. l. atrox*. It appeared to die out at the end of the Pleistocene epoch 10,000 years ago – no fossil evidence more recent than that date is known.[76] However, developing a suggestion first put forward by Mark Hall of Minnesota, Loren Coleman has postulated that the unexpected maned felids being sighted across North America today may actually be surviving male individuals of *P. l. atrox*; furthermore, he proposes that the equally mystifying black panthers discussed earlier in this chapter could be *P. l. atrox* females.[29,68]

In support of this theory, Coleman comments that the behaviour of these two types of American mystery cat compares closely with that of genuine lions elsewhere – with the maned beasts being proud but cautious, like typical male lions, while the pantheresque felids are less retiring and more aggressive, like typical lionesses. He adds that the classification of these two unidentified felid forms as the two sexes of a single species can explain those very occasional sightings on record of maned cats and panthers having been seen together.[29,68] Altogether a quite fascinating theory, whose scientific development could constitute a stimulating intellectual exercise. Sadly, however, in practical terms it suffers from a number of fundamental problems, some of which have been brought to public attention by Mike Grayson.[77]

First and foremost of these is the radical differences in pelage colouration between the maned and the panther-like cats. As Grayson has pointed out, if we assume that these do indeed comprise the two sexes of the same species, the exhibition of normal leonine colouration by the male whilst the female displays very pronounced melanistic tendencies would constitute an example of extreme sexual dimorphism totally without parallel amongst other mammalian species. The male-only mane of the lion is proof that this species is indeed capable of evolving a marked degree of sexual dimorphism, but even allowing for the fact that some lions have dark belly and neck manes, it is still exceedingly improbable that such dimorphism could aspire to the exceptional level required by the Coleman-Hall theory.[77]

Equally contentious is the total absence of sightings in modern America of mystery lion prides. As Coleman himself notes, lions are social[68] (and, according to felid specialist Dr Helmut Hemmer, the high degree of cephalization – brain development – displayed by the American lion makes it probable that this subspecies was too[75]), so if his *P. l. atrox* theory is true, why no records of prides?[77] And, indeed, why, out of all of the maned mystery cat records documented by Coleman, is there only a single episode which involves one of these felids and a pantheresque cat being seen together?

Also brought forward by Grayson is the undeniable fact that animals identical to America's black panthers are also being reported in regions of the world where survival of prehistoric lions is totally incongruous (such as Great Britain), as well as from regions where lions have never existed at any time (such as Australia).[77] In comparison with the escapee theory, the *P. l. atrox* explanation is inadequate here.

In addition to Grayson's comments regarding the *P. l. atrox* concept, another equally formidable and significant objection to this exists – namely, the blunt fact that, judging from reconstructions of the American lion in life based upon fossil evidence, it simply did not resemble the maned cats being seen there today.

In fact, *P. l. atrox* was once classed not as a lion at all but as a giant jaguar.[78] Only in more recent times have its close affinities with the lion been recognized. Moreover, some authorities, though accepting its leonine relationships, still prefer to class it as a separate species of lion – *P. atrox* – rather than considering it merely as a subspecies of *P. leo*.[79]

Thus, whilst America's maned mystery cats resemble modern lions both in overall size and in physical appearance, the American lion was very different indeed. To begin with, it was at least a third larger than the largest of modern lions – hence its earlier, alternative name of Great Cat. Furthermore, in relation to today's lions, the American lion's face was shorter, with a broader nasal region, and its limbs were notably longer – so much so, in fact, that it is considered to have been a truly cursorial felid, far more so than any modern lion.[79]

Arguing in favour of post-Pleistocene survival of *P. l. atrox*,

Loren Coleman notes[68] that only one American lion fossil skeleton has been recovered for every thirty of its sabre-tooth contemporary *Smilodon fatalis* from the famed tar pits of Rancho La Brea, near Los Angeles.[80] This is a startling ratio, one which has been put forward by many palaeontologists as evidence for the intellectual superiority of the American lion. Coupled with this is the fact that, relative to its body size, the brain of the American lion was larger than that of any Old World counterpart, either from the Pleistocene epoch or from the present day.[76] In short, it would be expected from this that *P. l. atrox* would stand a better chance of surviving undetected into modern North America than would *S. fatalis* (and certainly there is neither physical nor anecdotal evidence to suggest current survival here of the latter species).

Irrespective of the American lion's intellectual level, however, we still cannot ignore the seemingly irreconcilable morphological and behavioural problems noted above. Hence, although most certainly a captivating concept, the theory that America's maned and pantheresque mystery cats constitute a relict population of *P. l. atrox* is ultimately untenable – with the exotic escapee theory reasserting itself as the most plausible solution to these felid forms. But what of the single episode involving the maned lion- and panther-like cat being seen together by various eyewitnesses over a few days? The most reasonable explanation is that these were a couple of escapees (probably from a circus or private collection) originally reared and maintained together prior to their escape. This same solution could also explain occasional reports from Great Britain of dissimilar, large-sized mystery cats sighted together.

Santer – North Carolina's Mystery Cat

The santer is a largely forgotten feline anomaly which does not seem to slot readily into any of the three previous categories of American mystery cat. Hailing from North Carolina, this mystifying creature terrorized a number of communities in the state during the last years of the nineteenth century, featured in many reports by the Wilkesboro *Chronicle* and the *Statesville Landmark* and resurfaced in 1977 via a most interesting two-part article by Angelo Capparella III published in *Shadows* and quoting from many of the original newspaper reports.[81]

Initially it was treated humourously, but alarm generated locally by continued livestock killings inspired a more serious attitude to the santer in later newspaper reports. Sadly, very little was documented regarding its/their physical appearance (more than one animal seemed to be involved), hence it is not possible to arrive at a definite conclusion regarding identity. The *Chronicle* noted on 5 May 1897 that a lynx had escaped from a circus exhibiting in the area the previous year, and inferred that this might be the santer. On 9 June it announced that the santer had been caught – and that it resembled a large 'shepherd dog', but also recalled rumours of a second animal on the loose. And certainly all was not over, for on 20 October 1897 Charles Smoot alleged that he had recently seen a santer, describing it as 'striped from the end of its nose to the end of its tail'. And on 31 May 1899 a santer sighting was claimed by a Mrs Smoak, who stated that it was grey in colour and between a cat and dog in size.[81]

Due to the radical conflict in descriptions, it would seem that yet another cryptozoological composite had been 'created', by reports of various totally different animal types having been attributed erroneously to a single animal form. Capparella believed that, although some sightings were probably of non-felids, the real santer was a genuine large cat form. Moreover, the santer's alleged boldness and lack of fear when in the presence of humans suggested to him that a puma identity was also unlikely, and he leant instead in favour of the santer's being a currently unknown felid.[81] Yet the santer has failed to be reported since the 1890s (a mystery wild beast roaming around South Iredell in May 1934 was considered by locals to be the santer or an offspring of that beast, but no proof to support such claims was obtained[81]). It would seem more likely to have been based upon a single animal of unexpected form (an exotic escapee once again?), whose exploits set the scene for over-enthusiastic identification thereafter of *anything* large as the culprit. Shades of the Surrey puma-fox and the Shing Mun tiger-alsatian.

The final selection of North American mystery cats to be considered is a pot-pourri in which the unexpected and the unlikely are sometimes difficult to distinguish and disentangle from one another.

Blue Lynxes and Wampus Cats

Most people would be hard-pressed to believe in blue-furred lynxes – but, in fact, incontrovertible evidence for their existence is at hand. In 1938 Ernst Schwarz reported in the *Journal of Mammalogy* that the skin of just such a cat had been donated by Mrs Charles D. Walcott to the US National Museum (though, very regrettably, having been obtained through the fur-trade, all that was known about this most significant skin's origin was that it had come from somewhere in Alaska).[82]

Instead of exhibiting the familiar fawn colour of normal lynxes, its pelage was bluish-grey all over. True, it did possess the usual pattern of pale inner limbs and belly, but whereas the tail-tip and ear-tufts of typical lynxes are black, those of this specimen were simply a deeper shade of blue-grey – indeed, black colouration was totally absent. This demonstrates that it was not a chinchilla mutant. Instead, as Schwarz stated, it clearly represented a dilute mutant[82] (i.e. homozygous for the dense pigmentation gene's dilute mutant allele[54] – already proposed as the explanation for Fujian's blue tiger on p. 101, and responsible for the maltese shade in domestic cats). Enquiries made to the fur trade confirmed earlier unsubstantiated eyewitness accounts, for, according to various furriers, this mutant form occurs once or twice in every thousand lynx skins.[82] A drab blue lynx was also noted by Poland in 1892, together with a yellow specimen[83] for which Roy Robinson has suggested that the extension of black gene's recessive non-extension of black mutant allele is responsible (it replaces black pigment with yellow or red).[54] Poland listed examples of blue bobcats too, again evidently dilute mutants, plus red specimens that once more indicate the non-extension of black mutant allele.[54,83]

Equally intriguing is the felid featured in a frustratingly vague report which appeared on 3 August 1823 in Kentucky's *Louisville Courier* and in Boston's *New England Farmer*. It referred to a large, unidentified cat seen near Russelville, Kentucky, and described as '… a tiger of brindle color with a most terrific front – his eyes were as the largest ever on any animal around these parts'.[33,84] It was fired at from 50 yards/45.5 m, yet stood its ground for twelve shots before making off, apparently unhurt and at full speed.[33] An exotic escapee, a cryptozoological curio or a muddled misidentification? Sadly it is very doubtful whether we shall ever discover the answer.

If the existence of an aquatic sabre-tooth in tropical Africa seems improbable, how much more so an amphibious panther in central Missouri? This unlikely beast is the subject of numerous lofty legends recalled by the local inhabitants (especially in the vicinity of Roark Creek's valley), who refer to it as the 'gallywampus' and assert that it swims like a colossal mink and occasionally attacks terrestrial livestock.[8,85]

A land-living variation on the wampus cat theme is the whistling wampus. This, supposedly, is a huge black beast inhabiting Waldron in Arkansas, deriving its name from its beguiling whistling cry (said to sound like 'hoo-hoo') and possessing a notable appetite for lumberjacks.[8]

Not to be overlooked is the Oklahoma wowzer, for, according to fireside tales, this resembles a puma in colouration but is about five or six times bigger. One of these Brobdingnagian beasts allegedly destroyed an entire wagon-train in early pioneer days, killing more than thirty oxen in a few minutes (it simply bit their heads off) but not harming the people themselves.[8]

We should not forget the cactus cat either, reports of which supposedly originated from travellers passing through Tucson's cactus-bearing expanses during the nineteenth century. They described it as resembling a spiky-furred domestic cat but with the added attributes of a bifurcate tail and razor-sharp blades of bone on its forelimbs. It was said to use these to slash the base of large cacti in order to release the sap. Once the sap had fermented, the cactus cat would drink it heartily and then depart upon its inebriated way, screeching in drunken delight.[86]

Needless (although sad) to say, there is very little justification for believing that wampus cats, wowzers and cactus cats are anything other than terrors of the tall-tale variety. Nonetheless, there is one puzzling tie-in which merits investigation. In British Columbia, the Indians' totem poles sometimes depict a felid which they adamantly class as a real but completely separate form from the puma and which they refer to as the *how-how*.[87] Many native names for animals are onomatopoeic – is it just coincidence that *how-how* sounds remarkably similar to the 'hoo-hoo' cry of the whistling wampus cat?

And Finally ...

No chapter on North American feline mysteries and marvels would be complete without a mention of the celebrated cherry-coloured cat exhibited by that famed American showman Phineas Barnum. After having paid their money to see this wonderful animal, a few of its visitors later protested to Barnum that they had been both surprised and disappointed to discover that it was nothing more than an ordinary black cat. Barnum was quite unmoved by their remonstrance, for, as he reminded them, he had promised them a cherry-coloured cat and, after all, *some* cherries *are* black![88]

There's a lesson for cryptozoology in there somewhere.

1 Corbet, G.B., and Hill, J.E., *A World List of Mammalian Species*, second edition (Brit. Mus. Nat. Hist., 1986)
2 *Oryx*, Vol. 19, p. 172 (July 1985)
3 Purgavie, D., *Daily Mail*, 10 October 1987
4 Fisher, J., Simon, N., and Vincent, J., *The Red Book* (Collins, 1969); Banfield, A.W.F., *The Mammals of Canada* (University of Toronto Press, Toronto and Buffalo, 1974)
5 Downing, R.L., *Cryptozoology*, Vol. 3, pp. 31-49 (1984)

6 Wright, B.S., *The Eastern Panther* (Clark, Irwin, Toronto, 1971)
7 Golley, F.B., *Mammals of Georgia* (University of Georgia Press, Athens, 1962)
8 Randolph, V., *We Only Lie to Strangers* (Greenwood Press, Westport – Conn., 1951)
9 Wright, B.S., *Journal of Mammalogy*, Vol. 42, pp. 278–9 (May 1961)
10 Hardison, S., *Wildlife in North Carolina*, Vol. 40, pp. 15–17 (1976)
11 Sass, H.R., *Saturday Evening Post*, Vol. 226, pp. 31, 133–4, 136 (13 March 1954)
12 Nowak, R.M., *The Cougar in the United States and Canada* (1976), cited in Downing, R.L. (1983), op. cit.
13 Wright, B.S., *Animals*, Vol. 6, p. 85 (23 March 1965)
14 Young, S.P., and Goldman, E.A., *The Puma: Mysterious American Cat* (American Wildlife Institute, Washington, 1946)
15 Lewis, J.C., *Journal of Mammalogy*, Vol. 50, pp. 371–2 (1969)
16 Fegely, T., *Latrobe Bulletin*, 12 August 1987
17 Ricciuti, E.R., *The Wild Cats* (Windward, 1979); Denis, A., *Cats of the World* (Constable, 1964)
18 *The News*, No. 9, p. 16 (April 1975)
19 *Res Bureaux Bulletin*, No. 40, pp. 7–8 (9 November 1978)
20 Rickard, R.J.M.,*Fortean Times*, No. 28, p. 49 (winter 1979)
21 Coleman, L., ibid., No. 30, pp. 47–9 (autumn 1980)
22 Greenwell, J.R. (ed.), *ISC Newsletter*, Vol. 1, pp. 6–7 (spring 1982)
23 Cohen, D., *The Encyclopedia of Monsters* (Dodd, Mead & Co, New York, 1982)
24 Gordon, S., *PA Woods & Waters* (February 1987)
25 Hamilton, R., A Connecticut quarterly periodical – title unknown, p. 5 (summer 1987)
26 *West Virginia Advocate*, 14 September 1987; Ingram, B., *Virginia Country*, pp. 24–5 (autumn 1987)
27 *West Virginia Advocate*, 14 January 1988
28 Downing, R.L., Paper presented at the ISC Annual Members Meeting, University of Maryland, 14 May 1988
29 Coleman, L., *Mysterious America* (Faber & Faber, 1983)
30 *Doubt*, No. 17, p. 260 (1947)
31 Coleman, L., *Fate*, Vol. 24, pp. 48–54 (March 1971); Clark, J., and Coleman, L., *Fate*, Vol. 25, pp. 72–82 (June 1972) and pp. 92–102 (July 1972)
32 Coleman, L., *Anomaly Research Bulletin*, No. 23, pp. 5–8 (1978); Coleman, L., *Pursuit*, Vol. 12, pp. 61–2 (April 1979)
33 Clark, J., and Coleman, L., *Creatures of the Outer Edge* (Warner Books, New York, 1978)
34 Wright, B.S., *The Ghost of North America* (Vantage Press, New York, 1959)
35 *San Jose News*, 15 December 1973; *Arkansas Gazette*, 16 December 1973
36 Coleman, L., *Fate*, Vol. 30, pp. 62–7 (November 1977)
37 Hale, D., et al., *Daily Telegram* (Elmira, NY), 21, 25, 28 July, 18 August 1977
38 Hartley, T., *Sunday Telegram* (Elmira, NY) 8 January 1978
39 Crooks, S., ibid, 13 May 1979
40 Fuller, C., *Fate*, Vol. 38, pp. 26, 28 (January 1985)
41 Schaffner, R., ibid., Vol. 38, pp. 71–3 (May 1985)
42 *Tuscaloosa News*, 29 May 1987
43 Jenkins, R., *The Star-Ledger* (Newark, New Jersey), 23 June 1987; *Asbury Park Press* (New Jersey), 24 June 1987; Sipress, A., *Philadelphia Inquirer* 29 June 1987
44 Schaffner, R., *Creature Chronicles*, No. 12, pp. 4–10 (February 1988)
45 Hall, E.R., *The Mammals of North America*, 2 volumes, second edition (Wiley, 1981)

46 Nelson, E.W., *Wild Animals of North America*, revised edition (National Geographic Society, Washington 1930)
47 Langford, C., *Winter of the Fisher* (Manor Books, New York 1975)
48 Kelsey, P., *INFO Journal*, No. 41, p. 17 (October 1982)
49 Thomas, A.C., Personal communication (1984)
50 Ives, K.E., *INFO Journal*, No. 41, p. 17 (October 1982)
51 *Oryx*, Vol. 21, p. 123 (April 1987)
52 Lever, C., *Naturalized Mammals of the World* (Longman, 1985)
53 Ulmer, F.A., *Journal of Mammalogy*, Vol. 22, pp. 285–8 (1941); Paradiso, J., *Florida Scientist*, Vol. 36, pp. 215–16 (1973)
54 Robinson, R., *Genetica*, Vol. 46, pp. 1–31 (1976)
55 Coleman, L., *Carnivore Genetics Newsletter*, Vol. 2, pp. 209–11 (1974)
56 Cahalane, V.H., *Mammals of North America* (Macmillan, 1961)
57 Guggisberg, C.A.W., *Wild Cats of the World* (David & Charles, 1975)
58 McCabe, R.A., *Journal of Mammalogy*, Vol. 30, pp. 305–6 (1949)
59 *Pursuit*, Vol. 5, p. 12 (January 1972)
60 Goldman, E.A., *Proceedings of the Biological Society of Washington*, Vol. 45, pp. 143–6 (1932)
61 Merriam, H., *Journal of Mammalogy*, Vol. 1, pp. 38–40 (1919)
62 Day, D., *The Doomsday Book of Animals* (Ebury Press, 1981)
63 Nowak, R., *National Parks Conservation Magazine*, Vol. 49, pp. 10–13 (December 1975)
64 Taylor, W.P., *Journal of Mammalogy*, Vol. 28, p. 66 (1947); Hock, R.J., *American Midland Naturalist*, Vol. 53, pp. 324–8 (April 1955); Brown, D.E., *Southwestern Naturalist*, Vol. 28, pp. 459–60 (1983)
65 Fisher, J., *The Field*, Vol. 176, p. 224 (17 August 1940); Rabinowitz, A., *Jaguar* (Collins, 1987)
66 Coleman, L., *Fortean Times*, No. 31, pp. 24–7 (spring 1980)
67 Brandon, J., *Weird America* (E.P. Dutton, New York, 1978)
68 Coleman, L., *Fortean Times*, No. 32, pp. 21–2 (summer 1980)
69 *Newsweek* (New York), 27 March 1961
70 *Res Bureaux Bulletin*, No. 27, p. 6 (1977)
71 *Palm Beach Post*, 24 January 1978
72 *Res Bureaux Bulletin*, No. 50, p. 4 (August 1979)
73 Coleman, L., *Curious Encounters* (Faber & Faber, 1985)
74 *Express and Star* (Wolverhampton), 22 April 1988; *The Times* (London) 12 June 1988
75 Hemmer, H., *Worlds Cats*, Vol. 3, pp. 1–14 (1976)
76 Kurten, B., and Anderson, E., *Pleistocene Mammals of North America* (Columbia University Press, New York, 1980)
77 Grayson, M., *Fortean Times*, No. 36, pp. 58–9 (winter 1982)
78 Simpson, G.G., *American Museum Novitates*, No. 1,136, pp. 1–27 (1941)
79 Martin, L.D., and Gilbert, B.M., *Contributions to Geology, University of Wyoming*, Vol. 16, pp. 95–101 (1978)
80 Merriam, J.C., and Stock, C., *The Felidae of Rancho La Brea* (Carnegie Institution, Publication No. 422, 1932); *Illustrated London News*, Vol. 182, pp. 222–3 (18 February 1933)
81 Capparella III, A., *Shadows*, No. 4, pp. 1–3 (January 1977) and No. 5, pp. 1–3 (February 1977)
82 Schwarz, E., *Journal of Mammalogy*, Vol. 19, p. 376 (1938)
83 Poland, H., *Fur-Bearing Animals in Nature and Commerce* (Gurney & Jackson, 1892)
84 Schaffner, R., *Creature Chronicles*, No. 6, p. 6 (spring 1983)
85 Pipes, G.H., *Strange Customs of the Ozark Hillbilly* (Hobson Books, New York, 1947)

86 Headon, D., *Mythical Beasts* (Hutchinson, 1981)
87 Goss, M., Personal communication (1986)
88 Eldin, P., *Amazing Hoaxes and Frauds* (Octopus Books, 1987)

6 Onzas and Jaguaretes

Mexico and South America

> My own first impression of a living jaguar was not one of pure pleasure.... For it is his instinct to remain always hidden from the eye, and it confuses and maddens him to be held in place by bars and gazed openly at.
>
> W.H. Hudson (upon seeing a caged jaguar), *Harmsworth Natural History*

MEXICO

When the Spaniards invaded Mexico in the sixteenth century, they named its large cat forms after species familiar to them back home. Thus the puma *Felis concolor* was christened the *leon*, and the jaguar *Panthera onca* the *tigre* (names by which these two species are now known in many regions of Latin America). According to traditional zoology, no other large felid exists in Mexico.

Onza – Cheetah-like Puma or Puma-like Cheetah?

However, modern inhabitants of Sinaloa, the province running 400 miles/644 km along the Sierras down Mexico's western coast, acknowledge the existence there of a third large cat form, referred to by them as the *onza*. This name is found in records dating back again to Mexico's first Spanish settlers. Moreover, it is derived from the Latin word *uncia*, which refers to the Old World cheetah. Does this mean, therefore, that the Spaniards in Mexico encountered a cat form which reminded them of a cheetah? Apparently it does, for the Sinaloans describe the *onza* as being superficially puma-like but with a more slender body and notably long limbs.[1,2]

The most detailed *onza* narratives consist of *The Onza*,[3] a regrettably scarce book written by longstanding *onza* investigator Robert Marshall, and the reports and article written by ISC Secretary Richard Greenwell[1,2,4] (see also his forthcoming book *Animals Without Heritage*). These comprise the principle sources of information referred to in the preparation of the following *onza* history and should be consulted for further details.

What would appear to be the earliest known reference to this felid (though the term *onza* was not actually used here) was made by Bernal Diaz del Castillo, under the command of the infamous *conquistador* Hernán Cortés. In a report some time after having visited the famous zoo of the Aztec King Montezuma, Castillo recorded seeing 'tigers [jaguars] and lions of two kinds, one of which resembled the wolf'. In view of the wolf's long limbs and the corresponding characteristic of the *onza*, it is traditionally assumed that Castillo's 'wolf-cat' (known to the Aztecs as *cuitlamiztli*) was indeed the *onza*.[1-3]

In any event, by the eighteenth century '*onza*' was well established as the official name for Mexico's third type of large cat. And so the Jesuit missionary Father Ignaz Pfefferkorn – posted in 1757 to the remote, little-explored north Mexican province of Sonora – referred to 'the animal which the Spaniards call *onza*', describing it as being far less timid than the puma but of similar shape except for its rather longer, thinner body. Comparable *onza* descriptions, but this time from Baja California, were given during this same period by two other Jesuits, missionary Father Johann Jakob Baegert (working with the Guaricura Indians) and scholar Father Francisco Javier Claviego. Further *onza* reports and rumours were recorded during the nineteenth century, including the interesting belief of some Mexicans that the *onza* resulted from puma × jaguar matings.[1-3]

In the early part of the twentieth century, Dr George Parker discovered that the *onza* is a familiar but much-feared felid within the Mexican state of Durango. Its inhabitants informed him that the eyes of the *onza* were yellow and 'look like balls of fire in the night' and that this mysterious cat was held to be the most dangerous animal in the Durango mountains.[3,5]

Nevertheless, with a distinct lack of physical evidence to examine, zoologists paid little or no attention to such accounts, dismissing *onzas* as nothing more than misidentified or emaciated pumas.

In 1938 banker Joseph Shirk of Peru, Indiana, travelled to Sinaloa's San Ignacio district to hunt jaguars on La Silla Mountain, accompanied by hunting guides Dale and Clell Lee, renowned hunting experts from south-east Arizona. The higher altitudes of the San Ignacio district are relatively little explored, due to their extremely difficult terrain, and are characterized by a gradation from subtropical to semi-arid vegetation. According to reliable inhabitants of Sinaloa, this remote locality is home not only to jaguars but also to *onzas*.[1-3] Following their arrival, the Lee brothers were unable to locate any jaguar signs; however, they noted another form of cat there and hence set their dogs off in pursuit of this instead. Within a short time, a sizeable specimen of this unidentified felid was treed and later shot dead. Upon examining it, the Lees were greatly surprised to discover that, despite their very considerable hunting experience, they had before them the carcase of a cat form that they were completely unable to identify; for although it was reminiscent of a puma, its body was longer and much slimmer, and its limbs and ears were notably lengthier too. This animal was then measured and photographed, and the skull and skin were retained by Shirk.[1-3]

If only the remainder of the specimen had been preserved too (instead, it was butchered and disposed of), for when the Lees formally announced their exciting find upon their return home to Arizona, they were shocked and alarmed to receive nothing but ridicule and disbelief from the scientific world. Lacking a complete specimen as evidence that could be thoroughly examined, their case for a new form of felid collapsed, and the Lees avoided further publicity on the subject. The skull of their specimen was apparently deposited in an unnamed American museum during the 1960s, and its origins are now unknown, while the *onza* itself remained entrenched as a feline *persona non grata*.[1-3]

Indeed, this unhappy incident, coupled with the all-consuming events of World War II, might quite conceivably have jettisoned the *onza* into scientific obscurity forever, had its history not attracted the attention of another Arizonan hunter, Robert Marshall. Rather than pursuing the *onza* with rifle and eyepiece, Marshall chose to arm himself with paper, pen and travelling-boots and set about documenting every *onza* report, rumour and legend which he could uncover, and seeking out any *onza* relics which might exist. He eventually succeeded not only in amassing a very considerable stock of data concerning this mystery cat but also in discovering an incomplete skull (its lower jaw was missing) reputedly derived from an *onza* originating from Los Frailes, Sinaloa. His researches climaxed in 1961 with the publication of *The Onza*,[3] but science remained unwilling to admit to its subject's existence as a separate felid form.

The next significant step in the history of the *onza* – though it was not seen as such at the time – occurred in 1969, when P.C. Orr described a new species of fossil Pleistocene puma from a perfectly preserved skull, mandible (lower jaw), scapula (shoulder blade) and various vertebrae and ribs. He named this new cat *Felis trumani*.[6] Further finds in later years enabled palaeontologists to reconstruct a detailed picture of the cat's likely appearance in the living state, and they found that it bore a striking similarity to the

Old World, modern cheetah (as did, though to a rather lesser degree due to its larger head and overall size, its likely Pleistocene antecedent *Felis studeri*, another fossil puma, discovered in 1960[7]).

In the mid-1970s Dr Daniel Adams and co-workers from the University of California suggested that *F. trumani* was a specialized puma whose evolution had paralleled that of the cheetah, occupying in the New World the latter felid's niche in the Old World as a cursorial hunting-cat.[8]

By the end of the 1970s, after having analysed in great detail the *F. trumani* fossil remains so far uncovered and comparing them with those of the Old World cheetahs, Dr Adams had changed his mind. As a result of his studies, he announced a startling conclusion: that pumas and cheetahs were very closely related, sharing a common origin, and that *F. trumani* and also *F. studeri* were more than just pumas morphologically paralleling cheetahs – instead, they were genuine cheetahs themselves.[9] He based his belief upon numerous detailed and highly specific structural similarities between the American species (especially *F. trumani*) and the cheetahs of Africa and Asia, similarities which would not be expected if the New World cats were simply mimics rather than true relatives of the latter felids. Thus Adams removed *F. trumani* and *F. studeri* from the genus *Felis* (housing the normal puma) and referred them instead to *Acinonyx*, the cheetah genus, so that they are now known respectively as *Acinonyx trumani* and *Acinonyx studeri*. Suddenly the cheetah was no longer an Old World speciality – it was now a native American too.[9]

Adams' revelation meant that a remarkable situation now existed: that Pleistocene America possessed, in the form of *A. trumani* in particular, a bona fide cheetah whose appearance in life would have compared very favourably with that of a mysterious long-limbed cat of modern America whose native name of *onza* is derived from a word meaning 'cheetah'!

Needless to say, this formidable coincidence did not remain undetected for long. The German felid researcher Dr Helmut Hemmer of the University of Mainz was aware of the *onza* through reading Robert Marshall's book, and became intrigued by the close correspondence on a number of different morphological points between Truman's fossil cheetah and the alleged appearance of the *onza*. Following some researches on this subject during the early 1980s, Dr Hemmer formulated the daring hypothesis that these two cat forms were indeed one and the same species, i.e. that *A. trumani* had, in fact, survived beyond the Pleistocene epoch into the present day as the identity of the Mexican *onza*.[10]

Despite their apparent compatibility, this morphological

marriage of *A. trumani* and the *onza* was not destined to last. Hemmer's hypothesis had brought the *onza* to the attention of ISC Secretary Richard Greenwell, who became extremely interested in this cryptic cat and instigated his own personal *onza* investigations. He teamed up with puma specialist Dr Troy Best of the University of New Mexico to relocate the Shirk *onza* skull (he had already learnt that Robert Marshall still owned the Los Frailes skull). To date, their search has not been successful. However, whilst they were seeking this, another – hitherto unrecorded – *onza* skull was uncovered. It had been obtained in 1938 from Sinaloa's La Silla Mountain – the same time and the same location as for the Shirk specimen. Little wonder then that, when Greenwell and Best first received details of this, they assumed that it must be the long-lost Shirk skull. But eventual comparison of the newly located specimen – housed at Philadelphia's Academy of Natural Sciences – with good photographs of the latter skull revealed that the two were, in fact, separate specimens. Further investigations revealed that the newly identified *onza* skull had been obtained by R.R.M. Carpenter, another hunter who had been accompanied by the Lee brothers prior to World War II.[4]

Richard Greenwell's researches continued fruitfully with his visit during summer 1985 to Sinaloa. There he succeeded in locating a third *onza* skull – of a specimen shot during the mid-1970s by the late Jesus Vega (and once again in the very same location from which the previous specimens had been obtained). Greenwell visited Vega's son, Manuel Vega, and also fellow rancher Ricardo Urquijo, who now owned the Vega *onza* skull. Greenwell found it to be in perfect condition and brought it back with him to Tucson, on kind loan from Urquijo.[4]

With three skulls – Los Frailes (incomplete), Carpenter and Vega, all very similar to one another – now available for study, Dr Hemmer at last had the much-needed *onza* material with which to put his hypothesis to the test. This he did, by comprehensively comparing the morphology of these specimens with fossil skulls of *A. trumani*. And the result? Hemmer sadly concluded that, although the *onza* skulls did display certain interesting similarities to the latter, very notable differences also existed between the two forms, which clearly demonstrated that *A. trumani* and the *onza* were not one and the same species after all.[2]

Nonetheless, the possibility still existed that the *onza* was a close modern relative of the fossil species, transitional between this and the normal puma. But to determine whether or not this was correct, much more material than three skulls would be required – nothing less, in fact, than a complete specimen, for full scientific examination, anatomical and biochemical. Nevertheless, when seeking a creature as elusive as the *onza*, which inhabits terrain as notoriously remote and difficult as that of La Silla Mountain, such a requirement could quite conceivably take a lifetime or more to fulfil. In fact, thanks to a remarkable piece of good fortune, it took less than six months![1,2,11]

On the evening of 1 January 1986 rancher Andres Rodriguez Murillo, from Sinaloa's San Ignacio district, was deer-hunting in the vicinity of his house (in a valley behind Parrot Mountain) when he encountered a large, crouching cat which he assumed to be a jaguar. Fearing that it was about to attack him, he shot it. Examining the body, however, he found that it was not a jaguar after all, and appeared to be different from a puma too. Remembering Richard Greenwell's visit to the area a few months earlier, his interest in unusual cats, and his meeting with Manuel Vega, Rodriguez returned to his ranch with the carcase and contacted Vega forthwith. Vega arrived at once to examine the cat and identified it positively as an *onza*.[1,2] This initiated a rapid chain of communications which ultimately resulted in the specimen being preserved in excellent condition by freezing at a commercial fishery company. Greenwell was swiftly informed of its discovery, and on 19 February a scientific team headed by Greenwell, Dr Best and blood-tissues/electrophoresis specialist Ned Gentz arrived in the Mexican town of Mazatlan to dissect the specimen at the Regional Diagnostic Laboratory of Animal Pathology, an agency of Mexico's federal Ministry of Agriculture.[1,2]

The *onza* was a four-year-old female, of head-and-body length 113 cm (approx. 45 in), tail length 73 cm (approx. 23 in; very long relative to that of a female puma of comparable head-and-body length) and body weight 27 kg (59½ lb; notably less than that of a comparably sized female puma, even allowing for slight weight loss due to freezing). In overall appearance it did indeed resemble a very long-limbed, slender puma, but in addition it exhibited certain features not displayed by normal pumas, e.g. noticeably long ears, and small horizontal stripes on the insides of its forelimbs.[1,2,12]

Needless to say, with such an exceedingly valuable specimen, its external morphology was studiously examined prior to dissection. Only when it had been photographed from every imaginable angle and when every conceivable measurement had been recorded was the first incision made. Furthermore, even the dissection itself was videotaped to ensure that no vital detail escaped documentation. The major organs were preserved, together with a front and rear foot. Tissue samples from various organs were prepared for electrophoresis (a method of protein separation via passage of an electric current), whose result would then be compared with those obtained from other species to determine the taxonomic relationships of the *onza*. Hair and blood samples, again for interspecific comparison, were also taken plus selected skeletal material (including the skull and a set of limb bones).[1,2,12]

Among the most interesting discoveries resulting from the dissection and the first preliminary findings from the preserved material are the following. The body of the Rodriguez *onza* possessed adequate fatty tissue, thereby verifying that its gracility was natural, rather than emaciation brought about by prolonged starvation or metabolic disorders. In fact, it had been a very healthy specimen – even its parasite content was very limited – and had eaten a deer as its last meal (its stomach contained deer hooves). Moreover, its reproductive organs were normal, thereby discounting a hybrid identity. Its limb bones compared with those of adult male pumas; hence, if (as with pumas) the male *onza* is larger than the female, it is likely that male *onzas* are taller than male pumas.[1,2,12]

As announced by Richard Greenwell and Dr Best during their joint *onza* paper[12] presented at the July 1987 ISC Members Meeting at Edinburgh, research upon the Rodriguez *onza* is still in progress. This has been channelled along two principal lines – osteological (examination and comparison of its skeletal tissues) and biochemical (genetic and protein analyses of various tissue samples from the *onza* and from other cat forms, involving Dr Roy Mackal, a prominent biochemist and cryptozoologist from the University of Chicago).[12]

Thus the *onza* is currently at a stage of cryptozoological investigation similar to that of the Kellas cat. No longer is the determination of its actual existence the prime objective – now the search is on for its identity. The following possibilities exist: 1) an abnormal (mutant) puma; 2) a specialized puma subspecies; 3) a new species.

If it is found that *onzas* and pumas can both be born within a single litter, this will demonstrate that they belong to the same species and that the *onza* is nothing more than a mutant puma – at least at present (with its localized Mexican distribution and its morphological differences from normal pumas, one could perhaps speculate, as with the king cheetah, that it is evolving into a separate taxonomic form).

In view of the fact that a puma subspecies *F. c. azteca* already exists within the known Mexican distribution range of the *onza*, it would seem on first sight that a puma subspecies is an unlikely *onza* identity. However, if the lifestyle of the *onza* is such that it does not compete directly with the puma (comparable with the wildcat-Kellas cat situation?), this identity would be more tenable (i.e. implying sympatric speciation).

Even if it has originally descended from the puma, further researches into the anatomy, physiology and ecology of the *onza* may determine that it is now sufficiently distinct from the puma to warrant classification as a separate species. Indeed, it is possible that, with the Pleistocene extinction of the genuine American cheetahs *A. trumani* and *A. studeri*, the *onza* represents a sideline that evolved from the puma to fill the cursorial niche the cheetahs left vacant. And the reason why the *onza* apparently exists only in the mountainous regions of western Mexico rather than in the grassland regions of America with which one would normally associate a cursorial animal could be that it has been exterminated from such areas by man's rapid colonization of them.[1] And, of course, if the *onza* does come into contact with the puma but does not interbreed, this is very positive evidence in favour of its totally separate taxonomic status.[13]

What is particularly intriguing is the fact that two new cat forms – *onza* and Kellas cat – represented by specimens have been formally discovered since 1983 and that in both cases the most notable morphological feature is pronounced gracility. Is a fundamental genetic mechanism at work, capable of yielding gracile mutants in felids, regardless of species? This would be as significant a discovery as a new cat species. Only time, and continued research, will tell.

It is very rewarding to learn that Richard Greenwell is strongly opposed to any deliberate shooting of further *onzas*. Comprehensive treatment of the material preserved from the Rodriguez specimen should reduce the need for such activity. Moreover, with respect to osteological material in particular, it is quite possible that other *onza* remains are currently housed unknowingly in museums around the world, masquerading as puma relics. A rigorous examination of the latter – of the type currently in progress by Dr Troy Best[1,2,12] – may well result in additional *onza* remains.

I discovered one possible example of this during communications with Dr Ralph Molnar, curator of the Queensland Museum. Dr Molnar informed me that, whilst he was researching for his Master's degree at the University of Texas during the 1950s, a large cat specimen – a road-accident victim – had been found at the Texas-Mexico border and had been brought back to the university. As far as he can recall, it had been reduced by standard means to skeleton form for preservation before the researchers involved had realized that it was not a puma – until then, they had automatically assumed that it was a puma. Sadly, no further information was known to Dr Molnar concerning this, as by that time he had completed his course and had left the university.[14,15] If the researchers had thought that this mysterious cat was simply a puma, clearly in external morphology it must have closely resembled one, with its differences becoming apparent only from skeletal examination. This is the very situation that has been rife with the *onza*. Could this specimen have been an *onza*? Richard Greenwell is currently following up this incident. Perhaps another *onza* specimen waits to be unveiled.

Hunting Hyaenas and Man-Faced Felids

There remains one last item to consider regarding the *onza*: is it really the same creature as the 'wolf-cat' spied by Castillo in Montezuma's zoo? For, although one would naturally assume it to be the case, it is by no means conclusively established. After all, despite its long limbs, the *onza* does not really resemble a wolf to any degree. Is it conceivable that the Aztec 'wolf-cat' was actually some other, still unknown beast? I would be inclined to dismiss this idea totally – were it not for a certain tantalizing fossil species.

Though most closely related to cats, hyaenas are quite dog-like in outward appearance. Moreover, just like the cheetahs, though typically looked upon as Old World species, some hyaena forms did exist at one time in the Americas too, which leads us into the most fascinating aspect of this subject. Skeletons have been found in several different Mexican localities of a truly remarkable hyaena which lived during the Pleistocene epoch, i.e. a contemporary of *A. trumani*. However, this species, the hunting hyaena *Chasmaporthetes ossifragus*, shared much more than a geological time period and a geographical locality with the latter American cheetah, for *C. ossifragus* was a cursorial hyaena – possessing notably long limbs and a very gracile body.[16] In short, its appearance in life would have been the very epitome of the name 'wolf-cat'. Is it possible that *C. ossifragus* did not die out during the Pleistocene epoch but persisted at least to the time of the Aztecs in the more remote Mexican mountainlands? No reports of such a creature are known today, hence, even if it *had* survived to such a recent date, it is surely extinct now. I feel that it is less likely for Mexico's mountains to possess *two* mystery gracile carnivores than one in modern times, especially when they would most likely have competed with one another to some extent, having adapted to occupy much the same ecological niche. Nevertheless, it is certainly a thought-provoking coincidence that a creature fitting Castillo's description even more closely than the *onza* should have existed within this very country as late as the Pleistocene epoch.

As a final Aztec anomaly with possible pertinence to the *onza*, it should be noted that Castillo was not the only early Spanish visitor to describe a strange cat-like creature from Mexico. No less a personage than Christopher Columbus himself reported, in addition to pumas and jaguars, a third great cat – within his famous letter of 7 July 1503 to the King and Queen of Spain. In this he related:

> A cross-bowman slew a beast that resembled a large cat, but was much bigger and had a face like a man. He transfixed it with an arrow from the breast to the tail. Nevertheless it was so fierce that he had to cut off an arm and a leg. When a wild boar, which had been given to me as a present, caught sight of this beast its bristles stood on end and it fled with all speed ... Although the great cat was stricken to death and the arrow still transfixed its body, it immediately attacked the wild boar, encircled its mouth with its tail and squeezed it vigorously. With the one arm it had left, it throttled the wild boar's throat as one strangles a foe.[17]

The *onza* has a shorter face than the puma. Conversely, the seemingly prehensile tail of Columbus's beast is difficult to reconcile with an *onza* identity. Perhaps, as suggested by Herbert Wendt,[17] it is an unknown species of carnivore which has since become extinct. During the *conquistador* invasion of Mexico, the Aztecs' great libraries, containing numerous natural history tomes, were totally destroyed. The loss to cryptozoology of these irreplaceable sources of information may be beyond even the most grandiose of estimations.

Ruffed Cat

In any event, the *onza* may still share Mexico with one other mystery felid – though, to my knowledge, this second crypto-cat's existence is based solely upon a single account, by the late zoologist, cryptozoologist and writer Ivan T. Sanderson.[18] In this, no name was allocated to the creature. For reasons which will soon become clear, I shall refer to it here as 'the ruffed cat'.

During 1940, travelling alone through Mexico on a mammalogical collecting trip, Sanderson arrived at an unnamed mountain settlement in the state of Nayarit's Sierra mountains. These are totally separated from the neighbouring Sierra Madre Occidentale ranges and possess their own distinctive flora and fauna. At this settlement a few locals spoke Spanish, and Sanderson let it be known that he was seeking specimens of a particular form of squirrel. The locals promised to obtain some for him, and in the meantime they brought along a number of skins of other mammals, in the hope of selling these to him too.[18]

Amongst them was a large and very tough skin of a most

unusual cat. The skin measured just over 6 ft/180 cm from nose-tip to tail-base, with a further 1½ ft/45 cm for the relatively short tail. Of course, it is difficult to say how closely these measurements reflected the true length of the cat in life, as it would be virtually impossible to ascertain how much the skin had stretched or shrunk during drying. Intriguingly (in view of the *onza*), Sanderson recorded that, 'The legs appeared to have been rather long compared to, say, a house-cat or a puma.' The paws were still attached to the skin and were very large, well furred and splayed, most possessing the original claws, which were bright yellow in colour and very clearly retractile. The cat's face was short (again like the *onza*).[18]

The pelage itself was firm dorsally, soft ventrally and predominantly brown in colour. The head and shoulders lacked markings, but the flanks and upper limbs bore a series of wavy stripes in alternate light and dark shades of brown, whilst the lower limbs were very dark brown in colour, almost approaching black. The ridge of the spine running along its back was also dark brown, and (as far as Sanderson could recall) so too was the tail.[18] By far the most outstanding feature of the skin, however, was that the hairs sited just behind its shoulders appeared to grow forward to yield a large ruff encircling the neck and covering the ears from above and behind.[18]

Sanderson stated that he bought this skin and another, smaller pelt of this same cat form which was in poorer condition but with sharper stripes. Together with other mammal skins that he bought, these felid pelts (which apparently cost a lot more than any of the others) were sewn up in several layers of sacking and were finally stored in the government gaol of Belize, which Sanderson was using as a base. Tragically, however, during a subsequent trip, the gaol was lashed by a severe hurricane and, being at sea-level, was completely flooded out – the result being that everything not in bottles was totally ruined, including the skins.[18]

This is a most compelling but sadly rather intangible affair, as there is so little that can be followed up. The area itself is unnamed, the skins are lost and Ivan Sanderson, who travelled there alone, is no longer with us. The only hope is the possible existence still of the gaol – perhaps, if it does survive, records regarding the skins may too, which could add some details to the account left behind by Sanderson.

What could these cats have been? Lynxes have relatively long legs, large paws and thick fur around the neck region, which can look a little like a ruff, but no lynx possesses anything like the ruff described by Sanderson for the Mexican cat. Moreover, as a trained zoologist and a mammal collector, Sanderson would surely have compared it specifically with lynxes if it had appeared comparable with one. Instead, the detailed description which he gave does not fit that of any known felid.

The only sequel that I know of to this sorry saga is that Sanderson later saw another skin of this cat form on sale at a tourist store in the big market at Colima, at the south end of Nayarit's mountain block. Regrettably, however, the price which its owner was asking was far beyond that which Sanderson could afford.[18]

It would seem that the only way to follow up any aspect relating to the Mexican ruffed cat is to do what Sanderson suggested at the end of his article: '... pay a visit to the market in Colima. They may still have unknown cat skins for sale.'[18] They may indeed.

SOUTH AMERICA

During the late Cretaceous period (roughly 64 million years ago), South America became separated from North America, and it remained an island until the Pliocene epoch's close. During 62 million years of insularity, South America's mammalian fauna evolved along lines totally different from those of any other land masses, yielding many unique groups.[19]

At that time, no true felid existed there, but about 2 million years ago South America's independence ended when a land bridge formed, reconnecting it with North America. This enabled a great interchange of species to occur between the two continents, and amongst those mammals entering South America were the ancestors of all the true felids existing there today.[19] Of these, nine species are Small Cats, including their largest modern representative, the puma.[20]

Yet, without a doubt, the feline embodiment of South America's verdant vista is its single species of Big Cat, the jaguar *Panthera onca*. Owner of a magnificently marked pelage, the latter's elegance has tragically resulted in the jaguar being ruthlessly hunted into near or total extinction over much of its range. Formerly distributed throughout South America, it is nowadays confined largely to the Amazon basin, with a few highly endangered subspecies lingering principally in Ecuador, Peru, Bolivia and Argentina too.[21]

The lengthiest fully authenticated specimens on record are two which measured over 9 ft/270 cm in total length. At the other end of the scale, diminutive jaguars also exist, which in Honduras are referred to rather unflatteringly as 'rat-tigers'.[22] In comparison with the leopard, the jaguar occurs in a far smaller range of pelage varieties, but certain interesting forms are on record.

Paraguayan Ghost Jaguars

In many parts of South America, but especially Paraguay,[23] the natives fervently believe in the existence of pallid, ghost-like jaguars, occasionally glimpsed amidst the dense, shadowed jungle foliage. Needless to say, such tales were dismissed as myth and superstition by most Western travellers to those parts. However, the Spanish soldier and naturalist Don Félix de Azara described one jaguar skin shown him as being so pale in colour that the rosettes could be discerned only in certain lights[24] (a complete albino mutant?). Similarly, a greyish-white skin, bearing only faint markings on its flanks and belly, was revealed to J.R. Rengger, who was informed by the hunter concerned that its claws were white,[25] again suggesting a complete albino.

In contrast to these exceedingly rare (though clearly not mythical) white jaguars, melanistic individuals are rather more common. Referred to in Latin America as 'black tigers', they tend to be noticeably large, especially in the Mato Grosso.[21] According to various antiquarian zoology tomes and native Guyanan beliefs, however, a further type of black tiger would seem to exist within this continent, one which allegedly is very different morphologically from the typical melanistic jaguar. Nevertheless, its precise identity has never been satisfactorily ascertained.

Jaguarete

Nowadays a totally forgotten felid, this mysterious melanistic was referred to as the '*cougar noire*' by the eminent eighteenth-century naturalist de Buffon, and as the '*jaguarete*' (a less ambiguous name, which I therefore prefer and shall use hereafter in this book) by his equally eminent contemporary Thomas Pennant.[26] However, in the virtually verbatim version of Pennant's description which appeared in Thomas Bewick's *A General History of Quadrupeds*, S. Hodgson referred to it merely as 'the black tiger'.[27] Hodgson's choice of name would seem to imply that the *jaguarete* is truly nothing more than a straightforward melanistic jaguar. Yet neither the illustration which accompanied Pennant's description nor that (by Bewick) which accompanied Hodgson's is compatible with such an identity. To quote Pennant: 'Head, back, sides, fore part of the legs, and the tail, covered with short and very glossy hairs, of a dusky-color; sometimes spotted with black, but generally plain: upper lips white: at the corner of the mouth a black spot: long hairs above each eye, and long whiskers on the upper lip: lower lip, throat, belly, and the inside of the legs, whitish, or very pale ash-color: paws white: ears pointed. Grows to the size of a heifer of a year old: has vast strength in its limbs. Inhabits Brasil and Guiana [Guyana]: is a cruel and fierce beast; much dreaded by the Indians; but happily is a scarce species.'[26] In addition, Hodgson noted that it frequented the seashore and that it preyed upon a variety of creatures (including lizards, alligators and fishes) as well as devouring turtles' eggs and (rather curiously) the buds and leaves of the Indian fig.[27]

What could the *jaguarete* be? On first sight, a black jaguar identity seems most likely – in most specimens, the rosettes can indeed be seen as cryptic markings against the coat's abnormally dark colouration. However, the black jaguar is dark dorsally *and* ventrally, just like the black panther and other melanistic felid individuals, thereby contrasting markedly with the near-white underparts, lowers jaw and paws of the *jaguarete*. Of course, it may be that the *jaguarete* is nothing more than an inaccurate description of a black jaguar, but arguing against this is the statement in a footnote by Pennant that two *jaguaretes* were actually shown in London during the eighteenth century; hence their appearance would have been familiar to naturalists of that time. Another possibility exists – one which, though on first sight rather radical, is very compatible with the morphology of the *jaguarete*.

The mutant non-agouti allele is only one of two abnormal forms of the agouti gene. The second is a recessive form known as the black-and-tan mutant allele. In animals homozygous for this, the dorsal pelage is black, but the underparts are light or cream in colour (the nostrils and eyes and often the inside or back of the earlobes may also be outlined with pale fur).[28]

A jaguar homozygous for the black-and-tan mutant allele would correspond very closely indeed with the descriptions and depictions given by Pennant, Hodgson and Bewick of the *jaguarete*. An equally thought-provoking alternative to this is the possibility that the *jaguarete* may constitute a pseudo-melanistic form of jaguar, equivalent to the Asian and African pseudo-melanistic leopards described earlier. Again, these had very dark upperparts and much paler underparts.

So far, no pseudo-melanistic jaguar or jaguar specimen identified conclusively as a black-and-tan mutant has been revealed to science (at the same time, the jaguar has received far less scientific attention than the leopard). However, the presence of the *jaguarete* within the zoology tomes of two centuries ago suggests that one or other of these mutants may indeed be produced by the jaguar.

Warracaba Jaguars

The warracaba (or waracabra) tiger, as it is known to the Guyanan natives, differs from the typical jaguar in an extremely significant way with respect to behaviour: whereas the recognized jaguar (whether spotted or black) is a solitary hunter, the seldom-sighted warracaba tiger of Guyana allegedly hunts in packs, which in turn may contain dozens of individuals. Needless to say, any felid which hunted in this manner would be a very special kind of cat indeed.

Not surprisingly, therefore, the warracaba tiger has attracted considerable interest from travellers to Guyana. In an *Animal Kingdom* article,[29] William Bridges incorporated an impressive series of reports concerning this animal, dating back to the end of the last century, including the following selection.

In his book *Twenty-Five Years in British Guiana*, published in 1898, Henry Kirke noted: 'There is a mysterious beast in the forest called by the native Indians the "waracabra tiger." All travellers in the forests of Guiana speak of this dreaded animal, but strange to say, none of them appear to have seen it. The Indians profess the greatest terror of it. It is said to hunt in packs (which tigers never do), and when its howls awake the echoes of the forest, the Indians at once take to their canoes and wood skins as the only safe refuge from its ravages.'[30] Indeed, this was precisely the action taken by Indian attendants of C. Barrington Brown upon hearing (though not seeing) the approach of one such pack in an incident occurring at the edge of Guyana's Curiebrong River in the mid-1800s. On this occasion, a single boat was used as the means of escape, which Brown boarded too. Enquiring the nature of these evidently much-feared felids, Brown was informed by the Indians that, '... they were small but exceedingly ferocious tigers; that they hunted in packs, and were not frightened by camp fires or anything except the barking of dogs'.[31] Upon crossing the river, '... a shrill scream rent the air from the opposite side of the river, not two hundred yards above our camp, and waking up echoes in the forest, died away as suddenly as it rose. This was answered by another cry, coming from the depths of the forest, the intervals being filled up by low growls and trumpeting sounds, which smote most disagreeably on the ear. Gradually the cries became fainter and fainter, as the band retired from our vicinity, till they utterly died away.'[31] Brown remarked that these beasts' cry resembled that of the waracabra bird (better known as the grey-winged trumpeter *Psophia crepitans*, a predominantly glossy black relative of the cranes, coots and bustards), hence the name 'waracabra tiger'. These latter animals are called *y'agamisheri* by the Accawoio Indians, who state that they vary in both size and colour and that as many as a hundred individuals can comprise a single pack. Little wonder that Brown's Indian companions were so desperate to depart. The prospect of meeting up with a hundred or so jaguars all at once would surely daunt even the most courageous of human hunters!

In *Among the Indians of Guiana*,[32] published in 1883, Everard im Thurn alleged that he had actually encountered three warracaba tiger eyewitnesses but admitted that it was clear that the tale related by one of them was much exaggerated. Im Thurn also offered his own suggestion, that reports of these fabled felids had taken their roots from the fact that puma families occasionally travel together.[32]

During the early part of the twentieth century, Lee S. Crandall spent time working in Guyana and encountered many reports of the warracaba tiger. Once again, however, he never met an Indian who affirmed unequivocally that he had not merely heard but had also actually seen any of these mysterious creatures.[29]

This latter aspect is a frequent but notably perplexing component of warracaba tiger reports – the creatures are heard but never seen.

Consequently, as a solution to the mystery of the warracaba tiger and especially to this strange facet of the latter, Crandall proposed the following elegant explanation: that this beast was not a special form of jaguar at all; instead, it was simply some animal species which hunted in packs at night, yet which emitted such terrifying sounds whilst doing so that no Indian had ever been brave enough to investigate the identity of these sounds' originators – as a result of which the Indians had never realized that this aurally abhorrent animal was in fact already known to them by sight during the daytime. Crandall even named the species which he felt was responsible – an animal which is neither jaguar nor, in fact, any form of felid but is one of South America's most unusual species of wild dog, the bush-dog *Speothos* (formerly *Icticyon*) *venaticus*,[29] a very curious, little-known canid not closely related to other species. Measuring no more than 3 ft/90 cm in total length and a mere 1 ft/30 cm in shoulder height, in colour it is dark reddish-brown dorsally and virtually black ventrally (rather rare amongst non-melanistic mammals). The bush-dog's distribution extends from Panama and Colombia to Brazil, Guyana, Paraguay, Peru and northern Bolivia.[33] According to certain reports, it does hunt in packs[34] (indeed, it may spend its entire life in packs[35]), but in general behaviour is exceedingly secretive.[33]

Worth noting is the impression by botanist Dr Nicholas Guppy (who has spent much time in Guyana) that, whilst the older Indians still believe that packs of warracaba tigers exist in the more remote mountainous regions, the younger Indians seem more disposed to believing the Western identification of these as bush-dogs.[29]

And certainly, as far as its distribution, hunting behaviour and general elusiveness are concerned, the bush-dog does compare favourably with the legendary warracaba tiger (and, as the latter is not normally *seen*, morphological comparisons are superfluous). On the other hand, the famous hideous scream of the warracaba tiger contrasts sharply with the relatively feeble whine emitted by bush-dogs.[33] Also, it is rather difficult to believe that the Guyanan Indians, frightened or not, could really confuse – visually and/or aurally, singly and/or in packs – a bush-dog with any form of jaguar. The mystery of the warracaba tiger may not be solved after all.

Mitla – A Dog-like Cat or a Cat-like Dog?

The bush-dog has also been proposed as the identity of another mystery 'felid'. This latter crypto-cat is known as the *mitla* and was briefly referred to by the famous lost explorer Colonel Percy Fawcett in his book *Exploration Fawcett*. While describing various strange animals of the Madidi, Bolivia, he noted: 'In the forests were various beasts still unfamiliar to zoologists, such as the mitla, which I have seen twice, a black doglike cat about the size of a foxhound.'[36]

In *Searching For Hidden Animals*, Dr Roy Mackal suggested that the *mitla* could be the bush-dog,[37] which, as seen from the above description of this animal, is certainly a plausible possibility. In addition, I would nominate a further candidate, one which I have not seen put forward before in this capacity but which is eminently suitable for the role. The species to which I am alluding is a canid even more unusual than the bush-dog, the small-eared dog *Atelocynus microtis*.

This is a very aberrant but sparingly studied species known almost exclusively from various zoo specimens. Even its distribution range is undetermined. It has been recorded with certainty from Brazil, Peru, Ecuador, Colombia, Chile and possibly Venezuela. Its head-and-body length ranges from just over 2 ft/60 cm to 3 ft/90 cm, plus a further 1 ft/30 cm of tail, and it stands 1–1¼ ft/30–38 cm at the shoulder. Its pelage is black or dark brown dorsally, shading ventrally to a dull reddish-brown. But its most distinctive feature – and that most significant relative to the *mitla* – is its gait, for the small-eared dog moves with a strikingly feline grace and lightness, totally unlike the less agile movements of other canids.[33]

As it has been recorded from various of Bolivia's neighbouring countries, it is quite likely that, in the event of a formal research programme on the small-eared dog in the wild state being instigated, it will find that this species exists here too. Certainly its distinctively cat-like movements, in combination with its dark colour and overall size, constitute a notable correspondence with the mysterious *mitla*. Perhaps Colonel Fawcett's dog-like cat will ultimately prove to be a cat-like dog.

At the same time, the history of the *onza* suggests another solution. Perhaps, by referring to the *mitla* as 'dog-like', he meant that it had long legs (remember the 'wolf-cat' controversy concerning the *onza*?). If so, could the *mitla* be in any way related to the *onza*? The tantalizing fact is that *onzas* have been reported not only from Mexico but also from South America.[12] Perhaps Fawcett saw a dark-colour morph of the *onza*. But only future explorations of Bolivia's remote jungles (no easy matter even today) can provide the solution.

Siemel's Mystery Cat

During the earlier part of this century, the renowned hunter Sacha Siemel shot a very odd-looking cat in the Mato Grosso, whose identity has never been formally established. It was a heavily built animal in appearance, with a fawn pelage that bore brown spots and also a dark stripe along the spine.[38] What could it have been? Certainly no mere morph of some already known species – unlike, for example, rare red-striped ocelots on record[39] (which probably represent non-extension mutants of the normal ocelot[28]).

The most plausible suggestion is Siemel's own opinion, recorded by Richard Perry in *The World of the Jaguar*,[38] that it was a puma × jaguar hybrid. If so, this would be of very great zoological significance. Almost all mammalian hybrids (including the leopons and ligers noted earlier) are interspecific. However, if Siemel was correct, his felid would be an intergeneric hybrid (the puma belonging to the genus *Felis*, the jaguar to the genus *Panthera*). Moreover, virtually all intergeneric specimens have been bred in captivity as opposed to being wild-born.

Successful hybridization between pumas and jaguars in captivity has been alleged;[40] otherwise the only known intergeneric felid hybrids are certain puma × leopard crossbreeds – again bred in captivity. One specimen of this latter type was purchased in 1898 by Berlin Zoo from Carl Hagenbeck, and resembled a little grey puma but bore large brown rosettes;[41] and a similar animal has also been recorded by Dr Helmut Hemmer.[40] Judging from these, one would expect a puma × jaguar hybrid to bear spots on a puma-coloured background – which is precisely the appearance of Siemel's cat. Tragically his specimen has not been preserved, and the chances of a second puma × jaguar hybrid of wild-born origin being obtained are slim indeed; as noted by Perry,[38] the fact that two large felids co-exist within South America suggests that they do not compete directly (and hence do not come into contact to any extent with one another). Consequently a mating between these would be extremely rare.

Surviving Sabre-Tooths?

While it has been suggested that the New World lion *Panthera leo atrox* may still survive in parts of North America, its seemingly less intelligent sabre-tooth contemporary *Smilodon fatalis* is most assuredly extinct there. The principal reason for its demise is generally believed to be the disappearance of important prey species. If, however, as indicated by the discovery of sculptured *Smilodon* bones at Rancho La Brea,[42] this mighty felid was contemporary with man, human persecution may also have contributed to its extinction.

Certainly, overkill by man has been implicated as a prime reason for the relatively rapid disappearance of a number of large mammals in the New World.[43] Inoffensive and sluggish giant herbivores such as the South American ground sloths and armadillo-like glyptodonts would undoubtedly have been easy prey. Conversely, even the least intelligent carnivores, by virtue of their inherent powers of concealment and stealth (assisted enormously by this continent's dense rain forests), would have represented a far more difficult target. Moreover, South America possessed (and still possesses) considerably more species of ungulate and other herbivores than North America, yielding a plentiful and diverse source of prey for compatibly sized carnivores.

During the Pleistocene epoch, *Smilodon fatalis* existed not just in North America but also in Peru. In addition, an even larger species, *Smilodon populator* (sometimes wrongly termed *Smilodon neogaeus* – a *nomen nudum*) inhabited Brazil and Argentina.[16,44] Is it possible that amidst some of the more remote and inaccessible regions of this still little-known continent a last remnant of sabre-toothed cats still survives, avoiding the native Indians and remaining unknown to Western science? A few tantalizing reports exist which suggest that this exciting if startling suggestion may indeed be possible. Take the following examples.

In a paper concerning the stone cells of Chiriqui published in 1863, C.C. Blake documented this pertinent snippet of information: 'At Timana, in New Granada, sculptured stones have been figured by Mr Bollaert, representing a feline animal, the proportions of whose teeth slightly exceeded those of existing cats, and might possibly indicate a modified descendant of the extinct Machairodus [*Smilodon*] neogaeus of Brazil.'[45] Of course, the sculptures may be idealized, rather than literal, representations of the animal which served as their subject. At the same time, various ancient artistic works are known that depict animals discovered only relatively recently by modern science – the gerenuk, okapi, Grevy's zebra and Roxellana's snow monkey, for example.[46] Indeed, it is not unreasonable to suppose that clues to the existence of animals currently unknown to science still await discovery within further examples of ancient art ensconced within the world's myriad museums and art galleries.[47] So the stones of Timana should not be dismissed out of hand, especially as they are not the only pieces of evidence in favour of modern sabre-tooth survival in South America.

In his book *The Cloud Forest*,[48] Peter Mathiessen noted that, whilst he was in Paraguay, a wandering seaman named Picquet described to him 'a rare striped cat not quite so large as a jaguar and very timid, which is possessed of two very large protruding teeth'.[48] Picquet stated that this felid inhabited the mountain jungles of Colombia and Ecuador, and affirmed that he himself had spied it once. A most intriguing report – which stimulated Mathiessen to speculate whether: '... the sabre-toothed tiger, like the cougar, had long ago established itself here in a smaller subspecies and had thus survived the Ice Age extinction of its North American ancestor'.[48]

Many of today's carnivores, e.g. lion, cheetah, tiger, jaguar, brown bear and spotted hyaena, are smaller than their Pleistocene counterparts. There is no reason why the *Smilodon* line could not have undergone a comparable diminution of form. Indeed, a smaller body size coupled with a notably shy disposition would confer a great advantage upon any creature whose principal enemy was man, by facilitating concealment. Moreover, with the extinction of South America's herbivorous megafauna, a smaller felid requiring less food would be selected in preference to bigger forms (such as *S. populator* – larger than even the biggest of modern lions).

In an article published in *The Field* in 1942, Patrick Chalmers alluded very briefly to a cave painting discovered in South America which supposedly depicts a sabre-tooth attacking an odd-looking animal which palaeontologists consider to be a representative of the genus *Macrauchenia* (basically camel-like in form, though possibly possessing a short nasal trunk, and belonging to the extinct order of litoptern ungulates).[49] This painting was also referred to in Bruce Chatwin's book *In Patagonia* – he had been informed by the Patagonian polymath priest Father Palacios that it was approximately 10,000 years old and was located at Lago Posadas in Patagonia.[50] Most archaeologists believe that man entered the New World sometime between 30,000 and 15,000 years ago (with the latter date being most applicable to South America).[51] Consequently, if this painting depicts a genuine sabre-tooth and macraucheniid, we must assume that both of these species were still living *after* the close of the Pleistocene epoch (rather than having died out some time before, as palaeontologists currently think), in turn making the prospect of modern survival rather less implausible.

The most extraordinary report known to me that concerns an alleged surviving sabre-tooth in South America is one which was kindly brought to my attention by mystery cat investigator Phil Bennett. According to one of his own correspondents, a large felid weighing 160 lb/72.6 kg was shot in Paraguay sometime during 1975 and was referred to locally as a 'mutant jaguar'. However, a zoologist by the name of Juan Acavar is alleged to have examined its corpse, discovered that it possessed fangs measuring 12 in/30 cm in length and suggested that it could actually be a *Smilodon*. Nonetheless, to avoid disturbing the local people, the authorities apparently decided to stay with the mutant jaguar identity. If this remarkable account is valid, it would obviously rank as one of the greatest zoological discoveries of this century, but sadly all my attempts to trace Juan Acavar, the whereabouts of the specimen itself and any corroborating information to ascertain whether this incident really did happen in the first place have so far met with failure. Similarly, neither Phil Bennett nor his correspondent has succeeded in obtaining further details. Consequently, I clearly cannot vouch either for its authenticity or (assuming that it *is* authentic) its accuracy. Indeed, one readily apparent distortion in this account must surely be the fang (upper canine) measurement given. The longest upper canines so far recorded from any known felid type are from *Barbourofelis fricki*, a Nebraskan hoplophoneid (see p. 23) of the Pliocene epoch – yet even those formidable fangs attained a length of only approximately 8 in/20 cm.[52]

Nevertheless, in view of its tremendous significance if this incident *did* occur, it seemed wisest to include it here. Also, by bringing it to public attention, it is possible that the full facts (if any) will ultimately be uncovered. In any event, the other items documented above still remain to suggest the modern existence of a South American sabre-tooth. But what *type* of sabre-tooth?

Until now, *Smilodon* has received all the attention in this discussion. However, South America was once also home to a second, and completely different, sabre-tooth – a marsupial form.

Marsupials inevitably conjure up images of Australia, their present-day stronghold. Nevertheless, South America also houses a number of relatively small species: the opossums, rat-opossums or caenolestids and shrew-like microbiotheriid Back in the Miocene and Pliocene epochs, however, its marsupial assemblage was much more diverse and dramatic, as it included the wolf-like carnivorous borhyaenids. The most spectacular and specialized of these was *Thylacosmilus atrox*, for this formidable creature was a bona fide marsupial sabre-tooth. Occupying the same ecological niche here as that taken by the true sabre-tooths in North America, *Thylacosmilus* had evolved by convergence into a morphological duplicate. In total size it was comparable with a jaguar and possessed sturdy limbs but a relatively short tail. Its most striking feature, however, was its pair of upper canines, for, quite incredibly, these fangs were actually longer than those of *Smilodon*. Indeed, comparable with that of *Barbourofelis*, the lower jaw of *Thylacosmilus* was even equipped with a sizeable pair of flanges to serve as scabbards for these truly awesome teeth. By the end of the Miocene epoch, most of the borhyaenids and their smaller relatives had died out, but *Thylacosmilus* persisted through most of the Pliocene epoch before apparently following them into extinction.[53]

Dr Bernard Heuvelmans, however, has suggested that Mathiessen's mystery cat could actually be a modern relative of *Thylacosmilus*.[54]

The mountains of Colombia and Ecuador are inaccessible, little-explored regions which in effect constitute, by their discrete isolation from the surrounding lands beneath, islands undisturbed and unchanged for millions of years. If a marsupial carnivore could linger anywhere in South America up to the present day (avoiding competition with the more successful true felids that entered this continent from North America at the end of the Pliocene epoch onwards), these mountainlands must comprise some of the likeliest localities to sustain such survival. Naturally, however, the possibility that *Thylacosmilus* has persisted from the Pliocene epoch is much more remote than the possibility of *Smilodon*'s persisting from the Pleistocene. At the same time, there is no doubt that, whilst the discovery of a living *Smilodon* species would be a major zoological event, the finding of a modern *Thylacosmilus* would be nothing short of a scientific sensation. Let us hope that this most exciting enigma can be brought to a climactic conclusion in the near future, especially in view of the apparent rarity of the striped form from Colombia and Ecuador, so that this can then receive formal protection with all speed if it is truly a new species.

Water Tigers

In *On the Track of Unknown Animals*, Dr Heuvelmans painstakingly demonstrated the totally separate nature of two South American mystery beasts hitherto lumped together as a result of confusion and contradiction propagated by a number of scientific authorities at the end of the last century. One of the mystery beasts concerned – a cow-sized but harmless herbivorous animal known to the Tehuelche Indians and others of Patagonia as the *ellengassen* – could be a surviving ground sloth.[37,46,54]

The Iemisch – Aquatic Cat or Giant Otter?

The other unknown animal is very different – a puma-sized amphibious carnivore known to the Tehuelche as the *iemisch*, translated as 'water tiger' (and thereby corresponding to its modern Spanish name, *tigre de agua*).

Judging from the descriptions given by native Indians and also by Western observers of the *iemisch*, morphologically it compares most closely with a giant-sized otter. Moreover, such an identity has been put forward for it both by Dr Heuvelmans and by Dr Roy Mackal, who consider that it may even exceed in size the world's largest known otter species, the saro *Pteronura brasiliensis*. Measuring 5 ft/150 cm in head-and-body length, plus a further 3 ft/90 cm of tail, this magnificent animal is itself puma-sized but sadly appears to be extremely rare (confined to areas of Brazil, Guyana, Uruguay, Venezuela and northern Argentina.)[37,46]

There is one thorny problem to be faced when attempting to assign an ultra-large otter identity to the *iemisch*, namely the latter beast's notorious ferocity, which inspires terror in its human neighbours. While I agree that on morphological grounds the existence of a truly gigantic otter in parts of South America could solve the mystery of the *iemisch*, I find it very difficult to believe that any otter, regardless of its size, could engender such horror. An amphibious felid perhaps, but surely not an otter?

Yaquaru – The Real *Water Tiger?*

Other workers have similar doubts; after all, even the enormous saro is a notably shy creature. Consequently, Dr Heuvelmans and Dr Robert Lehmann-Nitsche have considered that such stories have arisen through confusion between the otter and traditional tales and memories of the jaguar (now extinct in Patagonia but formerly present there and known to the Araucan Indians as *nahuel*).[46,55] Heuvelmans cited the following accounts in support of this.[46]

The German Jesuit Martin Dobrizhoffer, in his history of a race of people known as the Abipones (inhabiting Argentina's extreme north), published in 1783, mentioned the *yaguaro*: 'In the deepest waters there usually hides an animal larger than any hunting-dog, called *tigre de agua* by the Spaniards and *yaguaro* by the Guaranis. It has a woolly hide, a long and tapering tail, and powerful claws.

Horses and mules swimming across these rivers are dragged to the bottom. Soon afterwards one sees the intestines of the animal, disembowelled by the tiger, floating on the surface.'[56]

In his book *A Description of Patagonia, and the Adjoining Parts of South America*, published in 1774, fellow Jesuit Thomas Falkner mentioned a brief personal sighting of a water tiger leaping into the River Parana. Though he provided no morphological details of this, he did supply a detailed water-tiger description given to him by the local Indians, to whom this is a familiar beast:

> It is called yaquaru, or yaquaruigh, which (in the language of that country) signifies, the water tiger. It is described by the Indians to be as big as an ass; of the figure the size of a large, over-grown river-wolf or otter; with sharp talons, and strong tusks; thick and short legs; long, shaggy hair; with a long, tapering tail. The Spaniards describe it somewhat differently; as having a long head, a sharp nose, like that of a wolf, and stiff, erect ears.... It is very destructive to the cattle which pass the Parana; for great herds of them pass every year; and it generally happens that this beast seizes some of them. When it has once laid hold of its prey, it is seen no more; and the lungs and entrails soon appear floating upon the water. It lives in the greatest depths, especially in the whirlpools made by the concurrence of two streams, and sleeps in the deep caverns that are in the banks.[57]

Heuvelmans noted that the large size, aquatic predilection, propensity for hauling horses and mules beneath the water, and fearsome claws of the above beast are all compatible with the jaguar.[46] True enough. However, there are various profound difficulties to be overcome in order to identify it categorically with the jaguar.

One concerns the water tiger's alleged inhabitation of the lower depths and whirlpools of rivers. The jaguar is a good swimmer and pursues its prey into rivers without hesitation. Nevertheless, it is not sufficiently adapted for an amphibious existence to be able to dwell in the underwater locales noted above for the water tiger. Equally, even allowing for the considerable flexibility and distortion associated with orally preserved legends, it is still rather hard to believe that in local myths the primarily terrestrial jaguar could be converted into a fully fledged aquatic carnivore. Additionally, if the jaguar *is* involved in the water tiger history, it is very surprising that no mention is made of its most striking rosetted coat. Instead, the feature concerning the water tiger's pelage which *is* mentioned is its long, shaggy hair – which is definitely not a jaguar characteristic. Similarly, although the jaguar does indeed possess rather formidable canine teeth, it would be a gross exaggeration to describe them as being in any way tusk-like.

In short, the *yaquaru* does not correspond very closely at all with the jaguar. Moreover, not only do the hirsute coat and prominent teeth of the *yaquaru* distinguish it from the jaguar, they also clearly separate it from any form of otter. In his book *In Patagonia*, Bruce Chatwin listed five different Patagonian mystery beasts and categorized the *yaquaru* (or *yaquaro*) as a creature separate from the *iemisch* (or *jemische*).[50] While discussing the *yaquaru*, he also referred to a section in George Chaworth Muster's memoir *At Home With the Patagonians* that mentioned the refusal by Muster's Tehuelche guide to cross the River Senguer for fear of encountering 'yellow quadrupeds larger than a puma'.[58]

So what can the *yaquaru* be, and how does it fit in with the already much-muddled mystery of the water tiger? Judging from the evident dissimilarity of the *yaquaru* relative to both the *iemisch* and the jaguar, it would appear that an amalgamation of creatures has occurred, but one which has not previously been recognized as such. Rather than the *iemisch* (surely some form of giant otter) having been combined and confused directly with the jaguar (as proposed by Heuvelmans and Lehmann-Nitsche), I suggest that an intermediate link between these two animals is present – which has hitherto remained unidentified yet which is the true water tiger. The identity of this middle-man is that mysterious mammal referred to as the *yaquaru*. From the above-documented descriptions, this can be seen to be a large and voracious carnivorous mammal that possesses a shaggy but non-patterned pelage, plus very large, tusk-like teeth (probably canines), and which, though less adapted for an aquatic life than the saro (unlike the latter it can move well on land), is far more so than the jaguar and hence can exist even in turbulent and deep stretches of water.

In short, a South American equivalent of the amphibious sabre-tooth cats of Africa – yet another example of evolutionary convergence of form resulting from two different species occupying the same ecological niche on their respective continents, the Old World Pleistocene sabre-tooths (e.g. *Megantereon*) in Africa, and the New World Pleistocene sabre-tooths (e.g. *Smilodon*) in South America. One South American sabre-tooth line may have remained terrestrial (explaining the Timana sculptured stones etc), while another became secondarily aquatic, yielding the *yaquaru*. The ferocity of the *yaquaru* has been assimilated into reports of its fellow aquatic carnivore the *iemisch*, whilst, by being a sizeable aquatic cat, the *yaquaru* has infiltrated the Indians' ancient memories of the now-extinct Patagonian jaguar, thereby even acquiring a similar name, despite its very different morphology and habitat. Suddenly the tangled tale is tangled no longer – three totally separate mammalian forms are at last well and truly separated.

Further support for the possibility of an aquatic sabre-tooth existing within modern South America is a letter written by a Guyanan missionary to his superiors in France during the eighteenth century, for in this he mentioned a mysterious animal called the *aypa*.[59] Most excitingly, this latter beast was described as being an aquatic creature whose head and neck greatly resembled those of a tiger in shape, size and fur but possessed jaws containing exceedingly large teeth.[59] Its body, anomalously, was allegedly covered in scales – but, as Heuvelmans has suggested in relation to the African *dingonek*, this may well be an optical illusion (see Chapter 4).

Maipolina – Mystery Marauder of Maripasoula

To bring this history of the water tiger to a close, one final South American mystery beast requires inclusion here – the Guyanan *maipolina*.

On 21 October 1962 a boy fell into the Maroni River, at Maripasoula. When his dead body was ultimately brought to the surface by local inhabitants and police, they immediately perceived that it had been partially devoured by some animal, and a doctor called to examine it confirmed this in his detailed report for the death certificate. The locals were adamant that the *popoké* was responsible – a most mysterious creature also referred to as 'the water-mother' (by the Creoles) and 'the *maipolina*' (by the Indians), and very greatly feared by everyone in the area. It is said to inhabit caves and hollows in the river bank and lies in wait for its prey within whirlpools and beneath the water surface. It will attack adult humans and even their boats, and at the time of the boy's death was held responsible for six other violent deaths within a few years, in the region of Maripasoula, Benzdorp and Wacapeu.[59,60]

Few people claim to have actually seen the *maipolina*, but Colonel René-Antoine Ricatte was able to interview one of these rare eyewitnesses, the Indian Amaipeti, son of Touanké, the Big Chief of the Roucouyennes. Amaipeti saw the animal one evening, about 500 m/550 yards from Touanké's village (roughly 30 km/18½ miles upstream of Maripasoula). It was lying on a rock and was estimated by Amaipeti to measure 3 m/9¾ ft in length, and 1 m/3¼ ft in width. Its feet were clawed – resembling the formidably taloned hind paws of the three-toed ant-eater *Tamandua tridactyla*, according to Amaipeti. Its ears were drooping, and he described its eyes as resembling those of a tapir (large, round, dark brown). The creature's fur was short; the chest was whitish, and a stripe of a similar colour approximately 10–15 cm/4–6 in wide ran down from the head along the animal's back, while the remainder of its pelage was fawn in colour. Its tail appeared to resemble that of a cow. Most significant of all, however, were its teeth, for, according to the description Amaipeti gave to Colonel Ricatte, they were comparable with those of a walrus.[59]

This last-mentioned feature is immediately indicative of a sabre-tooth. Its tail is also intriguing: if it resembled a cow's, we must assume that it was long and terminated in a tuft of hair, comparable, in fact, with a lion's tail. It certainly does not sound like that of any otter – hence an alliance with the *iemisch* would seem to be ruled out on this score as well as on that of its extraordinary dentition and drooping ears. A pelage paler ventrally than dorsally (countershading) is common in aquatic animals, assisting them to remain unseen from both above and below when submerged, hence this colour combination would be expected in an aquatic sabre-tooth. But if the *maipolina* is indeed such a felid, how can its short fur be reconciled with the woolly pelage of the *yaquaru*? Perhaps they comprise separate species, a long-haired form in Patagonia and a short-haired version in Guyana. Alternatively, they may constitute a single species, but one which is sexually dimorphic (i.e. the male and female differ notably from one another morphologically, as with the lion and lioness). Thus the *yaquaru* could be the male sabre-tooth, hirsute like the lion, while the *maipolina* is the female, like the lioness lacking this hairiness.

Of course, all of this is speculation at the present time – at least until a good photograph, if not an actual specimen, can be obtained for unequivocal identification. Nonetheless, there is good reason for believing that some form of aquatic sabre-tooth may well exist in various regions of South America, apparently alongside a truly enormous otter and a ground sloth of bovine build. Any zoologist willing to devote the time (and finance) in search of such creatures may well obtain a herculanean haul of major discoveries (not to mention a sliver of scientific immortality) for his labours.

A Last Mystery

In 1972 *Pursuit* reported that a person from El Salvador had alleged a few years earlier that he occasionally hunted Bengal tigers (*tigres Bengalis*) across the border in Honduras, explaining that they were descendants of tigers which had escaped some years earlier from a circus and had since multiplied.[61]

Now, I realize that, in *The Lost World*, Sir Arthur Conan

Doyle's ferocious if fictitious explorer Professor Challenger said of future zoological discoveries to be made in tropical America that 'Nothin' would surprise', but what would he have made of Bengal tigers?

1 Greenwell, J.R., *BBC Wildlife*, Vol. 6, pp. 354–9 (July 1987)
2 Greenwell, J.R. (ed.), *ISC Newsletter*, Vol. 5, pp. 1–6 (spring 1986)
3 Marshall, R., *The Onza* (Exposition Press, New York, 1961)
4 Greenwell, J.R. (ed.), *ISC Newsletter*, Vol. 4, pp. 6–7 (winter 1985)
5 Clark, J., and Coleman, L., *Creatures of the Outer Edge*. (Warner Books, New York, 1978)
6 Orr, P.C., *Bulletin of the Santa Barbara Museum of Natural History, Department of Geology*, Vol. 2, pp. 1–8 (1969)
7 Savage, D.E., *University of California Publications in Geological Science*, Vol. 36, pp. 317–44 (1960)
8 Martin, L.D., Gilbert, B.M., and Adams, D.B., *Science*, Vol. 195, pp. 981–2 (11 March 1977)
9 Adams, D.B., ibid., Vol. 205, pp. 1,155–8 (14 September 1979)
10 Hemmer, H., Paper presented at the Third International Congress of Systematic and Evolutionary Biology, University of Sussex, 7 July 1985
11 Bailey, M., *The Observer* (London), 16 November 1987; *Oryx*, Vol. 21, p. 56 (January 1987)
12 Greenwell, J.R., and Best, T., Paper presented at the ISC Annual Members Meeting, Royal Museum of Scotland, 26 July 1987
13 Colarusso, J., *ISC Newsletter*, Vol. 6, p. 10 (autumn 1987)
14 Molnar, R., Personal communications (1986–7)
15 Shuker, K.P.N., *ISC Newsletter*, Vol. 5, p. 11 (winter 1986)
16 Kurten, B., and Anderson, E., *Pleistocene Mammals of North America* (Columbia University Press, New York, 1980)
17 Wendt, H., *Out of Noah's Ark* (Weidenfeld & Nicolson, 1959)
18 Sanderson, I.T., *Pursuit*, Vol. 6, pp. 35-6 (April 1973)
19 Colbert, E.H., *Wandering Lands and Animals* (Hutchinson, 1973); Simpson, G.G., *Splendid Isolation. The Curious History of South American Mammals* (Yale University Press, 1980)
20 Corbet, G.B., and Hill, J.E., *A World List of Mammalian Species*, second edition (Brit. Mus. Nat. Hist., 1986)
21 Guggisberg, C.A.W., *Wild Cats of the World* (David & Charles, 1975)
22 Turnbull-Kemp, P., *The Leopard* (Bailey Bros & Swinfen, 1967)
23 Rabinowitz, A., *Jaguar* (Collins 1987)
24 de Azara, F., *Apuntamientos para la Historia Natural de los Quadrúpedos de Paragüay y Rio de la Plata*, 2 volumes (Madrid, 1802)
25 Rengger, J.R., *Naturgeschichte der Säugethiere von Paraguay* (Basle, 1830)
26 Pennant, T., *Pennant's History of Quadrupeds*, Vol. 1 (B. White, 1781)
27 Bewick, T., and Hodgson, S., *A General History of Quadrupeds* (E. Walker, 1807)
28 Robinson, R., *Genetica*, Vol. 46, pp. 1–31 (1976)
29 Bridges, W., *Animal Kingdom*, Vol. 57, pp. 25–8 (1957)
30 Kirke, H., *Twenty-Five Years in British Guiana* (Sampson Low, 1898)
31 Brown, C.B., *Canoe and Camp Life in British Guiana* (Edward Stanford, 1876)
32 im Thurn, E., *Among the Indians of Guiana* (Kegan Paul, 1883)
33 Bueler, L.E., *Wild Dogs of the World* (Constable, 1973)
34 Walker, E.P., *Mammals of the World*, third edition (John Hopkins Press, Baltimore, 1975)

35 Kleinman, D.G., *Journal of Mammalogy*, Vol. 53, pp. 791–806 (1972)
36 Fawcett, P.H., *Exploration Fawcett* (Hutchinson, 1953)
37 Mackal, R.P., *Searching For Hidden Animals* (Doubleday, Garden City 1980)
38 Perry, R., *The World of the Jaguar* (Taplinger, 1970)
39 Poland, H., *Fur-Bearing Animals in Nature and Commerce* (Gurney & Jackson, 1892)
40 Hemmer, H., *Veröffentlichungen der Zoologischen StaatsSammlung*, Vol. 11, pp. 1–121 (1966)
41 Haltenorth, T., *Zeitschrift für Säugetierkunde*, Vol. 11, pp. 349–52 (1936); Scherren, H., *The Field*, Vol. 111, p. 711 (25 April 1908)
42 Miller, G.J., *Los Angeles County Museum Contributions to Science*, Vol. 163, pp. 1–8 (1969)
43 Martin, P.S., and Klein, R.G. (eds.), *Quaternary Extinctions: A Prehistoric Revolution* (University of Arizona Press, Tucson, 1984)
44 Couto, C. de P., *Boletin Conselho Nacional de Pesquisas*, No. 1, pp. 1–30 (1955)
45 Blake, C.C., *Transactions of the Ethnological Society*, Vol. 2, pp. 166–70 (1863)
46 Heuvelmans, B., *On the Track of Unknown Animals* (Rupert Hart-Davis, 1958)
47 Janis, C., *Cryptozoology*, Vol. 6, pp. 8–23 (1987)
48 Matthiessen, P., *The Cloud Forest* (Pyramid Books, New York, 1966)
49 Chalmers, P., *The Field*, Vol. 180, p. 228 (29 August 1942)
50 Chatwin, B., *In Patagonia* (Jonathan Cape, 1977)
51 Martin, P.S., *Science*, Vol. 179, pp. 969–74 (9 March 1973); Gowlett, J., *Ascent to Civilization* (Collins, 1984)
52 Schultz, C.B., Schultz, M.P., and Martin, C.D., *Bulletin of the University of Nebraska State Museum*, Vol. 9, pp. 1–31 (1970)
53 Riggs, E.S., *Transactions of the American Philosophical Society*, Vol. 24, pp. 1–32 (1934); Kurten, B., *The Age of Mammals* (Weidenfeld & Nicolson, 1971)
54 Heuvelmans, B., *Cryptozoology*, Vol. 5, pp. 1–26 (1986)
55 Lehmann-Nitsche, R., *Zur Vorgeschichte der Entdeckung vom Grypotherium bei Ultima Esperanza*, cited in Heuvelmans, B., *On the Track of Unknown Animals*, op. cit.
56 Dobrizhoffer, M., *An account of the Abipones, an Equestrian People of Paraguay*, 3 volumes (London, 1822)
57 Falkner, T., *A Description of Patagonia, and the Adjoining Parts of South America* (1774; facsimile edition published by Armann & Armann, Chicago, 1934)
58 Musters, G.C., *At Home With the Patagonians* (John Murray, 1871)
59 Ricatte, R., *De l'Ile du Diable aux Tumuc-Humac* (Seusée Universelle, Paris, 1979)
60 Chapelle, R., *J'ai Vécu l'Enfer de Raymond Maufrais* (Flammarion, Paris, 1970)
61 *Pursuit*, Vol. 5, p. 12 (January 1972)

7 Queensland Tigers and Emmaville Panthers

Australasia

There in the bracken was the ominous spoor mark.
M. Harris, *The Tantanoola Tiger*

Present-day higher mammals (i.e. excluding the egg-laying monotremes), are split into two basic groups: 1) the metatherians or marsupials (named after the characteristic *marsupium* or pouch possessed by most species) and 2) all other mammals – the eutherians or true mammals. The marsupials and eutherians constitute two totally separate lines of mammalian evolution, but wherever the two groups have met, the marsupials have always been out-competed by the eutherians.

In Australia, however, the two groups did not encounter one another to any extent until relatively recently (via human introduction of various eutherians to the continent), for, by the time that Australia had become totally isolated from all other land masses (during the Palaeocene epoch, about 50 million years ago), marsupials had entered the continent but eutherians had not. Unlike South America (also once an island), Australia never again became connected with any other land mass.[1] Consequently, with the exception of a few taken up by monotremes (plus, much later, some small eutherian rodents and bats which found their way there prior to man's own arrival), those ecological niches compatible with mammalian occupancy were taken up exclusively by marsupials, a feat achieved by adaptive radiation – that is, the ancestral forms diversified via evolution into a vast array of different morphological types, each adapted to a separate niche. Moreover, they became so specialized within their niches that many marsupialian species actually came to resemble in external features their eutherian equivalents outside Australia – convergent (parallel) evolution.[2]

Marsupial counterparts of eutherians include the thylacine (paralleling the familiar eutherian wolf), carnivorous marsupial 'mice' (paralleling shrews), dasyures (mustelids and viverrids), marsupial mole (eutherian mole), wombats (marmots), phalangers (squirrels – there is even a flying phalanger which closely corresponds to the eutherian flying squirrel), hare wallabies (rabbits and hares) and kangaroos (deer and antelopes).

In view of such comprehensive morphological comparability of marsupial forms with eutherians, it is very surprising that no marsupial equivalent to any of the world's large eutherian felids (leopards, tigers etc) exists in Australia today (especially as there is an abundance of suitable prey). No marsupial felid exists *officially*, that is.

The Queensland Tiger

Nancy O'Brien of Cairns, Queensland, has good reason for doubting this zoological tenet, judging from her own experience with a strange animal, which she recounted in *Wildlife in Australia* in 1969: 'It was perched on my casement window top, and growling and snarling, and raking the air towards me with its right paw. Its eyes were wide open and a glittering green. So I sat up in bed and shook my walking stick at it and it leaped down. Being bright moonlight I saw the length of its body and that its tail was as long as its body and the stripes on it, from the small of its back to the butt of its tail. I immediately thought of it as a small half grown tiger.'[3] In her accompanying drawing, the stripes of her unexpected visitor were reminiscent of a thylacine's, but its head was unmistakably feline.

Nancy O'Brien is by no means alone in having reported such a creature – dozens more descriptions of large striped cat-like beasts have been recorded over many years from several north-western regions of Australia. Morever, Queensland has been a particularly frequent source of these reports – so much so, in fact, that the most commonly used names for this unclassified creature are 'Queensland tiger' and 'Queensland tiger-cat', even with sightings reported outside that state.

One issue which has been a common source of confusion regarding the Queensland tiger should be noted at this point to prevent any ambiguity arising hereafter. A *known* species of mammal exists which is also commonly called the tiger cat and which also inhabits Queensland. However, this latter creature (referred to scientifically as *Dasyurus maculatus* and belonging to the dasyure family of marsupials) is a much smaller beast than the unidentified Queensland tiger dealt with in this book, and is spotted, not striped, thereby having no bearing upon the reports noted here.

Following a familiar trend with mystery creatures, although unknown to science the Queensland tiger is anything but unknown to local inhabitants. For example, an Aboriginal painting from northern Australia has been identified by anthropologist Dr John Clegg which could possibly portray a striped cat.[4] And according to Dr Heuvelmans, such a creature has been known to the native Queensland Aborigines from the earliest times.[5] This is true for these regions' white inhabitants too.

As far back as 1705, a report from the Dutch East India Company at Batavia mentioned a tiger existing in Australia,[6] and in 1871 the Queensland tiger finally came to the attention of science when a letter from Brinsley G. Sheridan (Police Magistrate of Cardwell, Rockingham Bay, Queensland) was published in the Zoological Society of London's *Proceedings*. Sheridan described how, while his thirteen-year-old son was strolling along a path close to the bay's shore, his pet terrier took up a scent from some scrub near the beach and followed it, barking furiously, pursued by the son (who was well versed in bushlore despite his age). About half a mile/0.8 km from where the scent was first taken up, he observed an animal lying in the long grass, which he described as follows: 'As big as a native Dog [dingo]; its face was round like that of a Cat, it had a long tail, and its body was striped from the ribs under the belly with yellow and black. My Dog flew at it, but it could throw him. When they were together I fired my pistol at its head; the blood came. The animal then ran up a leaning tree, and the Dog barked at it. It then got savage and rushed down the tree at the Dog and then at me. I got frightened and came home.'[7] After listening to this account from his son, Sheridan made enquiries and learnt that such a creature had also been seen in the neighbourhood by other people, including Reginald Uhr, Police Magistrate at St George. Furthermore, Sheridan noted: 'Tracks of a sort of Tiger have been seen in Dalrymple's Gap by people camping there ... the country is so sparsely populated, and the jungles (or, as we call them here, "scrubs") so dense and so little known, that I have no doubt that animals of this kind exist in considerable numbers....'[7]

This compelling communication initiated a follow-up letter to the Society by Walter T. Scott from Cardwell's Vale of Herbert, published on 5 March 1872. In this, Scott reported that A.A. Hull, licensed surveyor, had recently been working with a party of five men on the Murray and Mackay rivers, north of Cardwell. While in their tents one night between 8 and 9 p.m., they heard a loud roar nearby and emerged with guns at the ready. Though unable to spot the creature responsible, they did note an unusual track (see the figure on p. 20), precisely formed in the soft ground. Scott also recalled that in 1864 a bullock-driver known to him had mentioned seeing a 'tiger' but was not believed at the time as, in Scott's words, 'He was a notorious liar.' Now Scott wondered whether he could have been telling the truth after all.[8]

A second letter by Scott was published by the Society a few months later, on 5 November, containing a further tiger incident: 'Mr Robert Johnstone, an officer of the Native Police, being in the scrub on the coast-range west of Cardwell with some of his troopers, had seen a large animal in a tree about forty feet from the ground, which on being approached sprang off to another tree about ten feet off, grasped it and descended tail first. The animal was said to have been larger than a pointer-dog, of a fawn-colour, with markings of deeper shade. Its head was quite round, and showed no visible ears; its tail was long and thick.'[9]

Many more sightings followed – and not just in Queensland. Some 'tigers' were even shot, but with disappointing results. The notorious 'tiger' of Tantanoola was identified as a calf, a second from Gippsland proved to be a feral pig, a third from Riverina was 'an escaped wild dog' (dingo?) and so on.[10] Happily, however, some convincing reports were also still emerging – especially from Queensland.

Take, for example, the following selection of excerpts from eyewitness reports collected by Queensland tiger researcher Janeice Plunkett and documented by Peter Makeig.[11]

In 1910 a Kuranda inhabitant (to whom such creatures were evidently nothing special) stated: 'Most of the tiger cats which I have killed were about four feet long and of fawn colour, with black stripes running across the body, which was fairly long, unlike an ordinary cat.' A fellow Kurandan noted in a separate incident some years later that: 'The creature ... had a round face and four exposed "tiger teeth" ... the other salient point in my opinion was the fact that big savage pig dogs were terrified of it.' A Tiaro dweller shot a supposed Queensland tiger in 1915, and recalled that such creatures were: '... slightly taller and heavier built than a domestic cat, with large head and strong shoulders. Also striped rings around the body. This specimen had a young one on each teat, approximately ten in all.' And according to a report from Bellenden Range in 1925, an animal '... about as large as a medium-sized dog rushed out and climbed a nearby tree. The animal was very savage. Its coat was beautiful and striped like a tiger.'

Of these, the Tiaro specimen is rather anomalous, for, while possessing the typical ring-like stripes, in comparison with most Queensland tigers reported it seems very small for an adult. Nevertheless, it is not the only diminutive specimen on record. For example, in a move from Queensland to Western Australia, Graham Soule noted that George Sumner of Port Hedland allegedly shot one such animal in 1905 near Katanning, south-west of Perth. It possessed a cat-like head and short-furred body striped with grey and black, and according to Sumner '... was not a domestic cat gone wild'.[12]

Back in Queensland, a similarly small striped creature was spied in or around 1900 by J. McGeehan. He had been walking through scrub on the Atherton Tableland behind his two dogs at about 4 p.m. when he heard a sound up ahead which suggested that his dogs were attacking some animal, something which was making a sound rather like that of a possum 'but harsher and more deeply intoned'. Upon his arrival on the scene, he saw a creature which '... partly resembled a large domestic cat, excepting for the body, which was rather light in build. The most striking part of its appearance was the well defined hoops of colour which encircled its body. These hoops or bands appeared to be about 2½ inches [6.25 cm] in width, and the colours were white and dun alternating in perfectly marked circles.'[13] As far as he could remember, this singular form of striping did not extend beyond the torso – its head, limbs and tail being dun-coloured. He described its head as being shaped more like that of a pomeranian dog than a cat's, but with smaller, pricked ears. Its eyes were dark, and its fur seemed finer and shorter than a domestic cat's. McGeehan estimated the animal's height at 12 in/30 cm; neck-to-tail-base length at 14 in/35 cm. Of particular interest were its teeth: 'I noticed that, when the mouth was opened, the top and bottom jaws, at the front, contained long fine fangs, but ... cannot now recollect whether the number on each jaw was two or four ... the fangs were in sets of two and about a quarter of an inch [0.6 cm] apart.'[13] McGeehan could not specifically recall the tail's appearance but felt that it matched that of a large domestic cat. He learnt in 1937 that similar animals had been seen in the scrubs of Babinda.[13] Sadly, he did not preserve the skin.

Another potentially significant episode on Atherton Tableland also ended negatively. After having seen a strange and sizeable striped creature near the Tully River's source, naturalist George Sharp later heard that a similar beast had recently been shot by an Atherton farmer. Naturally Sharp immediately made his way to the locality to examine the skin, which measured about 5 ft/150 cm from nose-tip to tail-tip; but it is no longer in existence.[5]

A supposed Queensland tiger was actually trapped alive by a Mr Endres of Mundubbera. It had a very short head and neck and was striped – though the stripes were not complete circles; it measured approximately 1½ ft/45 cm in height, and was the length of a large domestic cat – reminiscent of the McGeehan and Tiaro beasts. Once again, however, its pelt was not preserved.[5]

A particularly memorable encounter with a Queensland tiger was featured in the *Brisbane Courier* and later documented by Gilbert Whitley. Whilst riding between Munna Creek and Tiaro, G. de Tournoeur and his companion P.B. Scougall spied '... a large animal of the cat tribe, standing about twenty yards [18 m] away, astride of a very dead calf, glaring defiance at us, and emitting ... a growling whine'. As far as they could perceive through the torrential rain and approaching darkness, this formidable beast: '... was nearly the size of a mastiff, of a dirty fawn colour, with a whitish belly, and broad blackish stripes. The head was round, with rather prominent lynx-like [tufted?] ears, but unlike that feline there were a tail reaching to the ground and large pads. We threw a couple of stones at him, which only made him crouch low, with ears laid flat, and emit a raspy snarl, vividly reminiscent of the African leopard's nocturnal "wood-sawing" cry. Beating an angry tattoo on the grass with his tail, he looked so ugly and ready for a spring that we felt a bit "windy"...'.[5,10] Nonetheless, when the men rushed towards this creature and cracked their stockwhips, it bounded away.

Whatever this mysterious marauder might be, it was certainly no stranger as far as Australian writer Ion Idriess was concerned, for he claimed to have seen animals of this type on several different occasions in York Peninsula. He noted that it was '... as high as a hefty, medium-sized dog. His body is lithe and sleek and beautifully striped in black and grey. His pads are armed with lance-like claws of great tearing strength. His ears are sharp and pricked, and his head is shaped like that of a tiger.'[14] In a rather graphic account, Idriess told how he encountered one individual killing a kangaroo; in another, he recalled seeing a second such beast which this time was dead, lying alongside his famously fearless staghound, also dead – he did not say, however, what became of the tiger's body.[14]

As a pleasant change, this particular crypto-cat has also received favourable interest and attention from science. Indeed, in 1926 it was actually included within a formal tome on Australian fauna by A.S. le Souef and H. Burrell, who termed it 'the striped marsupial cat of York Peninsula' and described it as follows: 'Hair short, rather coarse. General colour fawn or grey, with broad black stripes on flanks, not meeting over the back. Head like that of a cat; nose more produced. Ears sharp, pricked. Tail well haired, inclined to be tufted at end. Feet large, claws long, sharp. Total length about five feet [150 cm]; height at shoulder eighteen inches [45 cm].'[15]

Reports concerning the Queensland tiger appeared in a scientific paper by G.H.H. Tate,[16] and Dr Ellis Troughton, former curator of mammals at the Australian Museum, included it within his definitive work *Furred Animals of Australia*, containing various of the accounts already given here. Summing up his section on this animal, Troughton commented that: 'Although there is some divergence concerning the size of the animal and the disposition of the stripes, there seems some possibility that a large striped marsupial-cat haunts the tangled forests of North Queensland.'[14]

Even the eminent British zoologist Dr Maurice Burton, noted for his scepticism concerning the Surrey puma and Loch Ness monster, looked favourably upon the possible existence of the Queensland tiger. Though this is most encouraging, one statement within an article which he wrote on this subject is certainly *not* – looking back, it now appears to comprise an unhappily accurate prophecy: 'It is possible that nothing more may be heard of the alleged "tiger-cat", that it may go down, or has gone down, before human settlement, or in competition with the wild dog and it is now extinct.'[17]

It is all too true that notably fewer reports of the Queensland tiger have emerged in recent years. One individual was described in a report from Mount Molloy in 1953, collected by Janeice Plunkett: 'The head was a good deal larger than an old tomcat, with teeth a lot like the extinct sabre toothed tiger (not size but shape).'[11] Note for further reference the remark concerning prominent teeth.

Well away from the centre of Queensland tiger country is the Otway Range – yet in the early 1960s, whilst driving along the road from Beech Forest to Gellibrand in this area, a man (name unknown) observed a tiger-like animal with a feline head and with dark stripes that travelled towards the creature's rear. As far as the eyewitness could tell, its coat's background colour was dark fawn.[12]

During this same period, a 2 ft/60 cm-high beast with a heavy head, slim hind limbs and small hind paws, marked with irregular black-and-white stripes on its body and its long blunt-ended tail, was spotted in the vehicle headlights of a man driving through Emmaville, Victoria[12] – a location now synonymous with another mystery felid, as will be revealed a little later.

In 1968 a strange creature sighted at Queensland's Mount Bartle Frere was described as possessing a head which '… appeared round and broad, its nose shorter and broader than a dog's. Some of its teeth appeared to protrude out and upward like tusks.'[11] Note the markedly prominent teeth again. This report is yet another collected by Janeice Plunkett, who became well known during the late 1960s in the Queensland tiger saga.

A secretary from Sydney, Ms Plunkett had developed a keen interest in this Antipodean anomaly – so much so that by 1969 she had amassed a hefty dossier of eyewitness accounts and had begun a personal campaign to track down a specimen to discover its precise scientific identity.[18] In September 1970 she led a three-month search team into the rainforest areas close to Queensland's Mackay, Maryborough and Cairns regions, visiting such locations as the Atherton Tableland, New England Tableland, Glen Innes and Toowoomba.[18] A piece of evidence in which she was particularly interested was the unusual four-toed print reported a century earlier by Hull, which became her expedition's logo.[18] Sadly, however, despite her determination and evident enthusiasm, the Queensland tiger eluded all her attempts to discover it.

During the 1972–3 winter, an alsatian-sized creature with tusk-like upper fangs, dirty grey coat and long tail was reported from the Daintree River's Cape Tribulation side,[19] and a long-tailed beast with a striped 2 ft/60 cm-long body, 1½ ft/45 cm tail, triangular head and feline gait was spied by three witnesses near Cairns' Herberton-Ravenshoe road junction one evening in January 1973 at about 10.15 p.m. (and also apparently in much the same area on 23 December 1972).[19]

By this time, however, various other mystery carnivores Down Under had begun to attract cryptozoological attention too, so that the Queensland tiger became increasingly overshadowed and overlooked. Reports still emerge intermittently, but hard evidence in support of its continuing existence is scarce indeed. In August 1982 a feline beast of leopard-like size and gait, with a heavily striped tail, was briefly seen at a distance of about 100 m/110 yards by Norwegian research scientist Dr Per Seglen whilst driving between Nambung National Park (near Perth) and Badgingarra.[20] And in 1983 a supposed Queensland tiger was killed at Craignish. Photographs of it which appeared in the *Maryborough Chronicle* depicted an animal with a long tail, lengthy fur and large canines.[21] It was identified by its dentition as a dog, by Janeice Plunkett, an identity supported by thylacine expert Dr Eric Guiler.[22]

Assuming that the Queensland tiger does still survive, what could it be? Eutherian tiger escapees from captivity offer no explanation, for its appearance bears very little similarity at all to *Panthera tigris*; even their striping patterns are different.

Conversely, in view of the overwhelming predominance of marsupials amongst native Australian mammals, it is hardly surprising that this order of pouched creatures provides both of the more plausible candidates for the Queensland tiger's identity.

1) Thylacine (Tasmanian Wolf)

The first contender is a creature which is itself currently playing hide-and-seek with cryptozoologists – the thylacine or Tasmanian wolf *Thylacinus cynocephalus*, a strikingly dog-like marsupial of roughly collie-size, with dorsal transverse stripes upon its posterior back region and tail base. The thylacine's history is a singularly sad one. During the nineteeth century, it carried a bounty on its head as a supposed sheep-killer and was shot on sight throughout Tasmania. By the beginning of this century, this once-common species – the largest living carnivorous marsupial – was already rare. A few specimens were exhibited in zoos, but no captive breeding programme was attempted. By 1936 the last zoo specimen was dead, and the wild population was utterly decimated. Ironically, the thylacine then became a protected species; in reality it appeared to be extinct. Expeditions were launched to rediscover it, and these have continued right up to the present day. A few promising sightings (albeit in the company of a much greater number of unconvincing ones) suggest that the thylacine may yet be holding on to existence by the skin of its polyprotodont teeth, but even so, it is without doubt one of the most gravely endangered of all mammalian species.[22,23]

On mainland Australia, its demise came very much earlier – the most recent fossils date at 2200 ± 96 years BP (before the present day).[24] Consequently, while the chances of a living thylacine being conclusively identified on Tasmania seem rather slim as the years roll on by, they would appear at first glance to be virtually non-existent on the island continent itself. Yet since the 1960s, in particular, many controversial reports have been recorded that describe creatures resembling thylacines being sighted in several different mainland locations (but notably within the western and south-eastern states).[22,25]

Even more puzzling is the Ozenkadnook tiger of Victoria. A photograph of this creature taken in the 1960s by Rilla Martin of Melbourne shows a dog-headed beast whose foreparts seem to bear white stripes upon a black pelage.[26] In view of its white rump and tail and the comparable whiteness of the surrounding foliage too, however, it is probable that these most unusual markings are merely shadow effects rather than actual stripes. Nevertheless, the identity of the animal itself is still a mystery. So too is that of the *yokyn* – the Aboriginal name for a strange dog-like beast of variable (sometimes brindled) colour and stocky muscular build, with long claws; it is familiar to Australian farmers and settlers, but not to scientists.[27] A mainland thylacine? Alternatively, as suggested by Dr Ralph Molnar, curator of the Queensland Museum, it could be a dog × dingo hybrid (Molnar, pers. comm.).

And how should we classify the *waldagi*? Dr. E. Kolig has reported three canine terms from the Wolmadjeri language in the

Kimberleys: *moran*, a dingo; *gunjar*, a domestic dog; and *waldagi*, a sinister dog-like beast.[28] Unlike many Australian mystery beasts referred to by the Aborigines, the *waldagi* is definitely not a spirit form. So what is it?

It is clear that there is a pressing need for detailed investigation of these varied dog-headed carnivores to identify categorically the creature(s) involved. It is equally clear that to rule out entirely the possibility that thylacines exist in Australia would be rash; for it seems most unlikely that all reports of mysterious dog-headed beasts here simply involve misidentified dingos, dogs or hybrids of these – which in turn brings us to the all-important question: is the Queensland tiger itself a mainland form of thylacine?

Though superficially promising – after all, the thylacine is (or was) a large striped carnivore native to Australia – there are several major problems with this identity. First and foremost, all known thylacines (Tasmanian and fossil mainland specimens, plus some remarkable mummified individuals preserved at Western Australia's Thylacine Hole) have unmistakably dog-like heads (hence its specific name, *cynocephalus*). Conversely, the Queensland tiger's head has always been described as being unquestionably cat-like. Can such a striking discrepancy be overcome? Victor Albert, a molecular biologist at Rhode Island's Brown University who has an especial interest in the Queensland tiger, has suggested that, although improbable, it would not be impossible for this mystery beast actually to be a short-faced thylacine form.[29] Ever since the mainland and Tasmanian thylacines were parted from each other by Tasmania's own separation from the mainland, the two groups could have followed very different evolutionary pathways, so that today their descendants may be very dissimilar morphologically from one another. Though possible in theory, the mummified mainland thylacines and contemporary fossils demonstrate that, as recently as about 2,200 years BP, no such change had taken place – and it is not very likely that anything so drastic has occurred since then.

Another fundamental problem to be faced when attempting to equate the Queensland tiger with a thylacine identity concerns tree-climbing, for, whilst the Queensland tiger displays feline arboreal agility, the thylacine is stoically terrestrial, like its eutherian canid counterparts.

Coat colouration is another area of conflict. The striking black-and-white hoop-like stripes totally encircling the tail and the underparts of much of the Queensland tiger's body certainly do not correspond with the shorter black stripes, upon the thylacine's brownish coat, which never extend downwards as far as the underpart and do not encircle the tail at all.

Then there is the question of spoor. It has been suggested that the strange four-toed print reported by Hull was really that of a thylacine or simply a domestic dog,[30] yet in the spoor of these latter beasts the toes are spaced well apart from one another, while those in the spoor noted by Hull were aligned very closely together. Intriguingly, as I learnt from fellow zoologist Malcolm Smith, an engraving of another print very similar to this in terms of toe spacing, but showing five rather than four toe impressions, can be seen at the Carnarvon Gorge, in a display of Aboriginal rock art which features numerous engravings of other animals' footprints too. Yet, unlike all of those, this particular example has never been identified with any known creature, native or introduced, living today in Australia (Smith, pers. comm.).

The Queensland tiger's exceedingly prominent tusk-like teeth and curved claws, so frequently reported, plus its leopard-like growl and its tail's very great length, are further features which serve well to differentiate it readily from the thylacine.

And as a final but highly significant point, we must take into account the fact that most reports of cat-headed striped beasts originate from Queensland, while dog-headed striped animals are most commonly reported elsewhere – as demonstrated by examining the geographic spread of mainland thylacine reports documented by Dr Guiler[22] and by Malcolm Smith.[31] If the two striped creatures are one and the same species, with the above-discussed differences in morphology and behaviour due merely to inaccurate reporting of sightings, we would expect a uniform distribution of both animal types. And so the logical (if unexpected) conclusion which must be drawn from this is that Australia houses not one but two types of striped carnivorous mammal unrecognized by science.

Supporting this solution to the situation on mainland Australia is the existence of an exactly comparable condition on New Guinea. Lord Rothschild reported that this island possessed a large striped creature with a cat-like head, thereby corresponding with the Queensland tiger.[15] At the same time, a distinctly dog-like form of unknown identity (but apparently separate from New Guinea's famous singing dogs, *Canis familiaris hallstromi*, related to the dingo) exists on Mount Giluwe,[32] close to areas in which fossil thylacines have been found.[33]

All in all, it would seem that, whilst the thylacine is a plausible contender for the identity of the dog-headed striped beasts of western and south-eastern Australia, we must look elsewhere for the solution to the mystery of the cat-headed tiger of Queensland – and thereby avoid (as pointed out recently by Victor Albert too[34]) the danger of lumping together two clearly separate forms of Australian mystery carnivore.

2) Thylacoleonid (Marsupial Lion)

This second contender is the one most vehemently supported by Victor Albert, by myself and by the great majority of other cryptozoologists too. It is a creature which was itself a profound mystery for many years, yet was first described (from fossils) as long ago as 1859, and by one of the world's most renowned palaeontologists, Professor Richard Owen. He formerly christened it *Thylacoleo carnifex*, 'the flesh-eating pouched lion', and pronounced that it had functioned as a bona fide marsupial felid.[35] Since then, other related fossil species have been disinterred and described, yielding an entire thylacoleonid lineage, of which *T. carnifex* was not only its most formidable but also (until recently) its most mysterious member. And all because of its teeth!

In eutherian felids, the canines are enlarged in size and the incisors very greatly reduced. In *T. carnifex*, however, the exact reverse was true, for, whilst its upper canines were very small, like eutherian felid incisors (its lower canines were absent altogether), its first pair of upper and lower incisors were huge, uniquely tusk-like structures that protruded from its jaws almost like a parrot's beak and were very reminiscent of eutherian felids' canine teeth. Nonetheless, virtually every palaeontological contemporary of Owen argued stridently that these immense incisors could not actually function as canines. However, these were not the only dental features which had suggested to Owen a carnivorous existence for *T. carnifex*. Its last pair of upper premolars and lower premolars possessed sharp blades (carnassials), a diagnostic feature of carnivorous mammals. Moreover, its eyes were set forward on its head, suggesting that it had binocular vision – again a notable characteristic of predatory species.[36]

Yet Owen's critics continued to deny flatly any possibility that *T. carnifex* was a meat-eater. The reason for this surprising scepticism rested with this species' ancestry, for the remainder of its anatomy had revealed unequivocally that its closest relatives were not the carnivorous marsupials already known (dasyures, thylacine); in stark contrast, they were the leaf-eating phalangers, fruit-eating possums and browsing macropods. Whoever heard of a flesh-eating phalanger? It seemed as incongruous as a carnivorous koala!

Consequently, every conceivable attempt was made to reconcile this bizarre beast's extraordinary dentition with (at best) a conformist vegetarian diet or (at worst) anything which did not include meat. Suggestions were varied and exotic, ranging from foliage and crocodiles eggs to cucumbers and melon.[37] None, however, provided a comprehensive explanation for its entire dental complement.

Indeed, this dietary dilemma was conclusively resolved only in recent times, courtesy of the scanning electron microscope (SEM), for it was discovered that by examining their surfaces via SEM techniques, teeth used for the chewing of flesh and those used for the chewing of plant material could be readily differentiated from one another by the pattern of scratches they bore. Here at last was a definitive means of uncovering the cryptic lifestyle of *T. carnifex*. Its carnassials were duly examined, and were shown to have been used for shearing,[38] which in turn supports the belief that its mighty incisors had assumed the role of canine teeth. After more than a century, Owen's belief had been vindicated: despite having descended from vegetarians, *T. carnifex* was indeed a carnivore, and hence a veritable wolf in sheep's clothing, so to speak.

Some near-complete, fossilized skeletons of this species have now been uncovered, so that we have a good idea of its appearance in life: namely, a leopard-sized, felid-shaped animal with a short, round head and powerful jaws housing those tusk-like, protruding upper and lower incisors. Despite having fairly long limbs, it may well have exhibited marked arboreal tendencies too, each forepaw possessing a pseudo-opposable thumb with a broad nail, which could have served it well in grasping branches (and probably even prey too), whilst its other toes each bore a formidable claw.[1,36,39] Moreover, it is very probable that its pelage was brindled or striped for camouflage purposes, like those of many eutherian felids.

Compare the above reconstruction of *T. carnifex* with the following description of the Queensland tiger, compiled from the eyewitness accounts given here: namely, a creature at least equal in size to a small leopard, with a feline build, longish limbs and a distinctly cat-like head whose jaws possess notably large, prominent teeth (actually described as tusk-like by some eyewitnesses); it also exhibits formidable claws, arboreal prowess and a striped pelage.

It scarcely needs to be said that these two descriptions match very closely – in fact, they could be two different eyewitness accounts of the same animal. Hardly surprising, then, that a surviving thylacoleonid (either *T. carnifex* itself or a modern descendant) is the favourite identity of most cryptozoologists for the Queensland tiger – a possibility which has gained very considerably in credibility since the recent revelation that *T. carnifex* was truly carnivorous.

Remains of *T. carnifex* have been discovered at several different sites across Australia, including Darling Downs in Queensland.

Most specimens are about 16,000 years old, but carbon-dating techniques carried out in the 1950s on a specimen unearthed at Lake Menindee, New South Wales, indicated that it died as recently as 6670–6470 BC.[40] Though such a date, if accurate, would be a great boon cryptozoologically, it is more likely to be an under-estimate, for dating-techniques used at that time were not as precise as those utilized today. All the same, certain Tasmanian specimens which *have* been dated recently have been found to be no more than 10,000 years old.

Yet if the Queensland tiger *is* a thylacoleonid, where are the missing fossils required to bridge the ten-millennium gap between itself and the Tasmanian specimens? Perhaps thylacoleonids *did* exist during this period, but in areas where fossil preservation is poor and where, in any event, palaeontological investigations are difficult to carry out – areas such as rainforests, for example. Certainly the diverse fauna typical of such habitats would supply more than enough prey to support a number of these carnivores. They would not even be in competition with the thylacine (either in the past or – if it still exists on the mainland – in the present), for the thylacine actually possesses a dietary preferance (medium/small-sized prey) very different from that of *T. carnifex* (large-sized prey).[41]

Victor Albert notes that the locality comprising Mount Bartle Frere in northern Queensland not only includes the largest (and one of the least explored) rainforest expanses in Australia but also has remained virtually unchanged for 30,000 years. Hence, if any thylacoleonids once existed here, it is possible that they are still doing so. Consequently, as Victor Albert also points out, it is particularly thought-provoking that this very area just happens to be one of the principal centres for Queensland tiger sightings; similarly, other major locations for such reports also have adjacent rainforests, e.g. Mackay, Maryborough, Cairns.[29,42]

It only remains to say that the morphological and behavioural correspondence between *T. carnifex* and the Queensland tiger is sufficiently striking for only the most narrow-minded and pessimistic of zoologists to deny out of hand any possibility that a thylacoleonid could still exist today.

One final point. What were the various 'mini' Queensland tigers reported earlier? Although some may have been bona fide cubs, the Tiaro specimen was clearly an adult individual (and hence not a Queensland tiger). According to Victor Albert, a freak striped variety of the known spotted tiger cat *Dasyurus maculatus* has been recorded at least once.[29,42] It is possible, therefore, that a creature such as this is responsible for the 'mini' tiger sightings noted here; the animals involved were all of dasyure size and build. Alternatively, they may even have been nothing more exciting than feral domestic cats with unusual markings that in turn led the observers concerned to wonder whether these animals were something special.

Australian Panthers and Pumas

As a land famed for its unique marsupial fauna and virtual absence of eutherian mammals, plus its separation from all other land masses for more than 50 million years, Australia must surely rank as one of the least likely places on Earth to house large feline creatures markedly reminiscent of Britain's Surrey puma and Exmoor beast, or North America's bona fide pumas and mystery black panthers. Nonetheless, reports of such beasts have indeed been documented from this island continent and have received an increasing degree of media attention in recent years. Furthermore, these felids are so similar to their UK and USA counterparts that, if locality names were omitted from the representative selection of Australian panther/puma incidents given below, it would be quite impossible to determine from which of these three totally separate regions the reports had originated.

The earliest of Australia's mystery panthers to attract widespread notice hailed from New South Wales, with the town of Emmaville as the epicentre of events and encounters. Inevitably referred to thereafter in New South Wales as 'the Emmaville panther' (even though, as will be seen, some sightings have been made far beyond this locality), it began receiving media coverage in 1956 and went on to establish itself for quite a few years as guaranteed headline material. From a sighting which he made of such an animal in October 1959, Sydney businessman Wallace E. Lewis described it as being jet black in colour and slightly larger in size than a greyhound, with a long tail and feline head[43] – a morphology reiterated in the many other eyewitness reports on record.

Though guaranteed to attract attention, the Emmaville panther's zoogeographically unexpected appearance was not a primary reason for its fame – or, more correctly, its notoriety. This was due to a much more serious and much less palatable matter, the concomitancy of its appearance with the wholesale slaughter of sheep and other farm livestock. A direct relationship or just coincidence?

As one example, between 1956 and 1957, 340 of Clive Berry's sheep were killed by some carnivorous animal on his 4,600-acre/1840 ha property at Pretty Gully, west of Uralla; more were killed in 1958. He dismissed the possibility that the culprit was either a dingo or a domestic dog, emphasizing that the manner in which his sheep had been killed bore the hallmarks of a felid rather than a canid attacker. He spent a very considerable time attempting to capture their killer but met with no success.[43] Mr Godley, one of Berry's neighbours, had also lost sheep to a mystery attacker of feline characteristics, so Mrs Godley made a plaster cast of the latter's spoor and sent it to Sir Edward Hallstrom (then chairman of the Taronga Park Trust) for formal identification. Sir Edward announced that, while not matching that of either dog or dingo (thereby corroborating Berry's view), it did correspond with that of a panther or tiger. This sparked off what was to become a deep interest of his own in this mystery creature – so much so that he offered a reward of £500 to anyone capturing it alive or dead *if* it indeed proved to be a panther or tiger, and double that amount if it actually turned out to be a marsupial felid.[43] Neither reward was ever claimed, but sightings and alleged panther killings of sheep continued in New South Wales throughout the 1960s.

In 1966, some miles north of Nowra, a black panther-like creature was attacked in one of Samuel Knight's paddocks by his two dogs, which were both badly hurt in the ensuing battle and fled, leaving their pantheresque adversary to escape into the surrounding bush. Interestingly, only a few months earlier, a circus truck had supposedly crashed whilst travelling between Nowra and Moss Vale, resulting in the escape of a black panther. If true, this could explain the origin of Knight's unexpected visitor, but in fact the whole circus incident appears to have been based upon local, unsubstantiated rumour rather than fact. In any case, it could not explain the welter of pre-1966 panther reports from that state.[44]

By 1969, the Emmaville panther's supposed crimes had become even more heinous – from sheep-killing to tourist-scaring. Consequently fifty expert rifle-shooters were set on its trail – but once again to no avail.[45]

By this time, moreover, reports of panthers on the prowl were emerging from other states too. In September 1972 farmer George Moir of Kulja, Western Australia, was shocked not only to discover several of his piglets dead with their hearts torn out and their throats ripped open but also to witness during this same period his panic-stricken sheep being rounded up, sheepdog-style, by two totally unfamiliar animals. As he drew nearer, he observed that they were uniformly black in colour, stood 2 ft/60 cm high at the shoulder and possessed a long, slender body with a tail of equal length. He realized that they were not dogs, appearing instead to be panthers that ran with a canter-like gait, the two forefeet coming down alternately, about 8 in/20 cm apart. They made their exit by leaping over two fences (one of these beasts failed to clear the first, falling to the ground but then, according to Moir, climbing over it like a cat), chased by Moir and fauna warden Don Noble, who were forced to give up the hunt after 5 miles/8 km, as the cats showed no sign of easing the furious pace of their flight. Moir subsequently learned that his neighbours Alan and Ron Johnson had lost fourteen of their own pigs to this (or another) pair of panthers, which they had seen on several occasions as well as having heard them give voice to blood-curdling cries.[46] Such sounds were already familiar to inhabitants of Emmaville and other New South Wales dwellers, such as farmer Ted Bell of Black Mountain, who recalled hearing such cries during the period when a mysterious large-sized felid had been reported in that area.[43]

Moir's unwelcome callers, or other creatures of the same type, paid a subsequent visit to his farm in November and were sighted by other inhabitants of the area, so that they ultimately became known as 'the Kulja panthers'.[46] News of them reached the state's Agriculture Protection Board, but it declined to intervene in the situation, its opinion being that these animals were not panthers at all but merely black kangaroo dogs.[47] One such dog *was* shot, but panther sightings continued.

During the mid-to-late 1970s, reports of black panthers intensified dramatically. In a *Fortean Times* article published in 1980, Paul Cropper examined a series of these from New South Wales,[44] while the Western Australian contingent attracted the attention of David O'Reilly, then a reporter for *The Australian*. Victoria had its share of panthers too; moreover, it was during this period and from this state that a further fact regarding Australia's out-of-place felids became widely known at last – namely that there was not one but two such forms of cat. In addition to accounts of jet-black pantheresque beasts, reports were also coming in concerning tawny-coloured puma-like cats. In truth, these latter felids had been sighted for many years, but until then they had failed to attract the degree of attention received by the more exotic and eye-catching panther type.

Demonstrating the clear dichotomy of form but evident overlap of distribution relative to these two felids is the following pair of sightings made during 1977. In April, whilst hunting near Horsham (about 200 miles/320 km north-west of Melbourne, Victoria) Neal Bothe, Ivan Bothe and John Spencer reported seeing a creature which they described as resembling a puma, observed at a distance of only 33 yards/30 m.[48] And in November a jet-black beast was sighted in the Wimmera outback (about 223 miles/360 km north-west of Melbourne), again at close range, i.e. less than 55 yards/50 m away, by Wimmera Lands Department officers Bert Bray and Alan Knight. According to their detailed description of the animal, it was about 40 in/100 cm in length with a long cat-like tail, and stood about 2 ft/60 cm in height. Its head was cat-like, with a very small nose and ears, its shoulders and rump were slender, and its coat was sleek.[49]

The presence in Western Australia of these two forms was highlighted by the writings of David O'Reilly, including two major reports on the subject which appeared on consecutive days in June 1978 in *The Australian*. In these, he boldly contrasted the orthodox scientific view (that such animals were simply feral domestic cats – or dogs) with those put forward by local inhabitants. With first-hand experience – including the all-too-available evidence of slaughtered livestock – these people were united in believing that Western Australia's mystery cats were genuine pumas and panthers which had escaped (accidentally or via deliberate release) from captivity and were now thriving in a naturalized state within the Australian bush, preying upon wild creatures such as kangaroos and making forays onto bush-bordering farms in search of sheep and other stock.[50] Furthermore, with sightings emerging as far afield within the state as Warburton, Healesville, Montrose, Neerim and Mt Evelyn in the past few years (and many of these too precise and well supported for an urban folklore explanation), it seemed evident that a fair number of these animals existed[51] – little wonder that the farming communities were so alarmed!

By 1981, David O'Reilly's personal investigations in the Perth area of Western Australia had brought in so much material concerning its out-of-place felids that he wrote it up in book form, entitled *Savage Shadow*.[47] Currently the only book devoted to these Australian anomalies, it contains numerous reports and eyewitness accounts documented chronologically and supplemented by data on physical evidence (claw marks, hair samples identified as feline, and animal kills – some represented by photos – bearing the unequivocal signs of a felid attacker).[47]

Sadly, however, what would have been the book's highlight proved to be as elusive ultimately as its subject. In *Savage Shadow*, O'Reilly recalled that a slide photograph supposedly depicting a wild Australian panther came his way during his investigations. Taken by a Mr Barry Morris, allegedly near Carnarvon, when blown up it revealed a cat-like beast with jet-black pelage and a tail that curled high in a semi-circle above its body. Unfortunately, the price Morris asked for the slide – $1,000 – was more than O'Reilly's newspaper bosses (and also those of all other newspapers to which Morris later applied) were willing to pay. Hence the photo apparently has never been published.[47]

During the 1980s, much attention has been redirected to Victoria, with sightings of tawny cats and jet-black cats being recorded regularly each year, with the former type becoming increasingly evident. As before, individuals of both colour forms are being seen in the same locations. For example, at Talbot, near Maryborough, a great tawny male cat was sighted in June 1985 by John Higgins and has seemingly been spied by others too in the vicinity of the forest behind Talbot, while at nearby Daisy Hill a pair of the black felids has been heard and seen on a number of occasions. Far more perplexing, however, is another revelation – that these two colour forms appear to belong to the same species, for, according to a detailed report published in the *Maryborough Advertiser* on 15 July 1987, a tawny-coloured female living in the forest near Majorca has a half-grown black cub. Moreover, in the mid-1970s, after having been flushed by staff from the vineyard at Château Rémy, a huge black cat returned later that day with its mate, a ginger-coloured individual.[52]

Most significant of all, the mystery cats, regardless of taxonomic identity, have finally achieved official status in the eyes of government officials; for the Victorian Government has actually added pumas to the list of predators which can attack farm stock,[52] something which, it seems, happened with alarming frequency in 1987 – so much so, in fact, that sophisticated American animal-snares are to be used by local researchers in an attempt to catch alive one of these elusive felids active in the Maryborough and St Arnaud regions. They are also to be made available to officers from the Department of Conservation Forests and Lands (staff from this department actually made their own sighting in July 1987 of a large-sized felid, news of which was passed on immediately to senior executives at Melbourne). As further proof of the new, serious approach to the subject by Australian officialdom, provision has been made at Melbourne Zoo for the accommodation of any mystery cat caught alive, and a dossier of material collected on apparent puma predatory activity in central Victoria is to be forwarded for evaluation to the United States Department of Agriculture.[53]

It seems likely that, if this policy of formal investigation and determination to secure a specimen of these animals is continued, the mystery will soon be resolved; they are also being sought by the Rare Fauna Group in the Grampians, with high-tech sound and camera equipment.[53] But what will they prove to be?

1) Feral Domestic Cat?

As already noted in earlier chapters, feral domestics do not normally exceed tame domestics in size (though in Australia they can weigh as much as twice that of their tame counterparts[54]), and they certainly never attain a sufficient size to be capable of killing sheep and kangaroos in the meticulously clean manner typical of mystery 'Big Cat' kills Down Under. Conversely, animals often seem larger than they really are when observed from a distance – hence some panther/puma sightings made a long way off could conceivably have been of feral domestics.

Supporting this suggestion is an incident recorded in the Sydney *Daily Mirror* on 15 November 1977. A large cat – described in the report as puma-like with protruding yellow eyes, a 2 ft/60 cm-long tail and fang-like teeth – had recently been shot dead by Tom Sega after stalking Tom and his father, Roman Sega, through the thick undergrowth on Cambewarra Mountain, near Nowra, New South Wales. Once dead, the creature was skinned by the Segas, who carried home its pelt but regrettably left its carcase behind on the mountainside.[55] Paul Cropper was most intrigued by this incident and visited the Sega family in 1979 to see the skin for himself but, upon examining it and even allowing for two years of shrinkage and other inevitable distortions, he was unable to convince himself that it had come from anything other than a large feral domestic cat. Worth noting, incidentally, is that, although in the report it was referred to as 'puma-like', Paul Cropper discovered that in colour its pelt was black (not tawny).[44]

If his identification of this specimen is correct, it serves well to show that even people familiar with a given area and its fauna can sometimes misidentify an animal encountered there if it is not seen clearly, so that the concept of a feral domestic cat being mistaken for a bigger felid is no longer so difficult to accept – unless, of course, it is offered as the explanation for *every* mystery 'Big Cat' sighting; after all, there is a limit even to misidentification. Similarly, although the idea that dogs and dingos (of which many black specimens have been recorded) are being taken for large-sized cats is very likely correct in some instances, all too often mystery cat eyewitnesses have expressedly stated that the animals which they have seen did *not* resemble canids; equally, spoor sometimes discovered after such sightings have not always matched those of canids.

So it would seem that, in a number of cases, the animals being reported really are very sizeable cats – but what can they be?

2) Native Eutherian Carnivore?

This is an immediate non-starter – with no fossil evidence to support the existence of eutherians in Australia prior to its isolation, any identity involving a native eutherian carnivore can be written off as exceedingly unlikely. Even the so-called native dog of Australia, the eutherian dingo, was introduced by man; it did not evolve there.

3) Unknown Marsupial Carnivore?

In view of Australia's marsupial dynasty, it is more reasonable to suppose that these so-called pumas and panthers, like the Queensland tiger, could be unknown marsupial carnivores. At the same time, whereas the Queensland tiger is markedly different in fundamental morphology from any other striped feline creature known in the world today, the Australian pumas and panthers appear identical in size, shape, relative body proportions and colour to those also reported from Britain, continental Europe and North America (as well as known pumas and panthers from their native lands), suggesting a common explanation for many (if not all) of these animals, regardless of locality.

4) Genuine Pumas and Panthers?

As already discussed in Chapters 1 and 5, an extremely plausible common origin does exist – as escapees from captivity. Still to be resolved, however, is their taxonomy. If two different species are involved, pumas and melanistic leopards would truly seem to be the most likely identities. Conversely, if only a single, dimorphic species (i.e. one having two distinct colour morphs) is responsible, inevitably we must look to the puma – certainly in relation to reports of pairs of Australian mystery cats which consist of one individual of each colour. In short, we must accept that naturalized black panthers do exist in Australia; and/or that pumas do too and have given rise either to a melanistic morph (a rather radical concept) or, more conservatively, to a very dark brown morph.

Many books mentioning Australian mystery cats comment that reports date back to the 1940s, which ties in nicely with the well-voiced rumours that during World War II American airmen stationed in various parts of Australia (notably the Western Australian coast) owned several puma and/or panther mascots which they subsequently released into the wild and which have bred amongst themselves to yield a notable number of individuals living there today. A very smooth answers-for-everything solution generally accepted by believers in Australia's feline anomalies – until the summer of 1987, that is, when the *Maryborough Advertiser* declared that this solution seemed to be little more than a cover-up; for its investigations of old reports had revealed that black felids and tawny felids were being hunted in the ranges on both sides of the highway around Victoria's Taradale and Kyneton as long ago as the 1880s.[52] Moreover, a lioness-like creature (puma?) was sighted in the hill country of Gunyah, near Trafalgar, by three men in November 1933;[56] puma-like cats were being reported from Bendigo properties prior to World War II;[52] and a creature described in the *Advertiser* as a black puma was actually killed at Kyneton in 1942[52] – all thereby pre-dating the American airmen's arrival.

No longer does the airmen origin for such animals stand. We must also look to the more orthodox sources of captive animals – zoos, private collections, homes – from which escapes can occur. Also to be considered is the possibility that some such cats have been released by people who smuggled them into the country and then decided to lose the evidence. Yet even this solution has problems.

The importation and quarantine laws in Australia are very strict. Additionally, even once inside Australia, livestock moving between states (as in circuses or other travelling shows, for example) has to be recorded on entry into a state and checked out when it leaves, making the possibility of an escapee's avoiding official notice a very slim one (Smith, pers. comm.). Nevertheless, despite all the improbabilities, mystery cats do exist in Australia. Perhaps the investigations taking place in Victoria will soon obtain the elusive solution – and preferably of the type which can be accommodated alive and well at Melbourne Zoo.

New Zealand Mystery Cats

In any case, not even the possibility of unidentified cats prowling Australia could be any more remote than the likelihood of mystery felids inhabiting New Zealand too, for, with the possible exception of the scientifically unrecognized *waitoreke* (a mystifying otter-like beast now most probably extinct),[5] New Zealand's only native mammals are two species of bat. All other furry fauna currently existing there have been introduced in recent times by man. Consequently it is extremely surprising to learn that reports have been intermittently documented from this dual-island country of large-sized, unmistakably feline beasts which elude all attempts at capture and even precise identification. The major outbreak to date of encounters with such animals occurred in 1977, as illustrated by the following selection.

On 8 July 1977 the *New Zealand Herald* reported that Graham Stevens, a Three Kings security officer, had been checking a building on his beat in the Auckland suburb of Mangere one evening when he saw at very close range a large lion with big yellow eyes, just in front of his van. Upon notification, the Otahuhu police searched the area but found no sign of the creature, and the manager of the circus that was currently in town maintained that none of his lions had escaped.[57]

Ten days later, New Zealand 1YA Radio announced that a tiger had been seen in Kaiapoi,[58] and during the last week of July various newspapers also carried news of this animal. It transpired that the sighting had been made by a Kaiapoi lady who allegedly observed the animal in her garden one morning at 4 a.m. At first the police discounted the report as a hoax, but then spoor and droppings were discovered in the nearby sandhills, close to Pines Beach.[58,60] As a result, a full-scale search was set in motion, involving a helicopter and men armed with guns, headed by Police Inspector W.J. Perring, who was quoted by the Sydney *Sun-Herald* on 24 July as saying that he was 'reasonably satisfied' that a large-sized cat, possibly a tiger, had indeed been in the area.[59] Nevertheless, the search was unsuccessful and was eventually called off, amidst rumours that the culprit was a tiger kept as a pet by a local man, which presumably had escaped and was later secretly recaptured.[60]

None of this, however, has been verified, and, as with so many mystery cat incidents, the animal concerned was simply never heard of again – nor, for that matter, was the Mangere lion.

Could they have merely been misidentified dogs? Quite possibly, although in the lion instance the animal was seen at very close range, making such an error rather more unlikely. No description of the Kaiapoi tiger's spoor or droppings was released, so we cannot use these to form any opinion regarding their owner's identity.

Feral domestic cats, descended from escapee pets, are very common in New Zealand and are rightly blamed for the demise of a number of this country's endemic bird species.[61] Even so, they could hardly be responsible for either of the large felids discussed here. The currently held maxims of palaeogeography and zoogeography dictate that New Zealand became isolated from other land masses long before either marsupial or eutherian mammals had the chance to reach it, and hence it would seem quite impossible for that country to be harbouring an undiscovered native species of large feline carnivore.

Thus we must fall back once again on the escapee theory for a plausible solution.

All the same, it would be a lot more reassuring if more than just a very occasional supposed escapee could actually be caught. Lewis Carroll devotees will fondly recall the Red Queen informing a bewildered Alice in *Through the Looking Glass*: 'Why, sometimes I've believed in as many as six impossible things before breakfast.' A cryptozoologist in the making?

Abbreviation: *PZSL* = *Proceedings of the Zoological Society of London*
1 Sutcliffe, A., *On the Track of Ice Age Mammals* (Brit. Mus. Nat. Hist., 1985)
2 Tyndale-Biscoe, H., *Life of Marsupials* (Edward Arnold, 1973)
3 *Wildlife in Australia*, Vol. 6, p. 54 (June 1969)
4 Brandl, E.J., *Australian Aboriginal Paintings in Western and Central Arnhem Land* (Australian Aboriginal Studies, No. 52, Australian Institute of Aboriginal Studies, Canberra, 1973); Clegg, J., *Archaeological & Physical Anthropology of Oceania*, Vol. 13, pp. 19–29 (1978)
5 Heuvelmans, B., *On the Track of Unknown Animals* (Rupert Hart-Davis, 1958)
6 Marchant, R.A., *Beasts of Fact and Fable* (Phoenix House, 1962)
7 Sheridan, B.G., *PZSL*, pp. 629–30 (7 November 1871)
8 Scott, W.T., ibid., p. 355 (5 March 1872)
9 Scott, W.T., ibid., p. 796 (5 November 1872)
10 Whitley, G., *Australian Museum Magazine*, Vol. 7, pp. 132–9 (1 March 1940)
11 Makeig, P., *North Queensland Naturalist*, Vol. 37, pp. 6–8 (1970)
12 Soule, G., *The Mystery Monsters* (G.P. Putnam's Sons, New York, 1965)
13 McGeehan, J., *North Queensland Naturalist*, Vol. 6, pp. 3–4 (1938)
14 Troughton, E., *Furred Animals of Australia*, eighth edition (Angus & Robertson, 1965)
15 le Souef, A.S., and Burrell, H., *The Wild Animals of Australasia, Embracing the Mammals of New Guinea and the Nearer Pacific Islands* (Harrap, 1926)
16 Tate, G.H.H., *Bulletin of the American Museum of Natural History*, Vol. 98, pp. 563–616 (1925)
17 Burton, M., *Oryx*, Vol. 1, pp. 321–6 (1952)
18 *Courier-Mail* (Brisbane), 2 and 31 August, 25 October 1970
19 *Cairns Post*, 17 and 18 January 1973
20 *West Australian*, 24 August 1982
21 *Maryborough Chronicle*, 2 February 1983
22 Guiler, E., *Thylacine: The Tragedy of the Tasmanian Tiger* (Oxford University Press, 1985)
23 Greenwell, J.R. (Ed.), *ISC Newsletter*, Vol. 4, pp. 1–5 (winter 1985); Park, A., *Smithsonian*, Vol. 16, pp. 117–31 (August 1985); Goss, M., *Fate*, Vol. 36, pp. 34–43 (July 1983); Beresford, Q., and Bailey, G., *Search For the Tasmanian Tiger* (Blubber Head Press, Sandy Bay, Tasmania, 1981); Brown, R., *Animals*, Vol. 15, pp. 416–19 (September 1973); Pycraft, W.P., *Illustrated London News*, Vol. 196, p. 564 (27 April 1940); Morey, G.W., *The Field*, Vol. 151, p. 822 (28 November 1931)
24 Lowry, J.W.J., and Merrilees, D., *Helictite*, Vol. 7, pp. 15–16 (1969); Merrilees, D., ibid., Vol. 8, pp. 39–42 (1970)
25 Ackman, P., et al., *Sunday Telegraph* (Australia), 8 August 1976, 27 March 1977; Douglas, A.M., *New Scientist*, Vol. 110, pp. 44–7 (24 April 1986); Rickard, R.J.M., *Fortean Times*, No. 49, pp..5–7 (winter 1987)
26 Harris, S., *Walkabout*, Vol. 34, pp. 28–31 (June 1968)
27 Fuller, C., *Fate*, Vol. 30, p. 34 (May 1977)
28 Kolig, E., *Mankind*, Vol. 9, pp. 122–3 (December 1973)
29 Albert, V.A., Paper presented at the ISC Annual Members Meeting, Royal Museum of Scotland, 26 July 1987
30 Krefft, G., *Annals and Magazine of Natural History*, Series 4, Vol. 11, pp. 315–16 (1873)
31 Smith, M., in Archer, M., (ed.), *Carnivorous Marsupials*, Vol. 1 (Royal Zoological Society of New South Wales, Sydney, 1982), pp. 237–53
32 Heuvelmans, B., *Cryptozoology*, Vol. 5, pp. 1–26 (1986)
33 van Deusen, H.M., *Journal of Mammalogy*, Vol. 44, pp. 279–80 (1963); Plane, M., *Journal of Australian Geology and Geophysics*, Vol. 1, pp. 78–9 (1976)
34 Albert, V.A., *Cryptozoology*, Vol. 6, pp. 119–20 (1987)

35 Owen, R., *Philosophical Transactions of the Royal Society*, Vol. 149, pp. 309–22 (1859)
36 Finch, M.E., in Archer, M. (ed.), *Carnivorous Marsupials*, Vol. 2, op. cit., pp. 537–51 (1982)
37 Cope, E.D., *American Naturalist*, pp. 520–2 (1882); Flower, W., *Quarterly Journal of the Geological Society of London*, Vol. 24, pp. 307–19 (1868); Krefft, G., *Annals and Magazine of Natural History*, Series 3, Vol. 18, pp. 148–9 (1866)
38 Wells, R.T., Horton, D.R., and Rogers, P., in Archer, M., (ed.), *Carnivorous Marsupials*, Vol. 2, op. cit., pp. 573–86 (1982)
39 Archer, M., and Dawson, L., ibid., pp. 477–94 (1982)
40 Daily, B., *Australian Museum Magazine*, Vol. 13, pp. 163–6 (1960)
41 Case, J.A., *Australian Mammalogy*, Vol. 8, pp. 45–52 (1985)
42 Rouse, R., *Gold Coast Journal*, 5 August 1987
43 Owens, B.L., *Australian Outdoors and Fishing*, pp. 17–19, 83 (April 1977)
44 Cropper, P., *Fortean Times*, No. 32, pp. 18–21 (summer 1980)
45 *Sunday Express*, 2 March 1969
46 Pash, B., *Sunday Times* (Perth), 12 and 18 November 1972
47 O'Reilly, D., *Savage Shadow: The Search For the Australian Cougar* (Creative Research, Perth, 1981)
48 *Sun* (Sydney), 28 April 1977
49 Forrest, B., ibid., 25 November 1977
50 O'Reilly, D., *The Australian*, 5 and 6 June 1978
51 *Pursuit*, Vol. 13, p. 94 (spring 1980)
52 Higgins, J., *Maryborough Advertiser*, 15 July 1987
53 *Maryborough Advertiser*, various reports, all from July 1987
54 Davies, W., and Prentice, R., *Wildlife in Australia*, Vol. 17, pp. 20–6, 32 (1980)
55 Field, A., *Daily Mirror* (Sydney), 15 November 1977
56 *Melbourne Argus*, 3 November 1933
57 *New Zealand Herald*, 8 July 1977
58 1YA Radio, New Zealand, early morning news item, 18 July 1977
59 *Sydney Morning Herald*, 23 July 1977; *Sun-Herald* (Sydney), 24 July 1977
60 *Fortean Times*, No. 25, p. 35 (spring 1978)
61 Fitzgerald, B.M., *Carnivore Genetics Newsletter*, Vol. 4, pp. 67–72 (1980)

8 Final Thoughts – Conclusions and Conservation

> How often have I said to you that when you have eliminated the impossible, whatever remains, *however improbable*, must be the truth.
>
> Sir Arthur Conan Doyle, *The Sign of Four*

After having eliminated the impossible relative to mystery cats – viz. that *all* reports of *all* such creatures result from dimly viewed dogs, manic mendacity, drunken delusion or mass hallucination – we are left with an initially improbable but ultimately inevitable conclusion: namely, that mystery cats of wide diversity and worldwide distribution do indeed exist. Their likely identities have been discussed individually in the previous chapters; when viewed collectively, it can be seen that three fundamental categories of modern mystery cats are present.

1) Felids comprising species or subspecies currently undescribed by science (or at least unknown to science in the living state).

These most probably include: the *mngwa, ndalawo*, machairodontid-like terrestrial and aquatic forms from Africa and South America, the Queensland tiger, Iriomote *yamamaya*, Ile du Levant and Irish wildcats, Bali leopard and spotted lions.

2) Felids comprising hitherto unrecorded morphs or other non-taxonomic forms of known species.

These most probably include: the black tigers and Fujian blue tigers, the king and woolly cheetahs and quite possibly the *jaguarete, damasia* and Transcaucasian black cat.

3) Felids comprising known species occurring in unexpected localities.

These most probably include: Britain's lynx-like cats, North America's maned leonine creatures, the puma-like felids of Europe and Australia, and the black pantheresque beasts of Europe, North America and Australia.

In addition, there are some felids, such as the Kellas cat and *onza*, which seem fated to straddle two categories until genetic studies can determine unequivocally their correct classification.

The official discovery of any of the mystery cats documented in this book will be of great scientific worth, but some will be especially significant. For example, although the accidental/deliberate introduction by man of certain small-sized known felids into foreign localities (e.g., feral domestic cats worldwide, jaguarundis into Florida[1]) is already officially acknowledged, the definite discovery of pumas living wild in Britain or black panthers in Australia, for example, would demonstrate that much larger known felids can and do survive in out-of-place localities too. Moreover, such a radical revelation would require urgent attention not only from zoologists but also from respective government authorities; for until now the only comparable situations concerning large mammalian carnivores involve packs of feral domestic dogs, which in Italy and the US, for example, have often occupied the ecological niche left vacant by those countries' wolves since their widespread eradication by man.[2,3]

Equally noteworthy would be the official discovery of dilute and/or black tigers, adding very considerably to our knowledge of pelage-related mutant forms exhibited by the felids. Similarly, it is possible that the genetic tests currently taking place with the *onza* and Kellas cat may reveal that these are actually abnormally gracile mutants of the puma and wildcat respectively, created by a hitherto unrecorded genetic mechanism.

And with respect to unknown taxonomic forms, the prizes on offer are exceedingly great. Felids such as the Ile du Levant and Irish wildcats, spotted lions and Iriomote *yamamaya* will most probably prove to be new subspecies, whilst the *mngwa* and Mexican *onza* could well be full species. Moreover, some may actually offer up even more to science than new species. If, for example, the Central African Republic's *tigre de montagne* proves to be a bona fide sabre-tooth, this will add an entirely new sub-family of felids to the list of animals known to be in existence in modern times. Furthermore, if the Queensland tiger is found to be a surviving thylacoleonid, a whole new family of living Australian marsupials will be included in that list. Most dramatically of all, if the large-fanged striped cat of Colombia and Ecuador actually turns out to be a living *Thylacosmilus*, a whole family of South American carnivorous marsupials hitherto believed to have become extinct at least 2 million years ago will be resurrected from the dead. Little wonder that mystery cats are starting to receive such serious attention from scientists throughout the world!

All the same, their scientific significance is not the only reason why every effort should be made to discover and document these animals with all speed. Another reason – equally important but far more urgent – also exists: their extreme vulnerability.

Felids have been persecuted mercilessly by man – for three principal reasons. Firstly: they are carnivores, and thereby a threat to man's livestock and (at least in the eyes of man, even if not in reality) to man himself. Secondly: by being fierce, the larger species in particular have constituted prized targets for 'sportsmen'. Thirdly: due to many felids' possessing highly attractive coats, they have been greatly sought after by the fur trade. The collective result of these depredations can be ascertained readily by reading the 1988 *IUCN Red List of Threatened Animals*. It classes no fewer than six full species of felid as vulnerable, a further two species and one subspecies as rare, together with four species and five subspecies as endangered.[4]

If this can happen to *known* species, how much worse is the likely fate of those not recognized by science? It can be plainly seen that an animal cannot receive official protection under conservation laws if it does not officially exist to begin with. Having said that, it is, of course, well known that the Loch Ness monster received a scientific name in 1975 in order for it to be classed as a protected species under British conservation laws,[5] but it must be remembered that the majority of mystery cat forms of likely taxonomic significance live in remote areas of the world where comparably overt attempts to secure their preservation are highly unlikely to occur.

One ray of hope for the future of mystery cats lies in the fact that they have eluded scientific discovery right up to the penultimate decade of the twentieth century, thereby demonstrating that they are very adroit (at least so far) at avoiding direct annihilation by men – for three reasons. Firstly: they are very elusive. Secondly: in the case of many tropical forms, the natives inhabiting their localities have often refrained from killing them out of fear or the imposition of taboos. Thirdly: 'civilized' man, whose armoury of guns and scant regard for 'primitive' customs could certainly pose a threat, is generally prevented from doing so by the frequently inhospitable and/or inaccessible nature of these cats' domains.

However, he can still decimate such creatures indirectly – by destroying their habitat and hence the delicate ecological web of existence into which, like all life forms, they are inextricably interwoven. Known cats, of course, have already suffered heavily from such activities in the past – and present. Most recently, for example, the Spanish lynx *Felis pardina* – a relict species lingering on from the Pleistocene epoch into present-day Europe and already greatly endangered – is now even more gravely threatened as a result of its last retreat, the Coto Donana (a stretch of pine forests, marsh and sandhills extending along the Guadalquivir delta), in turn being encroached upon by holiday developments.[6] Most devastating of all for mystery cats is the continued destruction of the world's rainforests, for these are home to the vast majority of the taxonomically significant mystery cats covered in this book.

Happily, the rainforests' *known* cats are receiving the earnest attention of notable international organizations, such as the Cat Specialist Group of the International Union for the Conservation of Nature and Natural Resources (IUCN), and the World Wide Fund For Nature (WWF). Smaller but no less dedicated groups are also carrying out very beneficial work. Very worthy of mention here is the Cat Survival Trust at the Marlind Centre in Welwyn, UK. Trust director Terry Moore is currently promoting the idea of establishing populations of various species of the smaller threatened felids (e.g. Geoffroy's cat, flat-headed cat) on uninhabited islands on the same latitudes as their normal localities.[7] Providing that such introductions do not pose a threat to these islands' native fauna, this comprises an exciting concept, greatly deserving not only of praise but also of attention and assistance from other conservation groups and sponsoring bodies. Equally commendable is the intention of the luxury motor firm Jaguar Cars to create a 150 square mile/388.5 square km, £50,000 jaguar reserve within the rainforests of Belize, in conjunction with the WWF and jaguar specialist Dr Alan Rabinowitz.[8]

But what can be done for the tropics' mystery cats? This is where cryptozoology can come into its own; for, although the discovery of a new species as a result of cryptozoological researches is in itself a great achievement, cryptozoology is uniquely able to accomplish an even greater one – the prevention of an animal species dying out before its actual existence is formally acknowledged. For by painstakingly researching and pursuing an animal form dismissed by traditional science as folklore or fancy, cryptozoology can not only bring about its discovery but also, in so doing, make it eligible for conservation consideration, thereby saving it from continued obscurity and ultimate extinction within habitats already threatened with destruction.[9]

Due to ignorance and arrogant disregard for travellers' experiences and natives' narratives, the tragic disappearance of creatures before they actually received official recognition (let alone protection) is certainly not without precedent. This is well demonstrated, for example, by the extinction of the Madagascan elephant birds and giant lemurs,[10,12] plus the enigmatic sea mink *Mustela macrodon* of New England and Canada.[12,13] Although known to the local people, these species were ignored by science until, through habitat annihilation and excessive hunting by man, they died out.

Many other species have also disappeared before having been formally recognized *to our knowledge* – but how many times has this occurred *without our knowledge*? Quite possibly a whole wealth of fascinating and irreplaceable species have been lost in this way, unknown and unrecorded, due simply to man's continued stubbornness and reluctance to take notice.

Consequently it is imperative that cryptozoology succeeds in its pursuit of mystery cats and mystery animals of every other kind. To date, no country provides funds for scientifically based cryptozoological research. Therefore it is especially to be hoped that a major cryptozoological discovery will be made in the near future – not only for that species' survival but also for the undoubted incentive it will provide to granting bodies for the provision thereafter of cryptozoological research funds, which in turn could lead ultimately to the protection of other, currently unknown species too. Perhaps the eventual identification of the Rodriguez *onza* specimen, for example, will provide the necessary impetus.

Though cryptozoology seems to be the only hope for engendering protection for mystery cats, if pursued too zealously it may actually have the very opposite effect. This has been recognized by ISC Secretary Richard Greenwell, whose statement that one *onza* specimen was enough for research purposes and that no more should be killed[14] cannot be commended highly enough. Similarly, the Bottriells are to be praised for their sterling efforts to attract positive scientific interest in the king cheetah and secure its protection.[15] Equally, with at least seven specimens of the Kellas cat already available for scientific research, I sincerely hope that the collection of further specimens of this intriguing felid will be deemed unnecessary and will not take place.[16] Instead, I believe that it is now time for formal scientific studies to commence in relation to the *living* Kellas cat, i.e. its ecology and behaviour (perhaps even involving, as suggested to me by the eminent mammalogist Dr Desmond Morris, the rearing and study of a kitten from an early age), to uncover its lifestyle and its ecological niche;[16] for only by understanding these can we hope to achieve what must surely be the ultimate goal of all work concerning the Kellas cat – to maintain the existence of this unexpected but most welcome addition to the British list of indigenous fauna.[16]

Happily it is quite possible that it will eventually be illegal to kill a Kellas cat. As part of the first five-year review of Britain's Wildlife and Countryside Act by the Nature Conservancy Council, the Scottish wildcat will hereafter receive full protection.[17] Consequently, if the Kellas cat is shown via genetic studies to be a wildcat mutant, race or subspecies, it will automatically be totally protected by law. Moreover, it is certain to receive protection if revealed to be a completely new species, and hence endemic to Britain.

It is time for cryptozoology to come of age. It continues to gain interest and respect; it must now accept a major responsibility. No longer should it be content merely to seek out new animals; it must also ensure that its discoveries are conserved and perpetuated. Otherwise its goals will be meaningless, its ideals empty.

Perhaps my documentation of mystery cat lore in this book may help, however slightly, to bring about the formal discovery of one such felid, whose 'official' status can thereafter work for it to acquire its protection and its habitat's conservation. Certainly I could not request a greater boon of my own existence than to assist in the accomplishment of such an achievement.

Take only memories,
Leave only footprints,
Kill only time ...

Trevor Beer, *Poachers Days*

1 Lever, C., *Naturalized Mammals of the World* (Longmans, 1985)
2 Hansen, J., *New Scientist*, Vol. 97, pp. 590–91 (3 March 1983); Boitani, L., *Acta Zoologica Fennica*, No. 174, pp. 259–64 (1983)
3 Beck, A.M., *The Ecology of Stray Dogs* (York Press, Baltimore, 1973)
4 IUCN, *IUCN Red List of Threatened Animals 1988* (IUCN, Cambridge, 1988)
5 Scott, P., and Rines, R., *Nature*, Vol. 258, pp. 466–8 (9 December 1975)
6 Clover, C., *Daily Telegraph*, 21 March 1987
7 Dunn, E., *The Mail on Sunday – YOU Magazine*, pp. 46–8, 24 August 1986
8 Kemp, M., *Daily Mail*, 16 April 1987
9 Shuker, K.P.N., *Swara*, p. 36 (January/February 1988)
10 Fuller, E., *Extinct Birds* (Rainbird/Viking Press, 1987)
11 Heuvelmans, B., *On the Track of Unknown Animals* (Rupert Hart-Davis, 1958)
12 Day, D., *The Doomsday Book of Animals* (Ebury Press, 1981)
13 Prentiss, D.W., *Proceedings of the US National Museum*, Vol. 26, pp. 887–8 (1903)
14 Greenwell, J.R., *BBC Wildlife*, Vol. 6, pp. 354–9 (July 1987)
15 Bottriell, L.G., *King Cheetah. The Story of the Quest* (E.J. Brill, Leiden, 1987)
16 Shuker, K.P.N., Kellas cat paper awaiting publication in *Cryptozoology* (written in 1986); Shuker, K.P.N., Paper presented at ISC Members Meeting, Royal Museum of Scotland, 26 July 1987
17 Clover, C., *Daily Telegraph*, 1 December 1987

Addenda

Rumour has it that a puma was shot dead and positively identified some time during 1987 in the vicinity of Greenwich Observatory, London; no further information is available.

An unidentified lynx-like beast has reportedly killed several pets in the Weymouth area of Dorset, England (*Daily Mail*, 17 November 1988); and a few days after a series of horrific sheep killings at Seasalter (between Canterbury and Whitstable), medical specialist Dr Sheila Drake sighted a large brown puma-like animal at close range in that same region (Pullinger, S., *Canterbury Adscene*, 20 and 27 January 1989).

On 20 December 1988, a 'lion' sighted by a motorist near a road in Nazeing, Essex, was swiftly tracked down by police – only to find that it was a 4 ft/120 cm-tall Irish wolfhound called Finn (*Daily Mail*, 21 December 1988).

Six months after the Hayling Island specimen, a second dead swamp cat *Felis chaus* has been found in Britain – this time by farmer Norman Evans, close to his home near Ludlow, Shropshire. It was very emaciated; a back injury (perhaps due to a collision with a car) may have prevented it from hunting (*Sunday Express*, 19 February 1989).

Omitted from p. 81, line 9: In 1917, N. Smirnov referred to *Felis daemon* as *Felis sylvestris caucasicus* aber. *daemon*, i.e. as an aberrant morph of the Caucasian wildcat.

A sighting of an unknown cat species at Hayuliang in Arunachal Pradesh, India, was reported by M.K. Ranjitsinh in December 1986 (*JBNHS*, Vol. 83, p. 653, 1986).

It has been suggested that the Bali tiger should be included within the Sumatran subspecies (Hemmer, H., *Zeitschrift für Säugetiere*, Vol. 34, pp. 216–23 (1969)), but most authorities still afford it separate subspecific status. The most recent Bali tiger review is that of J. Seidensticker (Tilson, R.L. and Seal, U.S. (eds) *Tigers of the World* (Noyes Publications, New Jersey, 1977)).

A former mystery cat of uncertain scientific status (Hayman, R.W., *Zoo Life*, Vol. 4, pp. 7–8 (spring 1949)), the servaline *felis servalina (brachyura)*, was eventually shown merely to be a speckled morph of the serval.

Despite their name, the various 'water felids' of North Amerindian lore (Meurger, M., and Gagnon, C., *Lake Monster Traditions* (Fortean Tomes, 1988)) are most akin to Nessie-type lake monsters.

Omitted from p. 181, line 36: A lithe, puma-like cat with freckle-like limb markings, identified locally as an *onza*, was trapped and shot some time prior to World War II in Mexico's Barranca de las Viboras by J. Frank Dobie (*Tongues of the Monte* (Doubleday, Doran & Co, New York, 1935)), but its skin was later destroyed by bugs.

The term *jaguarete* (from the Guarani *yaguarete*, meaning 'great beast') is nowadays used merely as a synonym for the jaguar, in contrast to its earlier, separate usage by Thomas Pennant for Chapter 6's white-bellied, black mystery cat.

A one-man expedition, undertaken by Jersey Zoo's assistant director Jeremy Mallinson, set out in September 1965 to seek the *mitla* in Bolivia (*Animal Life*, No. 39, p. 2 (November 1965)); to date, however, its identity is still unknown to science.

It should be noted that *Smilodon californicus* is merely a synonym of *S. fatalis*; it is *not* a separate species, as stated in certain other works.

A striking similarity between Ion Idriess's Queensland tiger eyewitness reports and the earlier, presumably fictional accounts in D.H. Lawrence's novel *Kangaroo*, has been noted by Dr Bernard Heuvelmans (*Cryptozoology*, Vol. 6, pp. 121–4 (1987)) among others.

After fifty-eight years of supposed extinction, the procurement of two specimens in 1986 marked the official rediscovery of the Corsican wildcat (Arrighi, J. and Salotti, M., *Mammalia*, Vol. 52, pp. 123–5 (1988)).

The International Society of Cryptozoology

Any reader wishing to learn more concerning mystery cats or any other mystery creatures should seriously consider becoming a member of the International Society of Cryptozoology (ISC). This society serves as a focal point for the investigation, analysis, publication and discussion of all matters concerning animals of unexpected form or size or of unexpected occurrence in time or space. It encourages scientific examination of all evidence related to these matters, and one of its principal objectives is the dissemination of cryptozoological information. This includes information concerning cryptozoological claims and concerning the analyses of evidence such as hair samples, photographs, sonar tracks, spoor casts and tissue samples. Governed by a board of directors comprising some of the world's leading biological scientists, the society also serves as a forum for public discussion and education and for providing reliable information to appropriate authorities and the news media. Society membership is open to all interested persons; membership includes receipt of the ISC's quarterly *Newsletter* and its annual scientific journal *Cryptozoology*. Membership enquiries should be addressed to: J. Richard Greenwell, The Secretary, The International Society of Cryptozoology, PO Box 43070, Tucson, Arizona 85733, USA.

Some Other Periodicals Regularly Featuring Information Concerning Mysterious Cats

BBC Wildlife: Broadcasting House, Whiteladies Road, Bristol BS8 2LR, UK

Carnivore Genetics Newsletter: St Stephens Road Nursery, Ealing, London W13, UK

Creature Chronicles: Ron Schaffner, PO Box 44062, Cincinnati, Ohio 45244, USA

Fate: Llewellyn Publications, Box 64383, St Paul, Minnesota 55164, USA

Folklore Frontiers: Paul Screeton, 5 Egton Drive, Seaton Carew, Hartlepool, Cleveland TS25 2AT, UK

Fortean Times: 96 Mansfield Road, London NW3 2HX, UK

INFO Journal: International Fortean Organization, PO Box 367, Arlington, Virginia 22210, USA

Pursuit: Society for the Investigation of the Unexplained (SITU), PO Box 265, Little Silver, New Jersey 07739, USA

Strange Magazine: PO Box 2246, Rockville, Maryland 20852, USA

Appendix

Scientific Classification of Living Organisms

The scientific method of classifying organisms utilizes a hierarchical system of categories, at the base of which is the species. Although there is still much dispute concerning its precise definition, generally speaking a species can be defined as one or more populations of organisms whose members can interbreed freely with one another and produce fit, fertile offspring. Whether or not such populations are separated from one another by geographical boundaries is of no concern; so long as members from each such population can, if brought together, yield fit, fertile offspring, they are classed as members of the same species (i.e. intraspecific) as, for example, in the case of Indian leopards and African leopards, or wildcats from Great Britain and from continental Europe. Members of populations belonging to different species (i.e. interspecific) can often mate and produce offspring too, but such offspring (called 'hybrids') are normally (though not invariably) sterile.

The system of nomenclature used in scientific classification is based upon that of the seventeenth century Swedish botanist Carl Linné (better known as Linnaeus), which allocates to every species its own unique binomial name, i.e. a name which is itself composed of two names. For example, the wildcat's scientific name is *Felis sylvestris*. The name *sylvestris* is the wildcat's specific name, while *Felis* is its generic name or genus (plural = genera). Unlike common names, which change from language to language, an organism's scientific name (of Latin and Greek origin) stays the same, thereby preventing any linguistical confusion about which species is being referred to in a given book, paper or article, etc.

Closely related species, though each possessing a different specific name, are grouped together within the same genus. Hence as the wildcat, sand cat, ocelot and lynx, for instance, are all closely related to one another, their scientific names are *Felis sylvestris, Felis margarita, Felis pardalis* and *Felis lynx* respectively. Less closely related to these – but very closely related to one another – are the lion, tiger, and leopard. Therefore, these share a different genus, *Panthera*, i.e. *Panthera leo, Panthera tigris*, and *Panthera pardus* respectively.

Just as closely related species are grouped together within the same genus, closely related genera are also grouped together within the same family – the next category on the ascending hierarchy of scientific classification. In the case of the wildcat, lynx, lion, tiger, etc., this is the cat family, known scientifically as Felidae. Equally, closely related families are grouped together within the same order, e.g. the cat family is included alongside the bear family (Ursidae), the dog family (Canidae), the hyaena family (Hyaenidae) and various others within the order Carnivora (carnivorous mammals).

Moving ever upwards in the hieararchy, closely related orders are grouped together within the same class. Thus, carnivorous mammals, along with rodents (order Rodentia), bats (Chiroptera), whales (Cetacea), elephants (Proboscidea), marsupials (Marsupialia), and all other orders of furry, milk-producing animals are grouped together within the class Mammalia (mammals).

Closely related classes are grouped together within the same phylum (plural = phyla), so that mammals (Mammalia), birds (Aves), bony fishes (Osteichthyes), reptiles (Reptilia), and all other classes of animals which, at some stage in their development, possess an elastic skeletal rod called the notochord are grouped together within the phylum Chordata. Finally, closely related phyla are all grouped together within the same kingdom – the topmost category in the hierarchy. Thus, chordates, along with ringed worms (phylum Annelida), jointed-limbed animals (Arthropoda), flatworms (Platyhelminthes), sponges (Porifera), and all other phyla of animals are grouped together within the kingdom Animalia. Other kingdoms include Plantae (plants), and Fungi (fungi).

It can be seen that each category contains a wider diversity of species than the one below it, e.g. the species all contained within the order Carnivora are more varied than those contained within any one of its families. This means that as the hierarchy of scientific classification is ascended, the relationship between the species involved becomes less and less obvious, e.g. mammals and birds (representing two classes) are less obviously related to each other than are cats and dogs (representing two families).

To make the classification system more manageable, various sub-categories are often employed too, inserted between the principal ones, and prefixed by 'sub- ' or 'super- '. For instance, a sub-family category is often used, and is inserted between family and genus, while a super-family category is inserted between family and order.

Also worth recalling is the subspecies, as described fully on p. 28. For a subspecies is given a trinomial (three-part) name, the third part being specific to the subspecies of a given species. For example, the tiger's Siberian subspecies is *Panthera tigris altaica*, whilst its Javan subspecies is *Panthera tigris sondaicus*.

Table 4. Scientific Classification of the Tiger *Panthera tigris*

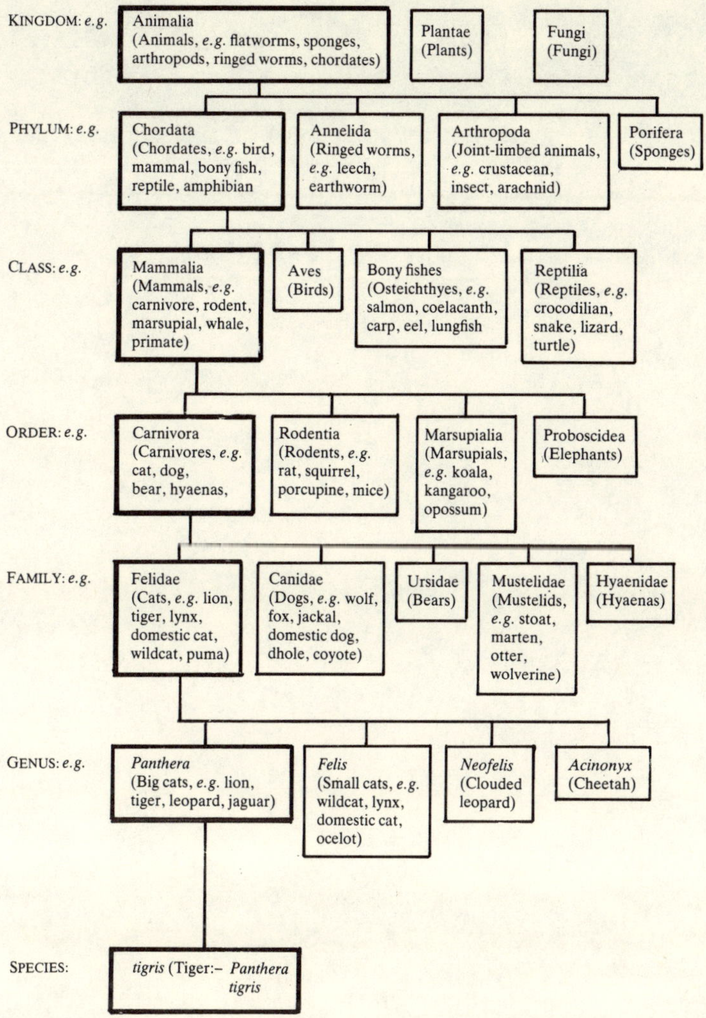

Glossary

Abundism: Abnormal multiplication of body markings.

***Agouti* gene**: Gene responsible, with grey or golden fur, for each hair of such fur being banded with yellow and black stripes.

Albinism: Abnormally pale colouration, resulting from absence or limited distribution of eumelanin and/or other melanin pigments; animals so affected are termed albinos (adj. = albinistic). See also p. 29.

Allele: One of a pair or series of alternative forms exhibited by a given gene; see also pp. 28–30.

Allopatric Speciation: When populations of one original species become geographically isolated from one another, with each population eventually evolving into a new, separate species; see **Sympatric speciation**.

Back-Crossing: Mating a hybrid with one or other of its pure-blood parents.

Bifurcate: Having two prongs, forked, or branching off into two separate parts.

Big Cat: In scientific sense, term denoting any cat species with a hyoid apparatus not composed wholly of bone, thereby enabling the cat to roar, but not to purr continuously, e.g. lion, tiger, leopard. See also p. 26.

Bipedal: Walking on the hind limbs only, as with humans, birds, bears on occasion, etc.

BP: Before the present day.

Canid: Any member of the family Canidae, e.g. dogs, wolves, foxes, jackals, bush-dogs.

Canine: (1) Adjective, applied to anything dog-like in appearance, behaviour, etc. (2) Noun, referring to the single upper and lower pair of fang-like teeth possessed by many mammals, and located just behind the incisors; used for seizing and tearing prey, and highly developed in most (though not all) carnivorous mammals.

Carnassials: Premolars and molars bearing sharp blade-like edges for slicing meat.

Chinchilla: In genetic sense, the *full colour* gene's recessive mutant allele responsible for absence of phaeomelanin in mammals, resulting in partial albinism; see p. 29.

Cross-breeding: Mating between animals of different species, subspecies, or breeds; also known as hybridization.

Cryptic markings: Dark body markings highly visible in normal individuals, but largely obscured in melanistic individuals by the abnormally dark background colouration of their pelage (as with the rosettes of black panthers, for example).

Cryptozoology: The scientific investigation of animals whose existence or identity has yet to be formally ascertained, e.g. this book's mystery cats, Loch Ness monster and other lake monsters, sea serpents, yeti, bigfoot, Congolese mokele-mbembe, etc.

Cursorial: Mode of existence based around fleet-footed activity, and characteristic of long-limbed animals, e.g. cheetahs, wolves, antelopes.

Dasyure: Name assigned to five species of Australian carnivorous weasel-like marsupial.

Dense Pigmentation **gene**: Gene responsible for inducing a mammal's normal degree of coat colour density.

Dilute: In genetic sense, the *dense pigmentation* gene's recessive mutant allele partly responsible for blue-coloured fur in mammals.

Dimorphism: The occurrence of two distinct morphs within a species.

Distal: The part of any structure furthest away from its point of attachment (see **Proximal**).

Dominant: In genetic sense, term applied to any allele of a given gene which can prevent the action of another allele of that same gene.

Dorsal: Appertaining to the upper side or upper surface of an animal (see **Ventral**).

Erythrism: Abnormally red colouration, resulting from excess of red-brown pigment phaeomelanin and/or chestnut-red pigment erythromelanin (adj. = erythristic).

Eumelanin: Blackish-brown pigment responsible for black colouration in mammals; often referred to non-specifically as melanin.

Eutherian: Any modern-day mammal other than monotremes and marsupials; characterized by development of placenta from embryo's waste-products sac (allantois), and a relatively long gestation period (during which the young can attain an advanced degree of development prior to birth).

Exotic: Noun or adjective, loosely applied to any animal currently existing in captivity and/or in the wild state within an area not contained in its normal, native range of distribution.

Extension of black gene: Gene responsible for normal distribution of eumelanin present in mammals' fur.

Felid: Noun applied to any member of the cat family (Felidae), e.g. lion, tiger, lynx, puma, domestic cat, cheetah.

Feline: Adjective applied to anything cat-like in appearance, mode of movement, etc.

Feral: Appertaining to animals which have lapsed from a domesticated into a wild condition e.g. populations of domestic cats now established and breeding in the wild.

Full colour **gene**: Gene responsible for inducing a mammal's normal complement of pelage pigment.

Gracility: the possession of a notably slender, graceful body and long, lithe limbs.

Heterozygous: Possessing two different alleles of a given gene; see also p. 30.

Homozygous: Possessing a pair of the same allele of a given gene; see also p. 30

Hybrid: The offspring of a mating between organisms of two different species, subspecies, or breeds. Often designated by the names of the two parent forms separated by an '×', e.g. wildcat × domestic cat = hybrid of a mating between a wildcat and a domestic cat.

Hyoid apparatus: Bony structure in throat region, whose composition influences the sounds made by cat species; see also p. 26.

Inguinal: Appertaining to the groin region.

Intergeneric: Appertaining to comparisons, interactions, etc., between individuals belonging to different genera.

Interspecific: Appertaining to comparisons, interactions, etc., between individuals belonging to different species.

Machairodontids: Sabre-toothed cats – a taxonomic group of felids characterized by extra-large upper canines and under-sized lower canines; supposedly extinct since the Pleistocene epoch.

Mandible: The lower jaw in cats and other mammals.

Marsupial: Any member of the mammalian order Marsupialia; most marsupial species are characterized by the possession of a pouch (and sometimes by a placenta derived from the embryo's yolksac), and by a notably short gestation period which results in the young being born in a very immature state, after which they make their way to the mother's pouch in which they then continue their development and suckle.

Melanism: Abnormally dark background colouration, as exemplified by that of the fur of the black panther, black jaguar, and other cat forms displaying this condition (see **Pseudo-melanism**); caused by excess of eumelanin (adj. = melanistic or melanic); see also pp. 28–30.

Metatherian: Alternative name for marsupial.

Monotreme: Any modern egg-laying mammal, i.e. platypus and echidnas.

Morph: One of two or more physically different (but not taxonomically different) forms of individual exhibited by a given species; e.g. the black panther is a melanistic morph of the leopard *Panthera pardus*.

Morphology: The physical appearance and structure of an animal.

Morphometric: Appertaining to analyses involving detailed measurements derived from an organism's morphology.

Mozaicism: Abnormal condition in which aberrant patches of pigment are distributed over an animal's body surface.

Mustelid: Any member of the family Mustelidae, e.g. weasels, otters, badgers, martens, skunks, wolverines.

Mutant: An individual exhibiting heritable characteristics which have arisen spontaneously (as opposed to gradually), and which differ from corresponding characteristics possessed by normal individuals of the species concerned.

Mutation: A change in the physical characteristics of an organism that results from a change in the structure or amount of that organism's genetic material (DNA).

Naturalized: Appertaining to any wild (but not domesticated) animal species which (by escaping from captivity or via deliberate introduction) has become established in an area to which it is not normally native (see **Feral**).

Nigrism: Abnormal fusion of body markings.

Nomen nudum: A published scientific name (for a given organism) which for various reasons is no longer accepted by science as legitimate, and hence should not be used, e.g. *Smilodon neogaeus* – see p. 197.

Non-agouti: In genetic sense, the *agouti* gene's recessive mutant allele responsible for melanism in many mammals; see also pp. 28–30.

Pelage: The furry coat of mammals.

Pers. Comm.: Abbreviation of 'personal communication' – term denoting that the information preceding it in this book's text is material obtained via personal communication with a correspondent, rather than from some published source or from personal research.

Phaeomelanin: Reddish-brown melanin pigment present in the pelage of many mammals.

Plantar pad: The pad present on the palm of a mammal's paw.

Pleiotropic: Appertaining to any gene responsible for a range of quite different effects upon an organism.

Polymorphism: The occurrence of more than two distinct morphs within a given species.

Primary guard hairs: Very long, coarse, stiff hairs (longer than normal – awn – guard hairs) scattered sparingly throughout a mammal's pelage, and sometimes differing markedly in colour from the predominant pelage colouration present.

Proximal: The part of any structure closest to its point of attachment (see **Distal**).

Pseudo-melanism: Condition mimicking melanism to some degree, but in which abnormally dark colouration results from abnormal fusion and multiplication of body markings (see **Melanism**).

Pug mark: The impression left behind by any pad on a mammal's paw that makes contact with the ground.

Race: Loose term, popularly used to designate local populations within a subspecies.

Recessive: Appertaining to any allele whose action can be prevented by that of another allele of the same gene.

Retractile: Capable of being drawn back or withdrawn (actively and/or passively) as in the case of the claws of most cat species. See also pp. 21–22.
Small Cat: In scientific sense, term denoting any cat species with a hyoid apparatus composed wholly of bone, thereby enabling it to purr continuously, but not to roar, e.g. pumas, lynxes, domestic cats, wildcats, ocelots. See also p. 26.
Spoor: Trail or track comprising an animal's footprints or pawprints.
Subspecies: A collection of morphologically similar populations of a species, inhabiting a geographical subdivision of that species' total distribution range, and differing taxonomically from other populations of that species.
Sympatric speciation: When populations of one original species evolve into new, separate species without first having been isolated geographically from one another (see **Allopatric Speciation**).
Taxonomic: Anything appertaining to the scientific classification of organisms; any characteristics of, or differences between, organisms which are considered to have bearing upon those organisms' evolutionary relationships to one another.
Taxonomy: The science of classification, as applied to organisms.
Thylacoleonid: Any member of the family Thylacoleonidae, comprising the supposedly extinct marsupial lions of Australia.
Ventral: Appertaining to the underside or lower surface of an animal (see **Dorsal**).
Vibrissae: A mammal's whiskers (often touch-sensitive).
Viverrid: Any member of the family Viverridae, e.g. civets, genets, binturong, fossa.

Index